Praise for *The Craft of* *Learning: A Guide for Faculty Development*

"This book and its accompanying Tool Kit will help us, the artisans of the craft of community-engaged pedagogy, do our work ethically and with competence. It is an exceptional and a much-needed resource for faculty development. This intentional, tangible, and interactive tool is a gift to community-engaged professionals. Thank you, Marshall and Star."

—***Lisa Georgiana***, *Director, Center for Community Engagement, Saint Francis University*

"*The Craft of Community-Engaged Teaching and Learning* is a competency-based blueprint for professional growth in engaged teaching and learning. As the authors say, 'This is a different kind of book' (p. 1). Welch and Plaxton-Moore's unique voices capture the essence of the foundational principles of engagement and the authors encourage and emulate best practices in teaching through the very way the book is written and the expectations for participation, co-learning and reflection by the reader. This book and its accompanying workbook will be my go-to guide for my work to develop faculty capacity—not just to teach community-engaged courses, but to become a community-engaged scholar and master of the craft of engaged teaching and learning."

—***Cathy Jordan***, *Professor of Pediatrics and Extension Specialist, University of Minnesota*

"As the work of higher education community engagement grows, what makes this book unique is the way which Plaxton-Moore and Welch frame community engagement as a kind of craft. The authors weave together the most vital foundational theories, applications, and knowledge in the field in a way that encourages and accompanies readers who wish to further hone their skills to participate in communities in creative, ethical, and effective manners. This is a timely and relevant book that will help anyone interested in deepening their practice, scholarship, and artistic expression of community engagement."

—***Chris Nayve***, Associate Vice President for Community Engagement and Anchor Initiatives, University of San Diego

"In *The Craft of Community-Engaged Teaching and Learning: A Guide for Faculty Development,* Marshall Welch and Star Plaxton-Moore invite their readers to a sustained dialogue. This dialogue is designed to help higher education faculty hone their 'craft' of community-engaged pedagogy, research, publication, and advocacy. Their book, with connected exercises, offers multiple entry points for higher education faculty to engage in this dialogue alone or in learning communities. For faculty needing an introduction to academic community engagement, this text begins with a useful history and the purpose of engaged scholarship with copious references to landmark texts. It then offers Welch's helpful OPERA model of course development. We have used this at my institution and found it a useful tool for both introductory and intermediate faculty development training. For more experienced faculty, the book invites a dialogue with the reader on how to advance one's career as a higher education civic professional and influence the home institution toward becoming a civically engagement campus. The concluding chapter, 'The Reflective Practitioner,' offers an inspiring image of the reflective character of the craft of community engagement faculty. This chapter invites readers to reflect on how best to weave together academic expertise, civic teaching and learning, community impact, and institutional change in service of civic professionalism."

—***James Peterman****, Professor of Philosophy and Director of Civic Engagement, Sewanee, The University of the South*

"Community-engaged teaching and learning has come a long way since the days of finding models in various disciplines to demonstrate its applicability in many (if not all) content areas. Yet, this is the first resource that brings the new advances into a guide for faculty development. Drawing on the most recent literature in the field and critical theory, as well as the knowledge of two seasoned practitioners, this book will help build faculty capacity for high quality community-engaged teaching and learning whether they are just starting to hone their pedagogical craft or seeking to deepen their practice. Faculty who use this guide to hone their craft will be not only better community engaged teachers but also better teachers."

—***John Saltmarsh****; Professor, Higher Education, University of Massachusetts; and Distinguished Engaged Scholar in Residence, Swearer Center, Brown University*

The Craft of Community-Engaged Teaching and Learning

Campus Compact is a national coalition of colleges and universities committed to the public purposes of higher education. Campus Compact publications focus on practical strategies for campuses to put civic education and community engagement into action. Please visit http://compact.org for more information.

The Craft of Community-Engaged Teaching and Learning

A Guide for Faculty Development

MARSHALL WELCH AND
STAR PLAXTON-MOORE

BOSTON, MASSACHUSETTS
Distributed by Stylus Publishing, LLC.

Published by Campus Compact
45 Temple Place
Boston, MA 02111

Library of Congress Cataloging-in-Publication Data
Names: Welch, Marshall, author. | Plaxton-Moore, Star, 1980- author.
Title: The craft of community-engaged teaching and learning : a guide for faculty development / by Marshall Welch & Star Plaxton-Moore.
Description: Boston, MA : Campus Compact, [2019] | Includes bibliographical references and index.
Identifiers: LCCN 2019008027| ISBN 9781945459078 (cloth : alk. paper) | ISBN 9781945459061 (pbk. : alk. paper) | ISBN 9781945459085 (library networkable e-edition) | ISBN 9781945459092 (consumer e-edition)
Subjects: LCSH: Professional learning communities. | Critical pedagogy.
Classification: LCC LB1731 .W4 2019 | DDC 370.71/1--dc23 LC record available at https://lccn.loc.gov/2019008027

13-digit ISBN: 978-1-7339028-0-9 Paperback
13-digit ISBN: 978-1-7339028-1-6 Hardback
13-digit ISBN: 978-1-7339028-2-3 Library
13-digit ISBN: 978-1-7339028-3-0 Consumer eBook

Printed in the United States of America

All first editions printed on acid-free paper that meets the American National Standards Institute Z39-48 Standard.

First Edition, 2019

Dedicated to the community partners, faculty, staff, and students we have had the honor and pleasure of working with over the years.

CONTENTS

PART THREE: ADVANCING THE CRAFT

FOREWORD

Scholars and practitioners come to community engagement from different fields, disciplines, and backgrounds. My own calling came during my undergraduate years at a state university, when I was a shy, somewhat sheltered student who was a bit naïve about the world. My undergraduate and graduate degrees in community health engaged me with the off-campus community, and I felt the relevancy of my academic studies and learned a great deal from the community members who served as informal educators. As a graduate student, I went on to conduct a qualitative study of the impact of service-learning on undergraduate students (Higher Education Research Institute, n.d.), with a focus on students enrolled in a course on educational theory and the role of social interaction in the development of cognition. In their interviews with me, students talked about how the course readings came alive for them when they were in the community tutoring children. The students felt that their learning had an impact on the children with whom they were working. As a result, these undergraduate students felt more compelled themselves to complete the readings and assignments for their own class. A few of the students spoke of how the practical application of their learning impacted the likelihood that they would persist with their own education.

For the last two decades I have served as the executive director of California Campus Compact, a statewide organization that builds the collective commitment and capacity of colleges and universities to advance civic and community engagement for a healthy, more just and democratic society (California Campus Compact, n.d.). In this position, I have had the privilege of leading a host of strategic initiatives designed to both transform the way we teach and encourage higher education administrators to build a campus culture that supports engaged scholarship.

Over time, I have used several resources to provide guidance to faculty wishing to teach a service-learning or community engagement course. This book by Star Plaxton-Moore and Marshall Welch is a unique and timely contribution. Their material draws on previous works, yet brings the pedagogy and practice of community engagement into the current day, incorporating and integrating multidisciplinary perspectives, social justice principles, and asset-based models.

Part One of this book provides a strong foundational basis for what it means to become a community-engaged faculty member. A great benefit of this set of chapters is that it creates space for faculty to consider the ways in which their values and goals impact how they teach their course and what they want their students to learn. Focusing on engaged pedagogy in theory and practice, the chapters provide an opportunity to reflect on—and perhaps rethink—how one engages with students and cocreates an educational experience with the community.

Part Two of this book delves deeper into the ways in which students learn and how faculty might design and implement community-engaged courses with student learning at the forefront. This part of the book is essential because many faculty have received, at best, minimal instruction on how to create, implement, and measure learning objectives or on how to design and facilitate discussions and reflection exercises. The section also includes a chapter on building partnerships and the importance of involving the community in all aspects of course creation. Creating and nurturing equitable and productive partnerships is one of the most important elements in ensuring a successful experience for all parties involved—students, faculty, and community members.

Part Three of this book frames the ways in which one can build a career as a community-engaged scholar. While there has been significant growth in community engagement as a field, there are still many institutions where an engaged faculty member may be the only one in the department who is teaching a community engagement course. Having a mentor or being part of a learning community, with intentional space to share practical teaching techniques and reflect on community engagement, can be extremely valuable. This section of the book is also helpful if one is seeking tenure or scholarly recognition of engaged scholarship. It highlights the importance of finding a supportive community to assist in improving the quality of one's work as well as navigating departmental or campus politics.

Overall, each section of this book offers a concise theoretical overview while also providing an additional "Advancing the Craft" discussion that delves deeper into each topic. This two-tiered structure acknowledges the varied developmental stages in which faculty might find themselves, allowing them the opportunity to obtain foundational knowledge and move into a deeper understanding of the work. The accompanying Tool Kits and workbook offer practical and structured guidance to assist in building a course. Thus, whether a faculty member embarks on the journey alone or in a learning community, this book and its accompanying workbook provide all of the components needed to design a high-quality community engagement course and to think about building a career as an engaged scholar.

This book provides a wealth of insights to aid faculty members and community engagement professionals whose work involves supporting faculty development at their institutions. At California Campus Compact we have found great value in creating a learning community of faculty, across multiple disciplines, and with faculty at different periods in their career trajectory. I can envision us using this book and its accompanying Tool Kits to create a learning community or faculty cohort experience over the course of a year or two. This book invites faculty to engage in an illuminating and valuable journey of discovery, reflection, creation, and implementation in creating a course or in crafting a career.

Elaine K. Ikeda
Executive Director
California Campus Compact

ACKNOWLEDGMENTS

We would like to acknowledge and thank friends and colleagues who helped with this project. We begin with Danielle Leek, who, while working with Campus Compact, enthusiastically embraced the concept and design of this book. We also appreciate the support of Maggie Grove and Clayton Hurd from Campus Compact as the project developed. We would like to thank Lisa Georgiana and her cohort of faculty at Saint Francis University who field-tested many of the chapters and Tool Kit workbook exercises. Thanks to Julie Hatcher and Mary Price at Indiana University–Purdue University at Indianapolis and Burt Bargerstock at Michigan State University. We wish to thank Elaine K. Ikeda for writing the foreword. Finally, Star would like to thank her spouse, Andrew, and her children, Jackson and Stella, for supporting her writing process even when it took her away from them some evenings and weekends.

INTRODUCTION

This is a different kind of book. As you will quickly see, you will be invited to engage and interact with us, the authors, and hopefully with colleagues through these pages. The narrative has been written as a conversation with you and, hopefully, with a community of learners with whom you are reading and working. Our research and our own experience in professional development show that a learning community is an effective approach to provide technical and even emotional support through a cadre of kindred spirits who share your enthusiasm and commitment for community engagement. We want to accompany and work with you as much as possible in this printed format. Therefore, we have created an online workbook with worksheets we refer to as a Tool Kit that can be downloaded from the Campus Compact website (https://compact.org/craft-companion/) to accompany you through these pages. We envision that you will download and print the PDF file of the Tool Kit worksheets for each chapter as you move through this book and sequentially compile them in a three-ring binder. In this way, you will be ready to complete the activities as you read the chapter. You may be tempted to forego these exercises, assuming they are just "add-ons" to this narrative. However, the workbook consists of a variety of exercises, case studies, activities, and even some short video clips of engaging conversations that are designed to reinforce what you read in this text as you create a blueprint for designing, implementing, and assessing community-engaged learning. As such, this book is not designed as a traditional narrative. Unlike other scholarly works, you will be invited to stop, think, write, and respond in your accompanying workbook and hopefully with colleagues.

We appreciate the utility of a workbook, as it is an intentional intellectual process that you work *in* and *with*, culminating with a tangible resource that you can keep and refer to over time. Each chapter and accompanying worksheets provide the blueprint, nuts and bolts, as well as the tools necessary to carefully *craft* a theoretically based engaged teaching and learning experience that will have an impact on not only your students but also the community and hopefully your institution and yourself. This workbook is the result and product of our extensive research on faculty professional development in the area of engaged teaching and learning (Welch & Plaxton-Moore, 2017, 2018) coupled with our own experience facilitating faculty development over a period of 20 combined years.

Let's pause here and now for your first invitation to interact with us by engaging in a Tool Kit exercise. As we all know, a tool kit is a collection of tools. One key tool that we use throughout this book, in the accompanying workbook, and in learning communities is critical reflection. As you will see and learn in much more detail in a later chapter, reflection is the intentional consideration of an experience in light of a learning objective (Hatcher & Bringle, 1997). We began this introduction by asserting that community-engaged teaching is a craft, and you are to become an artisan who must ply this craft with intentional and nuanced skill. Tool Kit I.1 begins our conversation and hopefully you will continue with colleagues in a learning community.

Tool Kit I.1—Refer to Exercise I.1 in your workbook. Take a moment to critically reflect on the concept of a "craft" and jot those ideas in your workbook. What is a craft? What does it consist of? How is it different (if at all) from the general idea and practice of construction or building?

Craft

Our embrace and use of craft as a concept provides continuity. As noted in their guidebook for community engagement professionals (CEPs), Dostilio and Welch (2018) argue a finely crafted house is much more than merely having the tools and knowledge of how to use them to build four walls and a roof. The same can be said of teaching—especially in the context of community-engaged teaching and learning that consists of multiple stakeholders and many moving parts.

We view *craft* as both a noun and a verb. It is both an artifact and a process integrating skill and art. As discussed by Dostilio and Welch (2018), Glover's (2010) conceptualization of craftsmanship resonates with us as it reflects a synthesis of skill and art that is relevant and readily applicable to teaching—it is

> the quality that comes from creating with passion, care, and attention to detail. It is a quality that is honed, refined, and practiced over the course of a career. . . . Craftsmanship, obviously, isn't something that just happens. It requires a great deal of time, patience and effort. . . . Craftsmanship is the difference between good design and great design. (para. 6)

We want to clearly acknowledge and articulate that the art and craft of teaching can take many forms. We do not mean to imply that community-engaged teaching and learning is the only or "best" way to teach. Likewise, we are not suggesting that all of your courses should incorporate this type of engaged pedagogy and scholarship. That would be quite a workload. We do, however, maintain that community-engaged teaching and learning goes beyond the four walls of a classroom and entails complex dynamics of working with community agencies and community members in *their* settings. As such, both instructor and students are invited into this setting as guests. This requires a unique set of skills and tools that are not necessary or typically applicable in traditional teaching and that most instructors did not obtain through coursework as part of their disciplinary preparation. But acquisition of these is not enough. An engaged scholar must be *competent* in the artful implementation of these skills and tools. So what exactly are these competencies? Before enumerating these tools and skills, let's first consider what we mean by the word *competency* and how this workbook is a competency-based curriculum in Tool Kit I.2.

> Tool Kit I.2—Refer to Exercise I.2 in your workbook. Reflect on your understanding of *competency*. What does that word or concept mean to you? What does that meaning connote? Regardless of your level of knowledge or experience, speculate and list possible skills and tools that are necessary to be competent as an engaged scholar.

Competency

We borrow from Dostilio and Welch (2018) as we articulate our understanding of competency. The Latin *competentia*, meaning "meeting together, agreement, or symmetry," comes from *competenes*, the present participle of *competere*, meaning "coming together or fitting together," which evolved over time to mean "sufficiency to deal with what is at hand" (Online Etymology Dictionary, n.d.). The Latin roots of competence, cognizance and responsibility (Rychen & Salganik, 2001), embed ownership and reliability in a standard of practice for those who exhibit competence. Rychen and Salganik (2001) conceptualized competencies as

> complex action systems that encompass not only knowledge and skills, but also strategies and routines for appropriately applying these knowledge and skills, as well as appropriate emotions and attitudes and the effective self-regulation of these competencies. (p. 8)

We also recognize that although many might embrace the notion of competency in principle, there is legitimate concern and even consternation over how competencies in other professions are used. In some professions, competency models are used only as preprofessional preparation rather than as a way of iteratively shaping and deepening practice. Unfortunately, a competency-based approach can often be corrupted into manifesting itself as a perfunctory list of "items" to "check off" in which a preprofessional merely goes through the motion of assimilating "steps" or "skills" to obtain a credential or license, rather than a deep appreciation and proficiency. However, well-conceived and articulated competencies can serve as a blueprint for professional growth and best practice. They must be artfully nuanced to create a craft as opposed to a product.

Effective Professional Development

Due to the complexities associated with community-engaged teaching and learning that will be examined throughout this book, we have an ethical obligation to articulate and adhere to a framework of competence for effective professional development. Effective professional and faculty development does not consist of or promote a plug-and-play approach of applying new tricks of the trade acquired in a brief one-hour brown-bag lunch workshop. This type of gathering is useful in many respects, but it lacks the depth and continuity required for honing a pedagogical craft. This carries over into a practice of "do no harm" that is borrowed from the medical profession. This tenet is critically important, as many well-intentioned instructors have unintentionally gone into the community with their students and actually done more harm than good as they attempted to employ poorly designed engaged learning experiences in authentic settings to meet instructional objectives of a course. Although a less-than-perfect experience may, in fact, be beneficial to the students, when done poorly, it can be at the expense of those we intended to serve. Therefore, if we are to do this work, we are ethically obligated to do it well and with competence. This book and accompanying workbook incorporate a set of competencies that have been identified by scholars and described in the professional literature (Axtell, 2012; Blanchard et al.,

2009). Additionally, we have included important components, skills, and practices that public scholars in the community have helped us to understand and assimilate. Their perspective and experience as coeducators in the community reflect reciprocal validity (Welch, Miller, & Davies, 2005) of equally valuable competencies that the professional literature may not include (see Table I.1).

You should note these competencies are framed in a scope and sequence that transition from a novice stage of practice to intermediate and advanced stages of practice. This book and accompanying workbook have taken these competencies and organized them into a three-part developmental scope and sequence:

- Part One: Laying the Foundations
- Part Two: Drawing the Blueprint and Using the Tools
- Part Three: Advancing the Craft

These integrate knowledge, skills, and application before, during, and after teaching a community engagement course. You and/or a learning community can move through all three sections, perhaps over the course of one academic year. We envision having the CE directing your community engagement center on campus to be participating and facilitating discussions as a group or with you individually. Experienced faculty with a history of teaching community-engaged courses may choose to review Parts One and Two and focus on Part Three to advance this work and your career. However, we originally envisioned the possibility of Parts One and Two of this book being examined over the course of one year, continuing with Part Three the following year after you've had some practical experience. The book and workbook were designed to help you move incrementally through developmental stages (see Table I.2).

Part One provides the foundations to engaged teaching and learning. Many faculty jump into teaching engaged courses without a background on the history and purpose of engaged scholarship. When this approach is taken, instructors are essentially moving through a set of steps of teaching rather than becoming engaged scholars. The foundations include key principles and tenets of community engagement. This portion of the narrative will also likely introduce you to new and perhaps even challenging information that faculty typically do not receive in their graduate work, let alone think about as they construct traditional courses. By understanding and incorporating these new concepts, you become an engaged scholar. Without this foundational grounding, you are an instructor teaching a community-engaged course. We believe there is a difference between these two approaches.

TABLE I.1
Competencies for Community-Engaged Scholarship

Skill Level	*Competencies*
Novice	Understanding of the principles and components of community engagement and community-engaged scholarship (CES)
Novice	Understanding of the various factors of community issues + developing strategies for promoting community capacity building and social change
Novice to Intermediate	Application of principles of CES in theory and practice (e.g., theoretical frameworks, models, and methods of planning, implementation, and evaluation)
Intermediate	Ability to work in and with diverse communities through cultural competency and intercultural humility
Intermediate	Ability to collaborate and problem-solve with various community-academic stakeholders and constituencies
Intermediate	Ability to write and obtain grants incorporating CES
Intermediate	Ability to disseminate new knowledge through peer-reviewed publications and presentations articulating CES procedures and products
Intermediate to Advanced	Ability to transfer skills to enhance community capacity and to share knowledge/skills with other faculty
Intermediate to Advanced	Knowledge and successful application of CES benchmarks, concepts, definitions, and principles to scholarly products, outcomes, and measures of quality
Advanced	Understanding of implications of CES and working with communities in translating the process into policy
Advanced	Ability to balance and integrate the academic trilogy into CES to meet academic cultural expectations within the academy
Advanced	Ability to articulate CES within the promotion and tenure process and ability to serve on promotion and tenure committees
Advanced	Ability to mentor students and novice faculty members in articulating CES in their professional portfolios

Note. Adapted from "Models for Faculty Development: What Does It Take to Be a Community-Engaged Scholar," by L. W. Blanchard, C. Hanssmann, R. P. Strauss, J. C. Belliard, K. Krichbaum, E. Waters, & S. D. Seifer, 2009, *Metropolitan Universities, 20*(2), pp. 47–65; cited in Welch, 2016.

Part Two of the book builds on this foundation using a metacognitive first-letter mnemonic device (Welch, 2010a) to help frame, include, and recall the basic components of designing and implementing community engagement courses. The five chapters in this portion of the book provide

TABLE I.2

Comprehensive Scope and Sequence of Faculty Development for Engaged Teaching and Scholarship

Characteristic	*Before*	*During*	*After*
Knowledge	Learn about the public purpose of higher education Learn about epistemology of engagement Learn about reflection Learn about intercultural humility	Continued professional development Participating in fellows program Participating in professional development learning community	Mentoring colleagues Serving on advisory committees Disseminating new knowledge Continued professional growth
Skills	Design and implement engaged teaching (e.g., service-learning) Design and implement engaged scholarship (e.g., community-based scholarship) Establish partnerships with community Design and implement scholarship on engagement	Community and trust building Reflection Intercultural humility Engaged research methodology Engaged teaching methodology	Preparing for promotion and tenure review
Application	Coordinate logistics and complete paperwork Join a professional learning community or have a one-on-one consultation	Incorporate new knowledge and skills Begin grant projects	Evaluating and assessing engaged teaching/scholarship for students and/or community Performing professional service in engaged scholarship Researching engaged teaching/scholarship

Note. From *Engaging Higher Education: Purpose, Platforms, and Programs for Community Engagement*, p. 166 by M. Welch, 2016, Sterling, VA: Stylus. Copyright 2016 by Stylus Publishing. Used with permission by the publisher.

a blueprint as well as the "tools" you'll need for your course and community partnerships. However, each chapter concludes with an invitation to take what has been presented and hone your craft by providing evocative questions to consider on your own or with a learning community. You will be invited to reflect on an array of ideas and practice that will transform not only your students but also yourself.

Part Three of the book further develops topics introduced in the previous two sections and is designed to advance the craft in your own professional trajectory and within the institution as well. Chronologically and developmentally speaking, this concluding section of the book presents "advanced" content to help progress as an engaged citizen scholar and civic professional (Hatcher, 2008). This includes exploring ways to disseminate your engaged scholarship in traditional scholarly venues as well as public spaces. This, in turn, is an important step as you prepare how to articulate and document this work in a performance review and for retention, promotion, and tenure. We continue exploring ways to advance engaged scholarship through working with colleagues and integrating your engaged scholarship with your role as a citizen to become a citizen scholar. We conclude by inviting you to continue this work as a reflective practitioner (Schon, 1983, 1987).

The Scholarship of Teaching and Learning

This book and companion workbook also employ important concepts from the scholarship of teaching and learning (SoTL), which is an entire field of study devoted to pedagogy. As discussed in more detail in chapter 2, most faculty are scholars within their own disciplines, incorporating disciplinary-based concepts into their research and practice. However, many are unfamiliar with and unaware of SoTL as it is not typically included in graduate preparation programs. Likewise, while completing discipline-based graduate work, most instructors have not had any theoretical training in the context of teaching or learning. Additionally, most faculty development programs may not be built on or incorporate theoretically based principles of adult learning. We have attempted to address both of these conundrums by basing the content and process of assimilating this content on theoretical principles of best practice.

Transformative Learning Model

To support and enhance what we see and do in this book and companion workbook, as well as in our approach to faculty professional development, we also incorporate principles of transformative learning theory (Cranton, 1996; Mezirow, 1991). In contrast to traditional didactic instruction of disseminating and acquiring information focusing exclusively on the "what" and "how," transformative learning includes consideration of the "why," inviting the learner to reflect on prior assumptions to form new meanings that guide new actions or behaviors. This is especially crucial to faculty considering community-engaged teaching and learning, as it requires a critical reflection and reframing of our preconceived notions of expertise and ways of knowing. As we will see in chapter 1, engaged teaching and learning involves a democratic approach of cocreating new knowledge with our students and community partners, whom we view as public scholars. In this way, instructors and students work *with*, not for, community partners to achieve mutually beneficial outcomes that not only foster students' learning but also build capacity in the community while contributing new knowledge to a disciplinary field (Saltmarsh & Hartley, 2011).

Metacognition

Metacognition is the psychological process of thinking about thinking (Bransford, Brown, & Cocking, 2000; Flavell, 1979; Tanner, 2012). This process helps retain and therefore effectively use information or procedures in new settings and circumstances long after the new knowledge was assimilated and without the coaching of a teacher or mentor. Many of us have used first-letter mnemonics as a metacognitive strategy to recall steps or lists (e.g., H.O.M.E.S. to recall the names of the Great Lakes—Huron, Ontario, Michigan, Erie, and Superior—in our junior high U.S. geography class). Part Two of this book and the accompanying workbook exercises are entirely based on a metacognitive first-letter mnemonic device (Welch, 2010a) to help frame, recall, and include the basic components of designing and implementing community engagement courses. This is not merely a simple "plug-and-play" approach to course development but rather a heuristic to help organize and understand the complexities associated with this form of pedagogy.

Learning Communities

This book, workbook, and format of professional development have been designed for use in and by learning communities (Cox, 2004; Lawler, 2003). Cox (2004) defined a *faculty learning community* as

> a cross-disciplinary faculty and staff group of six to fifteen members (eight to twelve members is the recommended size) who engage in an

> active, collaborative, yearlong program with a curriculum about enhancing teaching and learning and with frequent seminars and activities that provide learning, development, the scholarship of teaching, and community building. (p. 8)

Lawler (2003) characterized effective professional development for a community of adult learners as incorporating six components:

1. Creating a climate of respect
2. Encouraging active participation
3. Building on experience
4. Employing collaborative inquiry
5. Learning for action
6. Empowering the participants (pp. 17–19)

Faculty learning communities take a holistic approach and typically

1. meet for six months or more;
2. meet at a time and location conducive to learning;
3. facilitate individual projects through collective dialogue and shared ideas;
4. incorporate Kolb's (Kolb & Fry, 1984) experiential learning cycle;
5. promote empathy among members;
6. organically establish their own culture of openness and trust;
7. engage complex problems;
8. inspire and empower each other; and
9. have the potential to transform institutions into learning organizations (Cox, 2004).

Ideally, you are interacting with a group of colleagues and a facilitator as you work through this workbook. If not, it is our hope and intention that the interactive nature of this narrative and material will serve you in independently crafting an engaged teaching and learning experience. If you are reading this on your own, we encourage you to regularly meet with the CEP who coordinates community engagement on your campus to discuss the topics from this book and the exercises in the companion workbook.

Flipped Classroom Model

Finally, the invitation to read and engage with these passages *prior* to convening with colleagues incorporates the very aptly titled approach of the flipped classroom model (Lage, Platt, & Treglia, 2000). Learners are introduced to new information through readings and/or videos outside the classroom and before class sessions. This initial information is then assimilated through discussions, problem-solving activities, and simulations. This approach, coupled with the learning community model, generates rich dialogue and discovery as well as provides important technical and emotional support.

Honing the Craft

You, as an engaged scholar, are an artisan. Your craft is to artfully and strategically shape a holistic and transformative experience, not only for your students but also for community partners and those they serve. As such, you are preparing to craft an experience that transcends our traditional approach of teaching to learning that is focused on advancing social change by utilizing the knowledge of community partners as public scholars. Community-engaged teaching and learning must be carefully created with consideration for context, materials, design, impact, and purpose. Just like handicrafts, each community-engaged course is unique in form and function, in the way it manifests embellishments and flaws, and in the ways it unfolds in response to the work of multiple contributors. We conclude this introduction by inviting you to read and reflect in Tool Kit I.3 on the following quote by Parker Palmer (1998), who addresses developing a craft in a community of learners:

> The growth of any craft depends on shared practice and honest dialogue among the people who do it. We grow by trial and error, to be sure—but our willingness to try, and fail, as individuals is severely limited when we are not supported by a community that encourages such risks. (p. 144)

> Tool Kit I.3—Refer to Exercise I.3 in your workbook. To what extent do you think or feel these conditions or dispositions currently exist in higher education as a whole or at your institution specifically? Do Parker Palmer's remarks resonate with you? Why or why not? Are you ready and willing to enter into a setting and experience with others to collectively craft your engaged scholarship?

PART ONE

LAYING THE FOUNDATIONS

Chapter 1

BEING AN ENGAGED SCHOLAR AND DOING ENGAGED SCHOLARSHIP

We begin by reflecting on the words of Ernest Boyer (1997), who many consider to be the consummate voice of and advocate for community engagement in modern American higher education. In his remarks to the Association of American Colleges in 1988, Boyer argued:

> What we urgently need in the academy, then, are scholar-citizens—people who are committed to building an intellectual community, not just in the classroom but in the coffee shop, and committee room as well. And until scholarship in American higher education means not only publishing, but also designing integrated courses, serving on committees, and spending time with students, I am convinced that our efforts to renew the undergraduate experience will simply be time spent tinkering on the edges. (p. 65)

In another speech to the American Academy of Arts and Sciences in 1995, and later published in *Selected Speeches: 1979–1995* in 1997, Boyer described his vision of engaged scholarship:

> The scholarship of engagement means connecting the rich resources of the university to our most pressing social, civic, and ethical problems, to

> our children, to our schools, to our teachers, and to our cities—just to name the ones I am personally in touch with most frequently; you could name others. Campuses would be viewed by both students and professors not as isolated islands, but as staging grounds for action. (p. 92)

If you don't already have one, download a QR scanning app to your smartphone or tablet. Then, swipe your device over the video code in Figure 1.1 to see and hear a brief introduction of the late Ernest Boyer and then refer to Tool Kit 1.1.

Figure 1.1 Ernest Boyer video.

Note. Scan the QR code to access https://www.youtube.com/watch?v=4-TFN16faN0

> Tool Kit 1.1—Refer to Exercise 1.1 in your workbook. Read and respond to the questions regarding Ernest Boyer's conceptualization of engaged scholarship.

History and Public Purpose of Engaged Teaching and Scholarship

The public purpose of American higher education is, and always has been, to promote a democratic society (Saltmarsh & Hartley, 2011), taking a cyclical trajectory consisting of five phases, which is described in more detail by Welch (2016). The first phase occurred during colonial America when colleges were primarily Protestant institutions with faith-based service at their core to promote the common good and prepare young adults (men) to be meaningful members in a just and democratic society (Harkavy, 2004; Hartley, 2011). Later, in an effort to rebuild the country after the Civil War, the Morrill Act of 1862 created land-grant institutions to advance education, democracy, and agricultural science in rural communities (Harkavy, 2004).

The post–Civil War Reconstruction era also launched the second pragmatic phase, establishing the American research university when the German university model was adopted at John Hopkins University in

1876. Faculty began to focus on a narrow disciplinary specialization that generated greater loyalty to their discipline than to the broader public purpose of higher education (Benson et al., 2017; Benson, Harkavy, & Hartley, 2005). This led to generating an educational product that could be consumed by the government and business.

By the time of the Cold War, conditions stimulated a push toward big science that evolved into the entrepreneurial commodification of education (Benson, Harkavy, & Puckett, 2011). "Research parks" began to sprout on university campuses to generate products leading to patents that would financially sustain the institution. Grants were sponsored by government agencies and corporate entities, influencing the research agenda at universities. Although the resulting products make significant contributions to the economy as a whole, this trend contributed to a shift away from civic scholarship and the public mission of higher education. Meanwhile, many college campuses were the epicenter of the social movements and demonstrations related to civil rights, women's rights, protection of the environment, and the Vietnam War.

A malaise emerged after the turbulent 1960s and 1970s, when much of the country as a whole was simply worn out from the strife experienced through the Vietnam War and the civil rights movement. America shifted its attention to personal interest and gratification, often referred to as the "me generation," when many college students were essentially apolitical. Ironically, from this morass came the first inklings of a civic resurrection, on the part of students no less, supported by a handful of idealistic faculty and university presidents. This third phase was political, albeit a pragmatic political movement rather than a partisan political movement. By the 1980s, college campuses were scrambling to provide programmatic infrastructure that could support and sustain this new surge of student volunteerism.

The fourth phase, focusing on pedagogical purpose, began when college administrators and faculty took note of this growing trend of students' extracurricular civic volunteerism to integrate service with learning to arch back toward the original public purpose of higher education. By the late 1980s and early 1990s, professional associations and organizations such as Campus Compact were established as a scholarly scaffold to support this work. Research, publications, and conferences on the pedagogy of service emerged, creating the fifth phase of professionalization, in which the field of community engagement has emerged as its own field with its own research literature and professional organizations. Likewise, a new "community engagement professional" (Dostilio & Perry, 2017, p. 3) has taken on a growing leadership role on campuses to advance community engagement.

As such, it is important to realize and understand that civic and community engagement are really not new to higher education. Yet the public purpose and practice of engagement have largely been lost on many campuses and are not widely known or understood by many administrators or faculty within the academy (see Tool Kit 1.2). Although there has been a historical foundation for the public purpose of higher education, it has reemerged over the past three decades. The

> Tool Kit 1.2—Refer to Exercise 1.2 in your workbook. Find your institution's mission statement. To what extent does it align with Boyer's concept of engaged teaching and learning and the public purpose of higher education? To what extent does this mission of engagement exist or manifest itself on your campus?

Carnegie Foundation for the Advancement of Teaching has established an elective Community Engagement Classification that institutions can apply for and receive.

It is important for you from a pedagogical, philosophical, political, and pragmatic perspective to understand and be able to articulate how and why your interest and efforts in engaged teaching and learning align with your institution's mission. Philosophically, you embody the public purpose of American higher education through this work. Pedagogically, you are playing a role in shaping the minds of young adults and influencing change in the institution and community, as well as disseminating new knowledge to your field. Politically, your engaged scholarship advances social justice as well as confronts the neoliberalization of American higher education. Finally, and pragmatically speaking, as we will discover in more detail later in this chapter, it is imperative that you are able to integrate the academic trilogy as well as justify and articulate how your engaged teaching and scholarship falls within the mission of your institution as you prepare for evaluation and/or promotion and tenure, as discussed in chapter 12. In this way, whenever your engaged work is called into question, you are able to link it to your institution's foundational mission of engagement as you did in Tool Kit 1.2. But what exactly do we mean when we say "engagement" (see Tool Kit 1.3)?

Tool Kit 1.3—Refer to Exercise 1.3 in your workbook. What does engagement mean or look like to you?

What Do We Mean When We Say "Engagement"?

The term *engagement* conjures up many images. At the same time, many administrators and faculty assume they are using the same lexicon when talking about engagement. There is, however, a broad umbrella of experiential education under which a number of similar but distinct approaches and terms fall (Welch, 2017). In a general and very simplified way, experiential education can be thought of as learning that is experienced outside the traditional classroom in the community. This generic and narrow understanding has resulted in a somewhat careless exchange and use of words as synonyms when, in reality, they represent distinct approaches and purposes. The Carnegie Foundation for the Advancement of Teaching (2012) defined *community engagement* as "the collaboration between institutions of higher education and their larger communities (local, regional/state, national, global) for the mutually beneficial exchange of knowledge and resources in a context of partnership and reciprocity." Votruba (1996) characterized community engagement as academic activities that create, disseminate, apply, and preserve knowledge that serves various stakeholders in a variety of settings. Ehrlich (2000) succinctly described civic engagement as "working to make a difference in the civic life of our communities and developing the combination of knowledge, skills, values, and motivation to make that difference" (p. vi). Each of these characterizations reflects Boyer's principles presented at the beginning of this chapter. Likewise, although student learning is at the core, engaged teaching and learning transcends an academic focus to include benefit for the community at large. Traditional community-based experiential educational experiences are student-centric, focusing on assimilating discrete academic knowledge and demonstrating mastery of specific skills to earn professional credentials, licensure, or careers (Welch, 2016, 2017). As examined in much more detail in chapter 3, engaged teaching and learning reflect the tenets presented here and differ from traditional forms of experiential education that take place in community settings (see Figure 1.2).

Community engagement, in contrast, reflects the following key components enumerated by the Kellogg Commission (2001): (a) responsiveness to communities; (b) respect for partners; (c) academic neutrality; (d) access to the academy; (e) integration of the academic trilogy; (f) coordination of efforts through a common agenda; and (g) utilization of assets, resources, and partner groups in the community. Likewise, the Committee on Institutional Cooperation (2005) defined *engagement* as

> the partnership of university knowledge and resources with those of the public and private sectors to enrich scholarship, research, and creative activity; enhance curriculum, teaching and learning; prepare educated, engaged citizens; strengthen democratic values and civic responsibility; address critical societal issues; and contribute to the public good. (para. 5)

In essence, community and civic engagement generate new knowledge through the integration of research, teaching, and service that benefits society (Colby, Ehrlich, Beaumont, & Stephens, 2003; Kuh, 2008; Ramaley, 2010). Bringle and Hatcher (2011) summarize that engagement embodies the following characteristics: (a) it must be scholarly; (b) it must integrate

Figure 1.2 Community-based experiential education umbrella.

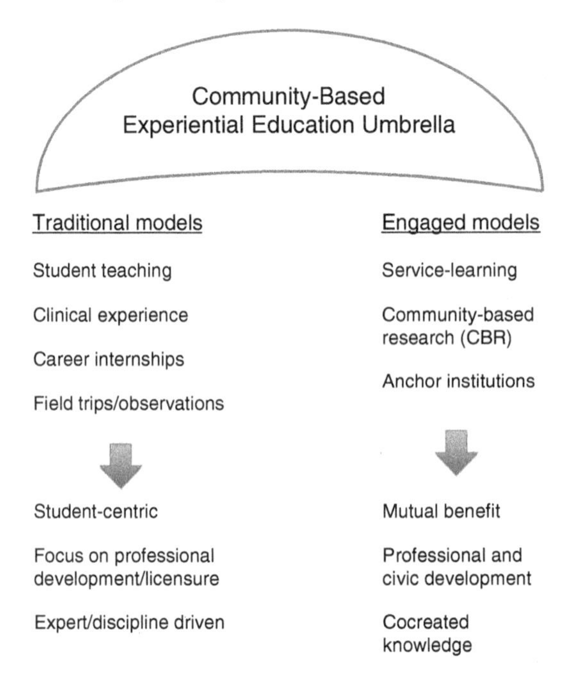

teaching, research, and service; (c) it must be reciprocal and mutually beneficial; and (d) it must encompass and reflect civil democracy. In a report to the Ford Foundation, Lawry, Laurison, and Van Antwerpen (2006) note,

> Civic engagement has become the rubric under which faculty, administrators, and students think about, argue about and attempt to implement a variety of visions of higher education in service to society. . . . There is near consensus that an essential part of civic engagement is feeling responsible to be part of something beyond individual interests. (pp. 12–13)

Engaged Scholarship

Engaged scholarship reflects Boyer's notion of using the rich knowledge and resources of higher education to address social and community needs through research, teaching, and service. Holland (2005) characterized engaged scholarship as the institution and its faculty applying their disciplinary expertise to address public purpose. Similarly, Furco (2005) argued that "engaged scholarship research is done with, rather than for or on a community—an important distinction" (p. 10). Research conducted in this context creates and disseminates knowledge that is beneficial to the discipline as well as the community. He goes on to suggest that the mutual benefit of this approach is that research and scholarship are enhanced and broadened through meaningful input, insight, and involvement by the community. In that light, Simon (2011) proposed that engaged scholarship "continually pushes the boundaries of understanding" (p. 115) through a synergistic interdependence between the institution and community that transcends geographic and socioeconomic boundaries. In this way, community partners bring their own unique public expertise and scholarship to the partnerships as public scholars (Saltmarsh & Hartley, 2011). We will examine engaged scholarship in much more detail in chapter 11. For now, consider possible new insights in Tool Kit 1.4.

> Tool Kit 1.4—Refer to Exercise 1.4 in your workbook. What new insights do you have about engagement? Have your notions about what it is changed at all? How?

Epistemology Versus Engaged Epistemology

We shift our attention to the interface of engaged epistemology within the context of community engagement. Epistemology is the process of how we *know* (Denzin & Lincoln, 1994). In academia, how we know has traditionally been grounded in theoretically based, positivist, and empirical approaches conducted and professed by professors (hence their title) who are experts in a discipline. This knowledge has been generated and tested over time. It is, indeed, important to incorporate sound information and methods in our scholarly work. That said, this approach, as important as it is, has limitations worthy of consideration.

First, our scholarly work is framed by our own personal and scholarly lens, which comes with its own bias and preconceived notions. Therefore, it is incumbent that we recognize not everyone shares that perspective and may view and experience the world in a very different way. A male, Euro-American perspective has dominated the traditional academic perspective; however, that has begun to shift as the professoriate is becoming more diverse. Second, the traditional and almost exclusive beneficiary of scholarship has been the disciplinary field as new knowledge is disseminated through peer-reviewed venues by other scholars with the same scholarly lens. As such, other stakeholders such as the community are often secondary in benefit, if at all. Third, the scholar's academic department and institution benefit from the reputation garnered through widespread dissemination of faculty scholarship. Although this is important, this reputation may come at a cost for marginalized participants and stakeholders. Fourth, the scholar, in turn, is recognized for their impact on the field and rewarded through the promotion and tenure process whereas important players in the process may not be acknowledged or positively impacted by the work.

To be clear, this scenario of traditional scholarship has its merit. Conversely, this epistemic approach can also be narrowly limited to the context of academia with little or no benefit or impact on the broader community outside the ivory tower and derived from the community in ways that are, at best, culturally insensitive or, at worst, exploitive and even oppressive, as we will consider in chapters 4 and 5.

Engaged epistemology, on the other hand, is a significant shift toward an inclusive approach of knowing that is grounded in critical theory (Kincheloe & McLaren, 1994) and critical pedagogy (Freire, 1970, 1998), constructivism (Freire, 1998; Guba & Lincoln, 1994; Schwandt, 1994), and democratization of knowledge (Benson & Harkavy, 2000;

Harkavy, 2004; Harkavy & Benson, 1998; Saltmarsh & Hartley, 2011), in which multiple ways of knowing are incorporated into our scholarship. These theoretical frameworks are briefly described in chapter 2. Engaged epistemology reflects and incorporates the essential tenets of community engagement and engaged pedagogy described previously. An engaged scholar implements engaged epistemology by recognizing, honoring, and using what "public scholars" know, as they are part of the community. These colleagues have a better sense of place and history of the community.

Finally, engaged epistemology addresses what Fricker (2007) calls *epistemic injustice* in which the legitimate perspectives of marginalized individuals or groups are ignored. The oppression and exploitation of these stakeholders are often unintentionally (or sometimes deliberately) perpetuated by scholars imposing traditional rational thought and ideas from academia in contexts and ways that may not be appropriate or useful in other settings and contexts. Engaged epistemology gives voice and agency to the community while making meaningful contributions to scholars' work.

Your Scholarly Identity

We have provided a historical pathway that has brought us to this point. We continue by reflecting on the traditional paradigm of scholarship (see Figure 1.3) that has separated research, teaching, and service operating as mutually exclusive endeavors that are primarily confined to a scholar's work within a departmental discipline with only a secondary ripple effect of impact on the institution and community as a whole (Welch, 2016). It is this existing academic trilogy and paradigm that has shaped your current identity as a scholar.

The main beneficiary of the research is our discipline as new knowledge is generated and disseminated within the disciplinary field through peer-reviewed venues such as journals and/or conference presentations to and for other scholars. This traditional, positivist approach manifests an array of values such as objectivity and identities such as expert, both of which are important. Likewise, traditionally we have had a rather narrow perspective of what teaching entails, with students being the exclusive recipients of knowledge disseminated within courses through lecture, readings, written assignments, and in-class discussions. Assimilating this new knowledge facilitates students passing the course as well as earning a degree with the hope of beginning a career. However, as we will see throughout this book and more specifically in chapter 6, teaching can and should go beyond these traditional roles and goals to include objectives that facilitate a broader, more holistic formation of our students as civically engaged professionals.

Finally, the traditional practice of service within the academic trilogy typically falls within two broad contexts, both important within the academy but with limited impact beyond the ivory tower. One context of service is within the institution in which the scholar is a "good citizen" by serving on various committees and governance boards such as curriculum committees. The second context of service is outside the institution but within the discipline by serving on editorial review boards or in leadership roles within disciplinary professional associations. Within this traditional paradigm, the community at large is a marginal beneficiary or collaborator, if at all. At best, the community becomes a setting where students are "placed" to demonstrate mastery of specific knowledge and skills related to course objectives and/or professional licensure requirements. At worst, the community serves as a laboratory to be experimented "on" by students and faculty with relatively little to no benefit for the community partners. As described in the following sections, engaged scholars broaden our notion of service by integrating the academic trilogy to serve multiple stakeholders in addition to our institutions and discipline.

Figure 1.3 Traditional scholarship paradigm.

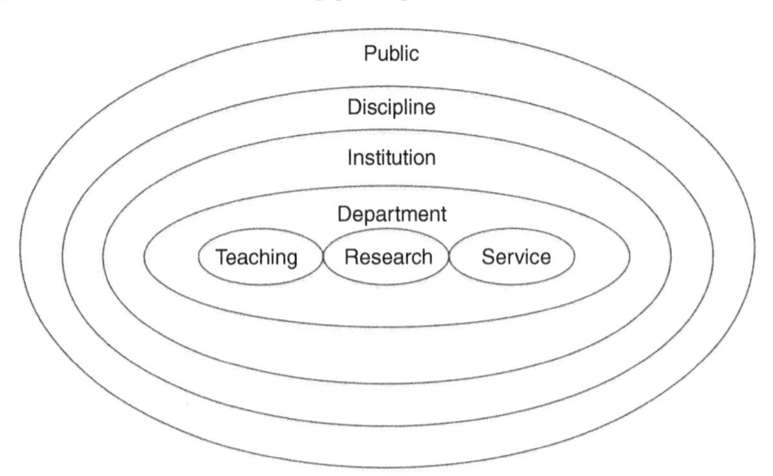

Note. From *Engaging Higher Education: Purpose, Platforms, and Programs for Community Engagement*, p. 56 by M. Welch, 2016, Sterling, VA: Stylus. Copyright 2016 by Stylus Publishing. Used with permission by the publisher.

Becoming an Engaged Scholar

As articulated at the beginning of this chapter and book, you are being invited to become an engaged scholar. It is important to understand this role is not in lieu of traditional responsibilities and expectations of a scholar. Indeed, the traditional role and responsibilities of research, teaching, and service remain, as does disseminating new knowledge within a disciplinary field. However, as an engaged scholar, the academic trilogy is integrated and broadened rather than viewed and actualized as separate and distinct domains. Likewise, contexts and stakeholders have been expanded to reflect a democratic and public approach whereby mutuality is extended to the community. In this way, students and representatives from the community are partners and coeducators, not only in the pedagogical frame of teaching and learning but also in terms of epistemology by reframing how we know and construct knowledge to include public knowledge (see Figure 1.4). The work articulated in this

Figure 1.4 Integrated paradigm: Engaged pedagogy, scholarship, and epistemology.

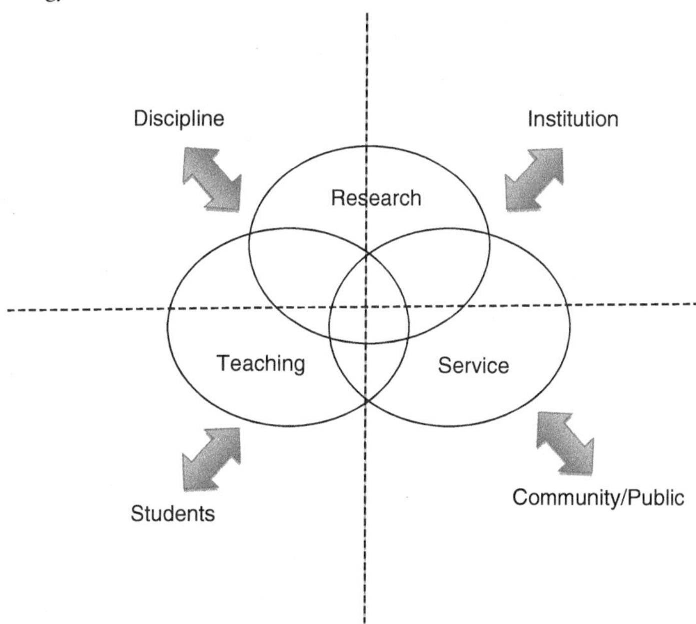

Note. From *Engaging Higher Education: Purpose, Platforms, and Programs for Community Engagement*, p. 56, by M. Welch, 2016, Sterling, VA: Stylus. Copyright 2016 by Stylus Publishing. Used with permission by the publisher.

book and workbook reconceptualizes the traditional paradigm into an engaged paradigm that integrates engaged pedagogy, scholarship, and epistemology.

We begin this identity shift by expanding the traditional perspective of academic roles that, in turn, spontaneously shape your identity and behaviors. Each of us takes on several identities or labels that define us. We do this by saying, "I am a . . . ," followed by filling in the blanks with various titles or identities. Some of these titles and identities, such as "sibling," "daughter/son," or "Latina/Latino," are given to us. Other identities are chosen. For example, one might say, "I am a sociologist, a Republican, a Lutheran, a Cubs fan, a vegetarian." Some identities, like racial heritage, are somewhat (but not always) apparent and others are not, perhaps even hidden, such as sexual/gender identity and preference. One could step back and for each and every one of those titles or identities ask, "What does that look like? What does that mean? What does that reflect or imply?" There would be any number of characteristics or behaviors that define a specific role and identity. Given certain circumstances and periods within our lives, the scope of these roles and responsibilities ebbs and flows as a result of values on a philosophical level and sheer logistical demands on our time and energy at a pragmatic level.

Our role and actions as scholars are shaped by and vacillate according to other contexts such as family, values, gender, heritage, economics, and politics, to name a few. Colleagues at the Office of Community Engagement at Indiana University–Purdue University Indianapolis (IUPUI) have included and incorporated useful approaches to mapping our personal, professional, and scholarly identities (Price, 2017). Building on their work, we now offer a similar opportunity in your workbook for you to reflect on your values and various roles that comprise your identity, in Tool Kits 1.5 and 1.6.

> Tool Kit 1.5—Refer to Exercise 1.5 in your workbook to reflect on your values and roles as a scholar.

> Tool Kit 1.6—Refer to Exercise 1.6 in your workbook to reflect on and map your present academic identity using the academic trilogy as a context.

An engaged scholar strategically looks at how to integrate research, teaching, and scholarship in multiple settings. This is a somewhat radical approach to how academics traditionally approach the academic trilogy. It is important to note that this approach does not necessarily mean "more work" but it does, as we will see in later chapters, require a different kind of work that is often "messy" because there are more moving parts, as depicted in Tool Kit Exercises 1.7 and 1.8.

Tool Kit 1.7 and Tool Kit 1.8—Refer to Exercise 1.7 and Exercise 1.8 in your workbook and read the case study as an example for integrating the academic trilogy as a form of integrated engaged epistemology. Then, identify and list the roles, values, behaviors, and products/impacts of the engaged scholar exemplified in the case study.

These case study examples illustrate how the traditional academic trilogy can be integrated to reflect the values and work of an engaged scholar. The remaining chapters and the Tool Kit exercises in your workbook are designed to help you continue the process of becoming an engaged scholar.

Honing Your Craft

So what does engaged scholarship look like? This will become clearer in the pages to come. For now, we refer you to the efforts of a working group sponsored by the Community-Campus Partnership for Health (Jordan et al., 2009) and the Office of Community Engagement at IUPUI (Price, 2017) who have adapted and expanded the six standards of scholarship developed by Glassick, Huber, and Maeroff (1997) into eight standards that serve as a rubric to assess and evaluate faculty members' engaged work as part of the promotion and tenure review process. However, we would also suggest that these standards could serve as more than just an evaluation metric. Rather, they can function as an ethos and a set of behaviors to guide your work as an engaged scholar. The following are Glassick and colleagues' (1997) standards:

1. Clearly articulated academic and community goals
2. Adequate preparation in disciplinary content area and grounding in engaged public scholarship
3. Appropriate methods that reflect and include rigor and tenets of community engagement

4. Significant results that impact the field and the community
5. Effective presentation and dissemination to both scholarly and community audiences
6. Reflective critique to identify and articulate insight to improve scholarship and community engagement
7. Demonstration and promotion of leadership and scholarly contributions coupled with agency and parity by all participants and stakeholders
8. Consistent ethical behavior coupled with cultural competence and socially responsible conduct

In Tool Kit 1.9 we invite you to reflect on the extent to which these standards of engaged scholarship are known and implemented in your setting.

Tool Kit 1.9—Honing Your Craft—Refer to Exercise 1.9 in your workbook. Reflect on the standards of engaged scholarship. To what extent are these known and implemented in your setting? To what extent do you already meet these standards? Do and can you envision these as not only a standard for assessing engaged scholarship but also possible benchmarks for scholarly identity and behavior?

Chapter 2

THEORETICAL FRAMEWORKS FOR ENGAGED TEACHING AND LEARNING

Theoretical frameworks were incorporated into our graduate programs to prepare us to be scholars in our respective disciplines. As such, nearly every field of study uses theory as a structure or plan consisting of concepts, constructs, or variables and the relationships among them that explain a phenomenon and that can be used to translate research into practice through process models consisting of implementation steps (Nilsen, 2015). The introduction to this book even describes the theoretical frameworks that shaped our approach to faculty development.

However, most faculty receive little to no pedagogical preparation on how to teach or on the dynamics of teaching and learning in traditional classroom settings, let alone in authentic settings through community engagement. In an unpublished white paper for the Pew Charitable Trust, Russell Edgerton, president emeritus of the American Association for Higher Education and visiting scholar at the Carnegie Foundation for the Advancement of Teaching, noted:

> The dominant mode of teaching and learning in higher education [is] "teaching as telling; learning as recall." . . . This mode of instruction fails to help students acquire two kinds of learning that are now crucial to their individual success and critically needed by our society at large. The

> first is real understanding. The second is "habits of the heart" that motivate students to be caring citizens. Both of these qualities are acquired through pedagogies that elicit intense engagement. (quoted in Swaner, 2012, p. 80)

Refer to Tool Kit 2.1 to reflect on Edgerton's statement and your formal teaching preparation, if any, during your graduate studies.

> Tool Kit 2.1—Refer to Exercise 2.1 in your workbook and reflect on Russell Edgerton's statement as well as to what extent you received any preparation on the dynamics of teaching and learning during your graduate studies. In essence, where and how did you learn how to teach in a college classroom?

Your intuition as an educator likely allows you to shape effective learning experiences, even if you aren't currently using a theoretical framework to do so. However, we argue that your community-engaged course will be even more effective if you integrate theoretical frameworks to maximize your course's academic potential as well as minimize the risk of exploiting community partners or inflicting hardship. This chapter is not designed or intended to "proselytize," or encourage you to "convert" to a specific theoretical model. Instead, this chapter is designed to inform your engaged teaching and help prepare you for articulating a theoretical framework of your engaged course to your students, community partners, colleagues, and later a performance evaluation review committee.

This chapter continues by providing a theoretical foundation for transformative education that promotes engaged teaching and learning. We also provide an overview of several theoretical frameworks that can and may inform your engaged teaching and student learning. This is not an exhaustive list nor is it a detailed description, as there is an array of frameworks to choose from that have entire books devoted to them. We draw upon an entire field known as SoTL, as previously mentioned. Potter and Kustra (2011) defined *SoTL* as

> the systematic study of teaching and learning, using established or validated criteria of scholarship, to understand how teaching (beliefs, behaviors, attitudes, and values) can maximize learning, and/or develop a more accurate understanding of learning, resulting in products that are publicly shared for critique and use by an appropriate community. (p. 2)

This chapter concludes with an overarching heuristic theoretical framework that incorporates the salient concepts presented here to inform and guide your engaged teaching and learning as an engaged scholar.

Transformative Education

As argued throughout this book, engaged teaching and learning can be a transformative educational experience. Harward (2012) characterized the gestalt of transformative teaching and learning as being composed of at least three dimensions. The first is epistemological, consisting of (a) a focus on "knowing that," meaning students learn information and facts to be studied (this typically dominates the teaching paradigm); (b) "knowing how to" in which students apply their assimilated knowledge and skills; and (c) "judgment," in which students discern a relationship between knowledge and action. We contend that the judgment component represents critical reflection that is explored in more detail in this chapter and chapter 9. Harward's second dimension of the transformative aspects of engaged teaching and learning is psychosocial in nature. Here, learning is integrated with the holistic development of the student to have an impact on their identity, dispositions, and behaviors. The third dimension is the civic dimension that emphasizes the integration of learning about the self with the common good of others and the community as a whole.

Theoretical Foundations

If there is a cornerstone to the theoretical foundation of engaged teaching and learning, it is most likely the work of John Dewey. Benson, Harkavy, and Puckett (2007) provide an extensive and exhaustive examination of his life and work in the context of community engagement. Written during the recovery from the horrors of the World War I, Dewey's salient points, focused on experience, democracy, and reflection, essentially frame what has become known as engaged teaching and learning. Early on, Dewey (1916) recognized and espoused the civic role education plays in advancing a democratic society in his landmark book *Democracy and Education*. His later books, *How We Think: A Restatement of the Relation of Reflective Thinking to the Educational Process* (1933) and *Experience and Education* (1938), introduced how experience and reflection on that experience shape learning. Likewise, he envisioned a *great community* developed and sustained through community schools. In 1899 Dewey espoused laboratory schools to provide hands-on learning to accentuate meaning-making and problem-solving through experience and reflection in his book *The School and Society* (Dewey, 1976). This approach, although not implemented in authentic community settings, became the theoretical premise for engaged teaching and learning. In sum, Dewey advocated reflective action, collaboration, and real-world problem-solving to advance a democratic society and foster intellect in individuals, groups, communities, and society as a whole (Benson et al., 2007; Benson et al., 2017).

A Taxonomy of Educational Experience

In contrast to Edgerton's characterization of traditional pedagogy consisting of "teaching as telling; learning as recall" (quoted in Swaner, 2012, p. 80) as described in the opening of this chapter, Bloom's taxonomy (Bloom, Engelhart, Furst, Hill, & Krathwohl, 1956) consists of a hierarchy of cognitive skills: (a) recall, (b) comprehension, (c) application, (d) analysis, (e) evaluation, and (f) creativity. The first two levels of the hierarchy reflect traditional didactic approaches of teaching and learning whereas the third level, application, is typically included within professional preparation programs or internships. The remaining three levels—analysis, evaluation, and creativity—are intentionally integrated within the learning experience through reflection and continued engagement in authentic settings. Similarly, Hart (2009) described a taxonomy of educational experience that shapes the consciousness of an individual in his book *From Information to Transformation*. The initial step or level is the pursuit and accumulation of information. Many students are at this concrete level, in which they equate acquiring factoids with learning. Much of the didactic approach of teaching perpetuates this format. It is essentially a transactional experience of paying tuition in exchange for a degree, which then presumably leads to a career. Hart continues by describing the second level as knowledge, in which direct experience leads to mastery of skills and concepts. Next comes intelligence, in which the learner integrates intuitive and analytic behaviors. The fourth level is understanding, followed by wisdom as the fifth level, which is characterized as blending truth with the ethics of what is right. Finally, this leads to transformation or waking up.

Experiential Learning Model

David A. Kolb and Roger Fry (1984) developed a learning model that reflects basic tenets of the scientific method and can be applied to community-engaged teaching and learning (see Figure 2.1). Their

Figure 2.1 Kolb's experiential learning model.

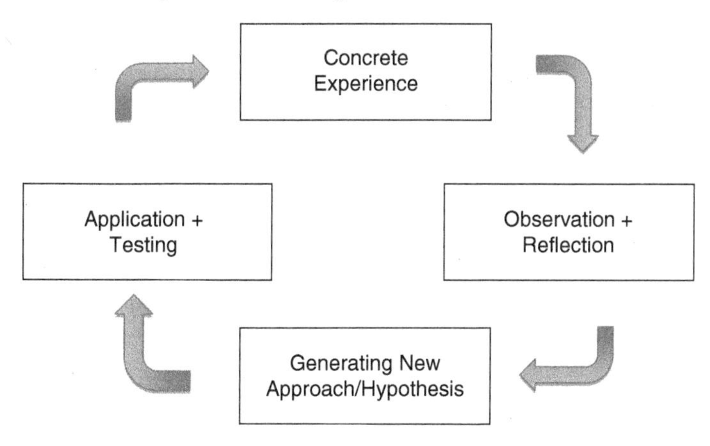

approach consists of four components and steps that can be initiated at any one of the four points. Incorporating Dewey's ideas, concrete experience is one of the four components, followed by observing and reflecting on what was experienced. The third step consists of generating new, abstract ideas or actions based on observation and reflection on the experience. These speculations or behaviors are then applied and tested in the fourth step. This continued spiraling process allows the learner to be actively engaged in the learning process as well as provides an opportunity to reflect on the outcomes.

Critical Reflection

Critical reflection is a key component to engaged teaching and learning. Influenced by Dewey and similar to Kolb and Fry's work, Schon (1987) described reflective practice as the process professionals use to gain insight into their way of knowing through experience. Coming from a background of design and organizational development, Schon viewed learning as having three components. The first consists of governing variables, which are factors that impact learning and behaviors. Second is an action strategy that people or groups employ to manage those variables. Third are the consequences of those strategic actions and decisions. The key here is the critical reflection that is involved in each of the three variables. He operationalized critical reflection in the following ways: (a) reflection-in-action, (b) reflection-on-action, and (c) knowing-in-action. Reflection-in-action is essentially engaging in a conversation with what is happening to seek insight and understanding. Reflection-on-action represents a post hoc summative analysis of the outcomes of what occurred. Knowing-in-action or tacit knowledge is the application of what has been derived from the reflection process in new or similar situations.

Mezirow's Transformative Learning Theory

Mezirow (1991, 1999, 2000) developed a transformative learning theory composed of 10 steps within 3 phases. The first phase represents cognitive dissonance or a disorienting dilemma when individuals encounter an experience that challenges their preconceived assumptions about the world. The second phase involves critical reflection through assessing the self and the sociocultural context in which individuals find themselves and the experience. The third phase is determining a course of action based on seeking, obtaining, and considering new information that can be applied to the experience or situation, resulting in transformation or change within the individual or the behavior. Students often experience disorienting dilemmas that challenge their assumptions during engaged coursework and their experience in community settings that differ from their own life's context. Reflection is the key to processing this experience in which an instructor does not rescue the student or "solve their problem" but, instead, accompanies them through what Welch (2010b) called the shadow-side of reflection to make meaning.

Pedagogy of Engagement

Colby and colleagues (2003) identified and described eight principles of best practice that constitute a pedagogy of engagement. Their principles are not limited to engaging with the community but certainly can be applied and transferred to that setting. Instead, this form of pedagogy entails active participation in the learning process rather than passively ingesting information from an instructor. The following are principles of best practice:

1. Learning is an active, constructive process.
2. Genuine and enduring learning occurs when students are enthusiastic about their educational experience.
3. Thinking and learning are active and social processes.
4. Knowledge and skills are shaped by the contexts in which they are learned.
5. Transfer of knowledge and skill occurs when they are learned in similar settings.
6. Intentional reflection and informative feedback is essential to learning.

7. Students have different levels and clusters of skills.
8. Genuine learning is facilitated by the ability of students to represent ideas and skills in more than one modality as well as moving to and from those various forms of knowing.

High-Impact Practices

Kuh (2008) suggested high-impact practices (HIPs) have six characteristics that can be used by instructors as pedagogical constructs to inform their teaching and students' learning. First, HIPs require students to spend more time and deepen their investment of energy in purposeful tasks on an almost daily basis. Second, students and faculty must interact on significant topics and activities over extended periods of time. Third, this type of activity typically provides opportunities for students to experience diversity in a variety of settings with an array of people who represent different backgrounds and experiences. Fourth, frequent feedback is generally provided. Fifth, students can apply and test what they are learning in the classroom in authentic settings off campus. Sixth, HIPs can provide transformative experiences as students develop and engage in meaningful interactions with faculty, other students, and other stakeholders from different contexts. Swaner (2012) argued HIPs can be considered as forms of engaged pedagogy because they promote students' developmental and holistic dimensions of thinking, feeling, and relating while integrating cognitive connections from course content with social contexts and communities.

These theoretical frameworks may be new to you. You may actually have been using them. We invite you to reflect on these theoretical foundations in Tool Kit 2.2.

> Tool Kit 2.2—Refer to Exercise 2.2 in your workbook to review and identify specific theoretical foundations presented thus far that resonate with you and/or that you have intentionally or unintentionally implemented in your teaching. Which, if any, of these concepts were new to you?

Theoretical Frameworks

Building on the theoretical foundation presented previously, the remainder of this chapter offers a cursory overview of a number of theoretical frameworks that can be used to support engaged teaching and learning.

Critical Theory

In many ways, Brazilian educator Paulo Freire might be considered the Dewey of critical theory, as his revolutionary ideas and concepts serve as a foundation in constructing critically engaged teaching and learning experiences. He viewed education as a political act and challenged mainstream pedagogy as a "banking" model in which knowledge is essentially "deposited" into the minds and consciousnesses of students and workers who were expected to be objective, impartial, and passive repositories of truth and facts intended to perpetuate oppression (Darder, 2015, 2017). As an alternative, Freire advocated for a critical consciousness to think skeptically about information and knowledge as well as its source. He described praxis as a pedagogy of reflection and action designed to empower the oppressed and bring about social change. Freire's concept of praxis argues that dialogue designed merely to generate and disseminate knowledge is not enough as it must also include critical reflection on the social construction of reality to bring about change (Freire Institute, 2018). This process requires listening carefully to all stakeholders (especially those whose voices have traditionally been silenced or ignored), engaging in authentic dialogue, and demonstrating respect through actions. This level of listening goes beyond receiving auditory factual information to include "hearing the story" of those telling their experience, generating an awareness of the affective and emotional dynamics of the context, and maintaining awareness of the "sense of place" embedded within a community setting.

Feminist Theories

Feminist theoretical and philosophical traditions afford another framework for organizing the community-engaged learning experience. Jane Addams, a contemporary of John Dewey, created a pedagogy of feminist pragmatism that recognizes that people are motivated by a combination of emotion and rationality and that cooperative and nonviolent challenges to power and injustice can lead to social change (Deegan, 2017). Contemporary critical feminists have further articulated theories that have implications for teaching and social activism. In her book *Teaching Community: A Pedagogy of Hope*, bell hooks (2003) reflects a spiritual approach of incorporating struggle, service, and shared knowledge and learning to create a "beloved community" (p. 35). Like prior feminist scholars and critical theorists, hooks views education as a political tool that can mobilize forces for liberation and equity—in this case, for African Americans from colonization by White supremacist systems. We also want to lift up contemporary women's studies scholars who have applied feminist theories directly to their service-learning and community-engaged courses. Seethaler (2015) argues that a feminist theoretical framework requires students to examine issues of power, privilege, and oppression in order to empower them to challenge social institutions and cultural practices that marginalize particular groups in their service-learning experiences. Further, Trigg and Balliet (2000) posit that for service (learning) to be effective it must adhere to principles of collaboration, respect, nonjudgment, and mutual transformation. Thus, we see implications for the design of course content as well as of the community engagement experience addressed in critical feminist theory.

Critical Race Theory

Though critical race theory (CRT) emerged from scholars in legal studies (Bell, 1980; Crenshaw, 1988; Matsuda, 1987; Williams, 1991) it can be applied as a framework for community-engaged learning. CRT explicitly names White privilege and White supremacy as oppressive forces that shape and confine the lives of Black Americans (and other people of color). This occurs through adhering to color-blind ideology, erasing the narratives of people of color in historical and contemporary educational texts and popular media, essentializing and stereotyping identity groups, and enacting macro- and microaggressions on people of color at the interpersonal, institutional, systemic, and cultural levels (Delgado & Stefancic, 2012). In terms of addressing the pervasive oppressions asserted by CRT, scholars emphasize counterstorytelling to affirm the validity, as well as the necessity, of the voices, perspectives, and experiences of marginalized and oppressed groups to gain insight into social construction of race and ultimately dismantle it as an oppressive construct (Delgado & Stefancic, 2012; Tate, 1997). This approach is especially important in the context of curating engaged course content as it calls educators to seek alternative sources of information from traditional academic texts to expose students to diverse and contentious perspectives on what students might have historically perceived as common sense. Further, this approach requires educators to prepare students to learn from the people they encounter and interact with in the community, and to see them as holders of valuable wisdom. Crenshaw (1991) extends CRT to illuminate the intersectional nature of "-isms" and how they magnify harmful impacts on people who hold multiple marginalized identities. CRT calls into question traditional colonial and positivist worldviews perpetuated in academia and how those translate into concepts and practices of education and service.

Social Development Theory and Constructivism

Vygotsky (1978) proposed a theory of learning that incorporates social interaction and social learning. A key component of his model that clearly reflects the importance of community partners as coeducators is his concept of the *more knowledgeable other* (MKO), who can be any individual who holds more knowledge or experience than a learner and is perceived as and takes the role of a coach or mentor. One might assume this to be the instructor but it can be students as well as community partners as public scholars. The MKO is then integrated into what Vygotsky called the *zone of proximal development* (ZPD), whereby the learner is allowed to develop or construct skills on their own, but with the guidance of the MKO. In essence, a student or a group of students is provided a set of tools to apply in the learning setting to "construct" their own learning experience. Vygotsky contended that the shared use of tools provides a sociocultural context that promotes social interaction through shared experiences. The metaphorical use of the words and concepts of *tools* and *constructing* has contributed to a related theoretical framework of constructivism in which learning and knowledge are thought to be socially constructed.

Constructivism is an alternative to positivist and objective inquiry in which knowledge is coconstructed through a variety of coordinated activities and human interactions (Schwandt, 1994). A heuristic and spiraling framework of iteration, analysis, and critique, followed by reiteration, reanalysis, and recritique, is essentially a form of reflection that is employed by multiple stakeholders or "knowers" to collaboratively create a construction that emanates or evolves from inquiry to determine if they "work" or "fit" with a credible level of understanding (Guba & Lincoln, 1994). This shared inquiry acknowledges and incorporates the values and perspectives of both the researcher and research participants. These constructions are used to interpret experience and make meaning. In the context of engaged teaching and learning, the concept of coconstructing knowledge in authentic settings *with*, as opposed to *for*, community partners reflects the democratic dimension of community engagement.

We now invite you reflect on these theoretical frameworks in Tool Kit 2.3 to identify which may resonate with you and why.

> Tool Kit 2.3—Refer to Exercise 2.3 in your workbook. Reflect on and discuss the premise and constructs of these theoretical frameworks. Which ones resonate with you and why? Which, if any, of these constructs were new to you? Are any of these applicable to the engaged course you are teaching or plan to teach?

A Triadic Theoretical Framework for Engaged Teaching and Learning

To summarize, we offer a very basic triadic theoretical framework for engaged teaching and learning that incorporates many of the salient pedagogical concepts presented previously. In essence, engaged teaching and learning are composed of the following components: (a) epistemology as multiple ways of knowing with an emphasis on the intellectual development of a student as well as generating new knowledge that builds capacity for society at large, (b) ontology as a way of being or doing in the world by applying what is learned and experienced, and (c) critical reflection to contemplate and make meaning of the learning and doing (see Figure 2.2). To simplify, this framework consists of and integrates the *head, heart, and hands*.

This framework incorporates tenets of experiential learning espoused by Hutchings and Wutzdorff (1988), whereby students bridge the

Figure 2.2 Integrated triadic framework for engaged teaching and learning.

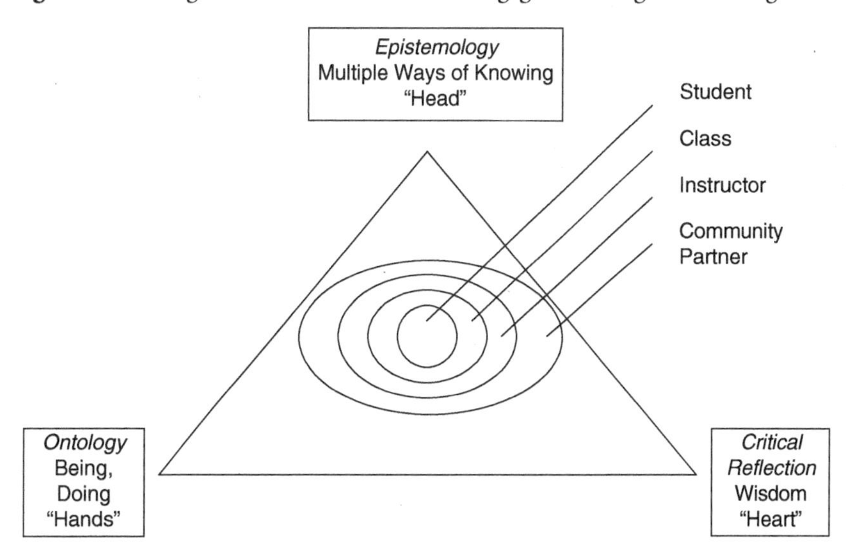

"knowing" or study of something with "doing" the subject, which is mediated through reflection. However, as discussed throughout this book and accompanying workbook, we advocate for and apply a democratized form of public scholarship that provides and allows for multiple ways of knowing and that includes the perspective of the community (Saltmarsh & Hartley, 2011). This expanded epistemological perspective offers multiple ways of knowing and includes an array of theoretical frameworks briefly described previously that offer alternative perspectives on and approaches to teaching and learning. Similarly, we argue that the ontological component of this engaged framework not only includes but also transcends application as a form of practicing assimilated knowledge and skills to promote a way of being an engaged citizen (Colby et al., 2003). Finally, critical reflection, as espoused by Dewey (1933), Schon (1987), and Mezirow (1999, 2000), provides an opportunity for students to intentionally consider and integrate their experience into what they are learning as well as how to function and be in the world to become what Hatcher (2008) calls a *civic-minded professional*. Each of the triadic components of this framework must be implemented to be considered as engaged teaching and learning (see Tool Kit 2.4).

Tool Kit 2.4—Refer to Exercise 2.4 in your workbook to discuss the triadic theoretical framework of engaged teaching and learning.

Honing Your Craft

We began this chapter by acknowledging that theoretical frameworks of teaching and learning are often somewhat unknown to many faculty members. Theoretical models are not merely abstract philosophical tenets to "believe in." They are, in fact, principles that guide our practice. They become, in essence, benchmarks for us to use to critically reflect on and assess what and how we're doing as we cocreate and codisseminate new knowledge with our students and community partners.

The constructs presented in this chapter may very well challenge our traditional assumptions regarding teaching and learning, including the notion that education can be a form of political action. In one respect, the civic dimension of engaged teaching and learning reflects Aristotle's depiction of *politika* as affairs of the state so students learn that they, as *politikos* or "citizens," are responsible for making decisions about the affairs of the state. In another respect, the critical theory described briefly here reflects overt and explicit political action to bring about social justice. The political aspect of critical theory may be more applicable to certain types of courses and disciplines than others. That said and as we will see through examples in later chapters and exercises in the workbook, even traditional "hard science" courses such as environmental studies and biology can explore political issues such as environmental racism and the implications it has on both the student as preprofessional and the policies that impact marginalized neighborhoods.

We also recognize and acknowledge that both of these political perspectives represent an alternative to a traditional notion of objectivity that is embedded in academic culture. Therefore, some of these ideas may be new, even creating what Mezirow termed a *disorienting dilemma* that challenges your previous assumptions about scholarship. Keep in mind that even the most seemingly innocuous act, such as choosing a textbook for a course, reveals our personal, professional, and academic preferences and biases. The notion of reciprocal validity (Welch et al., 2005) is a hybrid approach in which traditional positivistic approaches are combined with and enhanced by the voice and perspective of participant voices, such as students or community members, in ways that cause Baer and Schwartz (1991) to ask the provocative question whether "we [scholars] are presumed more rational than 'they' [practitioners or laypeople]" (p. 232). This approach allows scholars and teachers to determine if the theoretical foundations articulated in the literature and taught in classrooms are accurate and/or applicable (see Tool Kit 2.5).

Tool Kit 2.5—Honing Your Craft—Refer to Exercise 2.5 in your workbook to discuss ways of honing your craft by incorporating theoretical frameworks and constructs into your course.

Chapter 3

FORMS OF COMMUNITY-ENGAGED PEDAGOGY

Just as artisans must pay attention to the form and function of their handiwork, so too must you consider the various forms that your community-engaged course might take based on the desired function defined by you, your community partner, and your students. Before we jump in, we just want to say that, unless you are a sociologist or ethnic studies scholar, you may find some of the forthcoming information a bit new and somewhat challenging to integrate into your course. As discussed in the previous chapter, we understand that most faculty are not explicitly educated in community engagement or social justice pedagogies during their doctoral program formation. We recognize that much of what we, and other community engagement scholars, recommend is aspirational and not necessarily something that can be quickly and easily implemented. Likewise, this approach may not readily resonate with some departments and institutions. That's why we frame community-engaged teaching as a craft. There will always be room to grow, innovate, and strive for a better approximation of the ideal. Take a moment now to reflect on your understanding of community-engaged learning in Tool Kit 3.1.

> Tool Kit 3.1—Refer to Exercise 3.1 in your workbook to jot down your current understanding of community-engaged learning.

Community-Engaged Pedagogy Defined

Regardless of how your understanding of community-engaged pedagogies has developed, we hope you hold space for consideration of multiple forms and frameworks that fall within the rubric of community-engaged pedagogy. To begin, let's hear from a few faculty who describe community-engaged learning in their own words. Swipe your smartphone or tablet over the QR code found in Figure 3.1 and respond to the questions posed in Tool Kit 3.2.

Figure 3.1 What is community-engaged learning?

Note. Scan the QR code to access https://vimeo.com/207844757/77e23e45a9

> Tool Kit 3.2—Refer to Exercise 3.2 in your workbook. Watch the engaging conversation video clip to learn more about what community-engaged learning entails. Respond to the questions in your workbook about the video clip you viewed.

Dimensions of Community-Engaged Courses

Although the faculty in the video clip may make community-engaged learning sound simple and neat, the reality is that there's great complexity in plying this craft. The practice of community-engaged teaching requires one to work through a pragmatic process of cocreating student learning experiences and positive social change with multiple stakeholders. Given the requirement for flexibility, we eschew a narrow and uniform definition of *community-engaged pedagogy*. Instead, we offer three dimensions, or essential elements, that must be present in a course in some form for it to be classified as community engaged. The dimensions, while loosely framing the parameters of the practice, also allow for great flexibility in course design and implementation. In essence, a community-engaged course is defined by its purpose, process, and relationships.

Purpose

Faculty should design the course to equitably and harmoniously balance two goals (in addition to disciplinary learning outcomes):

1. Develop students' knowledge, skills, and dispositions for informed engagement in civic life and positive social change endeavors.
2. Contribute to building the capacity of community members and institutions to achieve a public purpose and foster the common good.

Process

Faculty should focus their attention on not only the outcomes but also the process by which activities are designed, implemented, and assessed. Essentially, faculty should do the following:

- Draw on student and community voices to shape learning and engagement activities.
- Infuse content and pedagogical practices that foster student learning about social justice issues, personal values development, and mechanisms for positive social change.
- Integrate guided critical reflection before, during, and after engagement to help students make meaning of intersections between academic content and community experiences.
- Include formative and summative assessment of student learning and community outcomes to improve current and future community engagement.

Relationships

Unlike a traditional classroom-bound course, the community-engaged course requires different faculty approaches, such as the following:

- Fostering reciprocal and authentic *relationships* that honor community partners as coeducators
- Reflecting shared leadership and solidarity with community over transactional relationships
- Prioritizing sustained community relationships
- Communicating expectations, limitations, ongoing feedback, and plans for addressing interpersonal and institutional challenges

Now is a good time to consider and develop a deeper understanding of the elements that comprise community-engaged learning in Tool Kit 3.3.

Tool Kit 3.3—Refer to Exercise 3.3 in your workbook to further consider the essential elements of community-engaged learning and develop a deeper understanding of them.

Foci, Forms, and Frameworks

We now turn our attention to the various foci, forms, and frameworks an instructor can incorporate when designing a community-engaged course.

Foci of Community-Engaged Pedagogy

Community-engaged pedagogy can be molded to integrate one or more areas of focus rooted in theoretical frameworks for learning. In this section, we've adapted descriptions of each known focus of community-engaged pedagogy from Heffernan's (2001) taxonomy. Note that these foci are not necessarily mutually exclusive and might sometimes be combined into hybrid courses.

Civic Focus

Civically focused service-learning describes a course in which the content and pedagogy are selected specifically to develop students' civic knowledge, skills, and behaviors. A number of individual scholars and faculty-driven councils have articulated specific civic competencies that can be used as blueprints for course and program development. One resource is *Civic Engagement Across the Curriculum: A Resource Book for Service-Learning Faculty in All Disciplines* (Battistoni, 2002). The book presents eight specific skills students need to be engaged citizens: political knowledge and critical thinking skills, communication skills, public problem-solving, civic judgment, civic imagination and creativity, collective action, community/coalition building, and organizational skills. In these courses, students learn about civic processes and democratic participation while also engaging off campus at organizations that contribute to the common good. This type of course may be interdisciplinary. The benefit of this type of course is the freedom to focus on covering content that directly contributes to students' development as civic actors. Further, it allows for a broad range of engagement experiences, including things like registering voters, canvassing, doing policy research, supporting advocacy campaigns, and so on. The challenge is that the course may not seem essential or rigorous by departmental standards. However, there are examples of high-quality courses, such as the Public Service and Community Engagement Capstone at the University of San Francisco. Students learn about theoretical frameworks of leadership and social change traditions while working collectively with a local nonprofit to complete a community-identified project. Students are simultaneously learning about ways they can play a role in strengthening community, practicing the skills needed to be effective in community change efforts, analyzing the implications of their participation, and investigating the role of organizations in addressing justice issues in society.

Disciplinary Focus

In engaged courses that have a disciplinary focus, a primary purpose is to facilitate student learning of disciplinary content. The instructor selects community partners who can provide experiences for students that animate, illustrate, and complicate disciplinary concepts and theories. Examples of disciplines from which these courses emerge include environmental science, communication studies, media studies, computer science, or biology. The benefit of this type of course is that the focus on disciplinary learning makes it easy to justify as an addition to a program. Also, students demonstrate a deeper commitment to courses that help them advance their competencies in their major field of study. However, accountability to disciplinary outcomes can sometimes be in tension with addressing the priorities and needs of community partners. Further, when instructors have a body of content that they have to cover to meet disciplinary outcomes, they have less flexibility to integrate civic content and opportunities for discussion and reflection about other inherent aspects of the community-engaged experience.

Project Focus

This form connects students to a project that addresses a community-articulated challenge. Like civically focused service-learning, this type of course thrives on interdisciplinarity, bringing together faculty and students from across disciplines to leverage their theoretical lenses, content expertise, and scholarly skills for the purpose of completing a project or contributing to an ongoing project that addresses a persistent problem. These projects tend to work when they are owned and guided by community-based organizations. The "engaged component" of project-focused courses will likely involve a combination of direct and indirect service. Examples of projects might include things like conducting a survey or implementing lead testing in local water sources. Students and faculty may need to immerse themselves in direct dialogue and interactions with community members and/or observation of the environment to gain information that will guide an intervention. One might expect to find courses like this in graduate programs in public affairs or nonprofit management or in undergraduate business administration courses.

A benefit of this form of engaged pedagogy is that it can replicate how working professionals come together across sectors to address social issues. It requires teamwork and deployment of individuals' complementary competencies toward a common goal. A fundamental challenge is time; it's extremely difficult to learn the landscape of a community, including its assets and challenges, and plan and implement a collaborative community-based project within a single academic term. Effective solutions require time, expertise, and an insider perspective to shape realistic interventions.

Competency Focus

There are a number of variations of this form, including practica, internships, fieldwork, and capstones. An important purpose of this type of course is to guide students to enhance and apply professional skills and disciplinary knowledge in a real-world setting. As such, most of these types of courses tend to be student-centric as the focus is on students assimilating and demonstrating competency of specific skills to receive professional licensure or credentials that may potentially detour the experience from mutuality of community partner goals, which is a key component to the tenets of community engagement (Welch, 2017). However, that is not always the case, especially when community partners such as school districts are actively involved in the development of preprofessional preparation experiences that include critical reflection and emphasize social justice or public purpose as defined by the partner (Welch, 2018). Courses usually involve a significant community-engaged commitment, with students on-site for around 8 to 10 hours per week. The benefit of these types of courses is that they are often a bridge between students' scholarly interests and a potential career trajectory. Relatedly, host organizations can benefit significantly from the contributions of interns or preprofessionals who make robust time commitments. Although there are several potential benefits, there's room for challenges to emerge. We will cover more of this in chapter 8.

An example of competency-focused community engagement is the University of San Francisco's Design Activism course. The instructor reaches out to community partners to collaboratively identify needed design projects, and then matches students one-to-one with a community partner and project. Students develop and practice their design skills by completing projects like composing a promotional video, developing the layout for an annual report, or creating a brand logo. Simultaneously, students learn about how organizations and movements rely on graphic design to communicate their messages to various audiences, and also examine how to make designs accessible to otherwise marginalized groups.

Solidarity Focus

A number of institutions offer credit-based courses that feature local or global immersions. Faculty lead students into communities affected by injustice for time periods that range from a week to a semester. Faculty prepare students for this experience, support their progression through it, and help them process the experience afterward by integrating academic content and reflection opportunities. The role of students in these community-engaged courses is usually that of participant observers. They may join in community events and activities, visit social service organizations, and meet with social change leaders and community residents. Pure immersions often intentionally don't include a traditional service component because one of the goals of this type of course is to dissolve the "us/them" or "server/served" binary that may be perpetuated when students engage in direct service activities. The benefit of this form of engagement is that it can be a transformative learning experience for students. In other words, they are pushed into a perpetual experience of discomfort as they navigate unfamiliar scenarios and integrate new information into their cognitive frames. The biggest drawback is that the course may not yield tangible benefits for the host community beyond building student awareness. Perhaps this may benefit the community in the future if the students choose to turn their awareness into action, but that's typically not an expectation built into the course. Thus, there's the concerning possibility that immersion courses may be no better than *poverty tourism*. One simple example of a problematic practice is when faculty take students on an "urban plunge" and provide a walking tour of underserved communities. Students cluster on the sidewalks, creating barriers for people trying to pass, and comment about the poverty. A better approach would be to work with an organization that trains youth in how to give tours of the neighborhood. Youth get to build public-speaking skills and feel pride in their community and in their own expertise about it. Also, they can take small groups of students to minimize the disruption to sidewalk traffic and act as a counterexample to students' deficit-oriented lens on the community.

Research Focus

Varying types of research-focused community-engaged courses have emerged from disciplinary fields, including community-based research, community-based participatory research rooted in scholarly traditions in public health, and participatory action research rooted in scholarly traditions of sociology and ethnic studies. All three types aim to engage underserved community members as researchers who define research questions, collect and analyze data, and disseminate findings in ways that contribute to positive social change. Strand, Marullo, Cutforth, Stoecker, and Donohue (2003) enumerate three essential principles that can apply to each variation of this type of engaged research and reflect tenets of engaged scholarship articulated later in chapter 11:

1. [It] is a collaborative enterprise between academic researchers (professor and students) and community members;
2. [It] validates multiple sources of knowledge and promotes the use of multiple methods of discovery and dissemination of the knowledge produced and;
3. [It] has as its goal social action and social change for the purpose of achieving social justice. (p. 8)

Faculty usually train community members in research methodology and support them through the life cycle of the project. When any of these forms of engaged research are connected to a course, students may be learning the methodologies and working on the research process alongside community members.

There are multiple benefits to this model. First, rigorous research has the potential to persuade policymakers to respond to community-identified concerns. Second, this is the ultimate example of how an institution can leverage faculty and student research capacities for a public purpose. Third, students develop advanced scholarly skills while also learning about justice issues and how social change happens. The major challenge is that projects usually extend beyond a single academic term, so the instructor must hold the thread of the project even if students come and go from the course each term. Further, if students and community members bump up against limits in their research capacities, instructors either have to build in more training or take up the tasks themselves. On a related note, the scale of this type of project requires major commitment from community members, but it may be hard to sustain their interest and involvement for a number of reasons. In sum, at its best, research-focused community-engaged pedagogy can contribute to community capacity building and the accomplishment of social change priorities, but its success is highly contingent on robust commitments from stakeholders. Tool Kit 3.4 provides an opportunity to identify which pedagogical focus your course might take.

> Tool Kit 3.4—Refer to Exercise 3.4 in your workbook to identify which pedagogical focus (or foci) your course may take.

Forms of Community-Engaged Courses

Many faculty new to community-engaged teaching initially visualize their students providing direct service like tutoring children or constructing trails in a wilderness area. However, the Haas Center for Public Service at Stanford University created and implemented a Public Service Pathways assessment tool and curriculum to help students explore six specific forms of service that could lead to careers (Schnaubelt & Schwartz-Coffey, 2016). These pathways can also be used as formats for shaping the service or engagement component of community-engaged courses (see Figure 3.2).

Figure 3.2 Examples of formats of community-engaged courses.

DIRECT SERVICE – Giving personal time, energy, or resources to address immediate community needs or priorities.

Marketing 126 Applied Marketing Research

The course provides a detailed overview of marketing research, strategic marketing planning, and the development of fully integrated marketing programs. Topics include market analysis, marketing mix strategies, product positioning, market segmentation, and related social and ethical issues. Student teams apply course concepts and best practices to create a marketing plan for local nonprofit organizations.

COMMUNITY-BASED RESEARCH/LEARNING – Connecting or producing scholarship with public and/or private sector resources that responds to community-identified needs or concerns.

(*Continues*)

Figure 3.2 (*Continued*)

Politics 116 Political Polling and Survey Research

This course explores the theoretical basis of modern empirical methods of investigating political behavior. The course stresses the development of empirical theories of politics through the formation and testing of hypotheses. Emphasis is on the use of survey instruments, polling techniques, and data analysis. Throughout the semester, students work in groups to complete a research project for a local nonprofit organization.

POLICY/POLITICS – Participating in processes of democratic self-governance.

Kinesiology 20 Facility and Event Management

This course is a study of the organization and supervision of recreation facilities as well as the concepts and methods of planning/producing sporting events. Course components include facility operations and management, policies and procedures, budgeting, staffing, event planning/management, crowd control and security, programming/scheduling, maintenance, and risk management. Trends influencing the design and operations of sport facilities will be discussed. Students work with athletic/recreation organizations to develop policy and procedures for program management.

PHILANTHROPY – The voluntary redistribution of resources by individuals and institutions.

January Term 069 Living Globally – Rwanda Rising, Land of a Thousand Hills

This course explores Rwanda as an example of broad-based development, human resiliency, and the power of reconciliation. As an added bonus, through the Kunwana Foundation, students will be given an *actual fund of $5,000* to create a portfolio of development projects that will benefit the people of Rwanda. At the end of the January term, students will be responsible for the approval of all project dollars to be allocated. In order to make informed choices about the fund, students will learn a holistic approach to development addressing five areas: health and human services, civic engagement, the arts, education, and the environment. They will witness how strategies in each area are implemented and contribute to increasing the quality of life for all Rwandans.

ACTIVISM – The process of involving, educating, and mobilizing individual or collective action to influence or persuade others.

(*Continues*)

Figure 3.2 (*Continued*)

January Term 063-01 The Metamorphosis of U2: Musically, Spiritually, and Politically

The course is built on the theological foundation of Walter Bruggeman's concept of orientation, disorientation, and reorientation of the Psalms that reflects the 30-year history and discography of U2 coupled with salient features of Catholic social thought and political activism. Specific social issues and social change organizations/activism addressed by U2's music will be examined. The class will collectively select from U2's ONE Campus Campaign "challenges" and form student teams to complete a service-learning project to organize a series of events and activities to promote consciousness raising for AIDS and/or African debt relief during the January term. The band's history and biographies of the band members will also be examined. The course will explore theological and spiritual contexts of U2's activism while learning and applying basic fundamentals of community organizing/activism using action plans to raise campus awareness of poverty and/or AIDS issues in Africa by establishing a campus chapter of the ONE organization.

SOCIAL ENTREPRENEURSHIP – Creating or expanding organizational structures that adopt ethical and effective business practices and/or generate market-oriented responses to solve social problems.

GRAD Level – GMAN 701 Managing and Leading Global Organizations (Overseas)

This class is conducted in the country of your assigned project, allowing your team to collect the appropriate primary data to complete your project. Students will also learn about the base of the pyramid operations and challenges through case studies, site visits, and industry/government lectures. You will develop skills essential for global managerial success through exercises in executive leadership, creativity, empowering people, communication, and team building in global organizations. Problems of motivation, leadership, job satisfaction, team dynamics, and organizational restructuring are addressed. You will also consider methods of changing organizational behavior by applying behavioral technologies. Activities include hands-on team-based games, managerial leadership exercises, self-assessment instruments, experiential exercises, personality inventories, and high-performance team building in global settings.

Social Justice Frameworks for Community-Engaged Learning

Now that we have a sense of the defining characteristics, foci, and forms of community-engaged learning, let us lean into the aspiration of designing courses that reflect a social justice orientation. We offer brief overviews of three contemporary frameworks from scholars who are attempting to redefine the field. These may seem unfamiliar, challenging, or even controversial depending on your academic discipline and professional experience. We ask that you dig into these frameworks with a mind-set of considering which aspects might be suitable and attainable for the course you have in mind.

Critical Service-Learning

Mitchell (2008) developed the critical service-learning model as an alternative to traditional forms of service-learning. She articulated concern about the harm that can come from service-learning that perpetuates students' stereotypes and replicates unequal power dynamics between campus and community. When courses don't integrate sufficient content to contextualize justice issues or adequate opportunities for students to critically reflect on what they are learning, students can easily leave class with their preconceptions reinforced. Thus, critical service-learning requires students to engage discursively with content about power, privilege, and oppression. Additionally, Mitchell challenges the practice of placing students with social service organizations that focus on addressing symptoms of social inequities. Instead, she advocates for working with groups that challenge root causes of oppression. Mitchell suggests that students might learn more, and contribute to more impactful efforts, if they work with groups that focus on advocacy and community organizing.

Liberating Service-Learning

Stoecker (2016) recently articulated a framework of liberating service-learning that prioritizes community change as the primary goal. He argues that community priorities and expectations should shape course content and format. Stoecker argues that students must learn to employ a sociological imagination to be able to effectively analyze and address the complexity of community issues. Further, courses should focus on building the knowledge power of grassroots organizing movements rather than partnering with direct service organizations. This allows students to engage in mobilization activities like research or canvassing rather than charitable activities. In this model, the role of the instructor is necessarily robust. They must not only hold a relationship with the community partner but also commit to being present with the community as an ally and a collaborator. Further, the instructor must be able to support students through what are likely new and uncomfortable opportunities to stretch beyond their current academic and interpersonal competencies. Finally, the instructor must be committed to the process of cocreating knowledge with community and disseminating it in ways that allow movements to leverage knowledge for change.

Decolonizing Service-Learning

Yep and Mitchell (2017) advanced the framework of decolonizing service-learning, which entails "unmasking hegemonic power structures and fostering autonomy and self-determination" (p. 295) for traditionally underserved and marginalized communities. If we trace the genealogy of community-engaged learning back to its student activist roots, then decolonizing service-learning embodies a return to the principles embedded in struggles for racial equity. For example, the Student Nonviolent Coordinating Committee (SNCC), Third World Liberation Front, and Black Panther Party combined political education, solidarity in action, and community service (Oden & Casey, 2007; Yep & Mitchell, 2017). Movement leaders required participants to be educated about policies and laws, theories of change, and strategic resistance practices so they could effectively advance the cause of liberation. Yep and Mitchell (2017) advocate for extrapolating these decolonizing practices from liberation movements to the design and implementation of community-engaged courses. Specifically, decolonizing service-learning means deferring to communities to set the agenda for community engagement projects, honoring the diverse epistemologies of community members and social change leaders, examining interpersonal and institutional power dynamics, and committing to community empowerment and equitable social transformation as ultimate outcomes of community engagement. You now have an opportunity to consider which of these frameworks aligns with your vision of your course in Tool Kit 3.5.

> Tool Kit 3.5—Refer to Exercise 3.5 in your workbook to start testing out which frameworks align with your vision for your course.

Putting It All Together

Now that you have some foundational information about what community-engaged pedagogies entail, you can begin to weave together the components of your course. Note that much of what was shared represents an aspirational template, so don't expect that you'll be able to integrate the most critical and complex practices in your first attempt. Start with elements, forms, and frameworks that are manageable for you. From here, you will build your capacity to implement more justice-oriented forms and frames over time. For now, begin drafting how you would articulate what *community-engaged pedagogy* is in your syllabus in Tool Kit 3.6.

> Tool Kit 3.6—Refer to Exercise 3.6 in your workbook to start drafting language about community-engaged pedagogy that will be incorporated into your syllabus.

Honing Your Craft

At a basic level, a community-engaged course provides students with an opportunity to "do something good" with the community and complement their classroom learning with real-world experience. Although we hope it is true that your course will facilitate student learning and positive contributions to community, the options for how you structure this experience are vast and hold important implications for *what* students learn and contribute.

In this chapter, we invited you to move beyond seeking a succinct definition and checklist-style guidelines. Rather, we are asking you to tap into your own values, beliefs, and notions of how educational institutions and their constituents might deploy an array of community-engaged courses designed to advance a social justice agenda. Depending on your institution, discipline, and prior professional experience, you might feel trepidation about adopting an explicit social justice agenda for your course. We know there are some contexts where certain foci, forms and frameworks would be perceived as inappropriate. Thus, part of honing your craft is reading your context and determining a course design that accounts for existing limitations but also manifests a vision that strives toward the aspirational power of community-engaged pedagogy. Tool Kit 3.7 presents a scenario and provides an opportunity to consider how you articulate (describe) and then implement or introduce (realize) the public purpose of community engagement.

> Tool Kit 3.7—Honing Your Craft—Refer to Exercise 3.7 in your workbook to explore how you would respond to a scenario in which you and your students talk about what constitutes community engagement for a public purpose.

Chapter 4
COMMUNITY

In the field of community engagement, the term *community* is used quite often, but rarely discussed in a way that elucidates a shared understanding. Individual relationships, like the partnerships you'll form with public scholars, are situated within a broader community context. Indeed, the entirety of your course will be influenced by community dynamics. We're guessing you may not have spent much time pondering what *community* means, so let's take a moment for you to do a little reflection on it in Tool Kit 4.1.

> Tool Kit 4.1—Refer to Exercise 4.1 in your workbook to consider your own understanding of community.

At a superficial level, it is easy to conceptualize community as any place off campus. But the geographic and sociocultural dimensions of community factor heavily into where, how, and with whom we engage. The geographic dimension matters for both practical and ethical reasons. The logistics of students being able to travel to and from their engagement site can define the limits of where community engagement might occur. If the partner community is far from campus and inaccessible except by car, students might be required to use their institution's shared ride arrangements or mass transit, which has implications for when and how long they can be in the community. Further, location can determine the extent to which students and community members feel a common purpose. If the community and the institution share geographical space and are subject to the impacts of historical and contemporary forces in similar ways, there's a foundation for building on common purpose. If the community where students do engagement does not share a common fate with the institution, it may be more challenging to establish and maintain a relationship of reciprocity and interdependence.

The geographic element of community engagement is also integrated with a sociocultural dimension. Typically, colleges and universities don't establish partnerships with middle-class or affluent communities for community-engaged learning. Thus, when the term *community* is invoked in this pedagogical realm, it usually references underserved, marginalized, oppressed, working-class, and low-income communities. Again, depending on geography, these communities might also be described as communities of color, racially minoritized communities, ethnic diasporic communities, or newcomer communities. Thus, we see how intersections of class, race, ethnicity, and other aspects of identity factor in. Yet we are guessing that when you came up with your analogy for community these particular descriptors did not come to mind. Why, then, do they become a defining factor in the term *community* when it is linked to *engagement* and situated in institutions of higher education?

This chapter attempts to reframe and hopefully even complicate our notions of community relative to our endeavors as academics to simultaneously educate students and contribute to the common good. We begin by challenging the common tendency to regard community as a monolith and the pitfalls of acting in accordance with this mythical conception. Then we move to suggest various definitions of *community* that hold space for reconceptualizing individual and institutional relationships. Recognizing that the way we imagine and convey the work of engagement relies heavily on language, we examine the simple use of prepositions in describing our actions and goals for community engagement. We conclude by exploring the transformative paradigm of the "beloved community" as described by Martin Luther King Jr.

Community: The Myth of the Monolith

Given the way we generally talk about community-engaged learning, there is potential for us to dangerously default to seeing community as a singular organism whose component parts function harmoniously in service to the whole. We invoke the word to describe a particular location or group of people. But in both cases, the term *community* glosses over the diversity of roles, desires, perspectives, and needs of the people and institutions that are part of the community. It belies the inevitability of existing solidarities, alliances, tensions, struggles, and visions. Entering into community engagement with this naïve and limited perception can lead to significant challenges and potential to do harm.

Thus, it is imperative to examine the complexity of community both as a concept and as a realized embodiment of the people and places you are hoping to engage. To begin, we invite you to consider how historical and contemporary economic, political, and social forces shape, and are shaped by, community spaces and demographics. Let's explore a case study in Tool Kit 4.2 that demonstrates how diverse and competing community forces might affect a community-engaged learning experience.

Tool Kit 4.2—Refer to Exercise 4.2 in your workbook and read the community case study and respond to the questions.

Defining *Community*

A substantial and growing body of literature emerging from a range of disciplinary traditions and interdisciplinary scholarship seeks to define *community*. We have chosen to home in on particular definitions that feel most applicable to community-engaged learning as we've presented it. At the same time, we feel compelled to share definitions that both complement and contest each other.

Human Connection

The definitions that resonate most with us center on human connections and account for the realities of the modern world, including forces like globalization and the rise of technology. Indeed, many contemporary scholars describe community as solidarity, or a feeling of being bonded with other people (Bhattacharyya, 2004; Bradshaw, 2008; Kempers, 2001). Parker Palmer (1987) goes even further into the essentialness of human connection by claiming "what makes community possible is love" (p. 25). Although this is an attractive line of thought in the sense that it makes community feel very quaint and nurturing for constituents, the tenet of solidarity is not reflected in all communities. We need only to look at rapidly gentrifying neighborhoods in urban centers to see the tensions and divisions within community. Nevertheless, Palmer's vision holds value in representing an aspiration for what community could be.

Recognizing that a more complex definition is needed, we turned to the interdisciplinary scholarship of faculty administering community engagement programs at institutions around the world. Thakrar, Kenn, and Minkley (2014) set out to explore the deep and rich meanings imbued in the term as articulated by multiple constituents involved in community engagement. They espouse principles of community engagement in which "data" emanate from stories and voices that are not often raised up in higher education community engagement practices. They also contend that the term should be personalized, examined, and even contested by those who identify as part of community. In other words, they reject traditional academic and rational notions of objectivity when it comes to visioning and practicing the work of community engagement. Indeed, each of the authors provides a brief autobiography that illustrates the evolution of their thinking about community and offers up their understanding of the term in ways that raise important questions about the cognitive constructs, and social realities and aspirations, that we convey through this term. Thakrar, a management faculty member who teaches in South Africa, proposed that the term *community* should be replaced with another term (perhaps *people*?) that more effectively articulates "the idea that there are . . . differences, disagreements, and perhaps even dissenters; that [people's] origins, and identities are not easily classified; and . . . [that] 'common substance' is not confined to racial or spatial relations" (Thakrar et al., 2014, p. 777).

Kenn, a law professor in upstate New York involved in legal defense connected with her institution's place-based initiative, conceptualizes community as a "dynamic, layered, fluid force that grows and contracts with each individual and can expand to encompass communities within communities . . . [like a] helix, spiraling out from an ever-expanding center" (cited in Thakrar et al., 2014, p. 781).

Minkley, as a White South African faculty member, interrogates how community is defined differently by the state than it is by the people. He argues that the state operates on the definition of *community* as a population whose location (physical and social) allows it to be controlled through a combination of political, economic, and cultural interventions, whereas Black South Africans see community as the sum total of shared experiences of oppression and exploitation, but also resistance and liberation (Minkley, as cited in Thakrar et al., 2014).

These authors also conducted a qualitative analysis of 63 definitions of *community* provided by students, community leaders, government officials, and CEPs. Several themes emerged from their analysis, further illuminating the essential aspects of community. These themes were (a) the existence of a "common substance" (p. 787) among individuals, (b) an emotional connection or sense of belonging to the group, and (c) a geographic or spatial location (Thakrar et al., 2014). We propose that these themes are a starting point for reframing the work of community engagement away from generic technical interventions and toward prioritizing relationships, seeking common purpose, and holding reverence for the sacredness of place as a site of dynamic experiences of oppression, struggle, and resilience. Consider ways to use your own story of community in Tool Kit 4.3.

Tool Kit 4.3—Refer to Exercise 4.3 in your workbook to explore ways of tapping into your own story of community.

Sense of Place

The fields of anthropology, geography, and psychology have examined and provided insight into the phenomenon referred to as sense of place. This goes beyond physical borders and boundaries to encompass cultural and social dynamics that define a group. It is important to consider and incorporate these dynamics as we endeavor to establish partnerships outside the academy. Place or locus of attachment occurs when there is an emotional bond between a geographical location and an individual or a group (Altman & Low, 2012). A sense of place can also manifest when an individual or a group ascribes symbolic meaning to a place. Contextual culture in the form of attitudes, values, and traditions that are collectively shared creates meaning for those in this setting. These influences can have either a positive or negative impact on the pride and identity of a community (Theobold, 1997). Therefore, there is a reciprocal relationship between a geographical location and those within it, each informing and influencing the other (Buttimer & Seamon, 2015). As engaged scholars, we must be cognizant of the potential constructive, as well as destructive, impact our work may have on this important relationship.

When Students Are Members of the "Engaged Community"

We must bring your attention to the likely reality that some students may be from the community with which you intend them to connect, or from very similar communities in terms of demographics, culture, resources, and challenges. Consider how these students may experience the discourse that you facilitate and the way you contextualize community. Your words and actions, including how you design and facilitate the course, will have specific ramifications for students from the "engaged community." If they perceive your conception of community as paternalistic, shallow, or inaccurate, this will have a negative impact on how the students feel and act in your course. On the other hand, if your curriculum, course discussions, and community engagement activities reflect respect for the assets of the host community, it will send a positive and inclusive message to students.

For example, if you describe the community strictly in terms of deficits and struggles, students will likely take this personally and feel that you are defining them in the same way. You may want to invite multiple guest speakers from the community, including community services staff and local residents, to provide diverse perspectives on the community's resources, gifts, challenges, and struggles. Similarly, you may assign students to read articles, blog posts, public declarations, poetry, and so on that provide a range of views on the community. In this way, you are providing a comprehensive introduction to community instead of a single description or perspective.

Another common mistake in regard to engaging students from the host community is tokenizing them as spokespeople for the community. This is a heavy and unrealistic burden for students to bear, especially because their perspectives and lived experiences are not universal to all community members. The dangerous potential for tokenization and marginalization can be mitigated in a number of ways, including by explicitly stating and modeling the belief that each person experiences community in ways that are particular to one's lived experience and cannot necessarily be generalized. To be clear, though students should not be asked to speak as "the voice" of their communities, their individual perceptions and definitions of community should be honored and respected alongside the voices of others in the community. Refer to Tool Kit 4.4 to consider how to include and incorporate student perspectives in appropriate ways.

> Tool Kit 4.4—Refer to Exercise 4.4 in your workbook to explore ways to invite students' perspectives without tokenizing or generalizing them.

Prepositions Matter: From *For* to *With*

One obvious manifestation of our conception of community in the context of community-engaged learning is the preposition we use when talking about this work. Traditional understandings often reflect a charity or service orientation and are conveyed through use of the prepositions *for* or *to*, as in "we are advocating *for* the community" or "we are providing services *to* the community." Use of these prepositions implies that community is an object to be acted upon or a laboratory for our own research and learning. This mind-set perpetuates problematic relationships of paternalism and imperialism. For example, a research methods course might require students to find an organization that will allow them to conduct interviews with clients. The organization staff obliges, thinking they will get to use the interview data to inform their program evaluation and improvement process. However, after the student collects interviews from clients and uses them in the final paper, the student never shares back the raw data or analysis with the organization, meaning staff don't benefit from the research access they provided to their clients. The dynamic of using the community as a laboratory or placement site is so common in certain communities that residents will actively resist interventions from higher education institutions, pointing to disempowering and exploitive past experiences with research studies, service projects, and other collaborations that resulted in no positive impact on the community.

The prepositions *to* and *for* deny the reality that the community and its constituents have agency to raise themselves up, but if we look at the history of social movements, we see that it is communities of marginalized and oppressed people that have led social transformations to improve their own lives and our world. And so, when we think about community engagement, we would be wise to use the preposition *with*, as in "partner with community organizations" or "work in coalition with community change agents." In this way, we communicate respect for the capacity of the persons and institutions that compose community. To illustrate this approach, consider the slogan "Nothing about us without us," which was made popular by disability rights activists in the 1990s in response to discriminatory public policies. This simple and powerful statement was a call for self-determination, and a rebuke of a status quo that denies direct participation of particular communities in policymaking processes that affect them. When applied to community-engaged learning, the phrase calls us to be accountable to the desires, priorities, and needs of community, as articulated by its constituents, when determining our engagement activities. This approach embodies and reflects a true partnership, and we can look to recent scholarship to help us shape our understanding and practice in regard to working with community partners. Now it is time for you to further explore this concept and practice in Tool Kit 4.5.

> Tool Kit 4.5—Refer to Exercise 4.5 in your workbook and complete the activities that illustrate the concept and practice of "Nothing about us without us."

Partnership Versus Placement

Despite raising concerns over assumptions regarding the true meaning of "community partners" as opposed to the predominant practice of "community placements," Pearson (2002) suggested any form of partnerships, whether in business or in our personal lives, should include ongoing face-to-face conversation, a shared plan, resource sharing, and sustained communication. Beere (2009) characterized partnerships as comprising the following key elements: involvement of two or more individuals or groups, a relationship shaped by mutuality, and a commitment to a common purpose or goal. Holland (2005) articulated best practices of campus-community partnerships that remain germane today. These include exploring and expanding separate and common goals; understanding capacity, resources, and expectations of all partners; reflecting mutual benefit through careful planning; sharing control of activities and decisions; and continually assessing process and outcomes. The Carnegie Foundation defines *partnerships* as "collaborative interactions with community and related scholarship for the mutually beneficial exchange, exploration, and application of knowledge, information, and resources" (Carnegie Foundation, 2012).

We now look to a well-known model as we craft our courses in alignment with an aspiration toward working *with* communities, in all their complexity, toward a greater approximation of the common good.

Beloved Community: The Ideal

To expand our examination of community beyond the higher education institution as a frame of reference, let us invoke what

Martin Luther King Jr. described as the "beloved community." He provided a vision for how Black people, engaged in the struggle for civil rights, could make and remake community as a healing and renewing space in the face of systemic oppression and state violence. The trope of the beloved community is rooted in philosophical and theological traditions. Philosopher Josiah Royce is credited with coining the phrase and providing a definition of the concept, which has evolved over time. Royce described *beloved community* as the achievement of a transcendent connection among people that grows out of a love powerful enough to transform individuals to embrace their identities as members of community over the social influences that guide people toward individualism (as cited in Jensen, 2016, p. 246). Theologian Howard Thurman described *beloved community* as a "harmony that transcends all diversities and in which diversity finds its richness and significance" (as cited in Jensen, 2016, p. 246).

King's understanding of beloved community formed from his upbringing in the Black church and direct experiences with Black suffering from, and resistance to, oppressive systemic forces. Many scholars argue that King's definition of *beloved community* evolved over his time as a minister and civil rights activist, starting as an articulation of the absence of fear and oppression, but becoming more sophisticated and visionary in the later years of his involvement with the movement. Toward the end of his life King articulated a vision for beloved community that can be summarized as the manifestation of "divine love" in our relationships with each other, a love that grows through reconciliation and redemption and the alleviation of injustice (Jensen, 2016). For generations since, many have drawn on King's vision of beloved community to organize for positive social change. Listen to Eran Thompson, a community organizer in Billings, Montana, describe how this vision has shaped his life and work by swiping your smartphone or tablet over the QR code in Figure 4.1.

Taken together, the musings of these scholars and activists can help us channel a comprehensive vision of beloved community to shape our

Figure 4.1 The beloved community—Eran Thompson.

Note. Scan the QR code to access https://www.youtube.com/watch?v=EIFdPjKC6_s

community-engaged courses. To clarify, we are not suggesting that we should appropriate a concept that has been primarily connected to historical and contemporary movements for racial equity and justice. Rather, we suggest using this concept as our "north star," to create a vision of community that will build authentic relationships among people, proliferate a culture of care and love for humanity, foster a commitment to a collective cause, honor diversity in all its forms, and lay the foundation for reconciliation for injustices. Consider ways of seeking exemplars of beloved community in Tool Kit 4.6.

Tool Kit 4.6—Refer to Exercise 4.6 in your workbook to explore ways of seeking exemplars of beloved community.

Honing Your Craft

At this point, you might be asking, "What does this mean for me and my (fill in the discipline) course?" How do I integrate the concept of beloved community into physics? Marketing? Engineering? In response, we can look to educator and activist Parker Palmer (1987), who aims to "connect concepts of community to questions of epistemology" (p. 21). Given that higher education institutions are primary sites for generating and disseminating knowledge, they should be drawing on the diversity of the world's epistemologies and including community as a subject to be learned and practiced. Palmer calls for the following kinds of love when cultivating connections between community and epistemology in academic spaces: (a) love of learning and (b) love of learners. Indeed, this aligns with characteristics of beloved community in that it names the importance of both the ideological aspect of creating community and the interpersonal aspect. Regardless of the subject you teach, community-engaged learning has the potential to accomplish Parker's vision, precisely because it calls students to interact with public scholars and each other as knowledge holders and to work *with* diverse people to achieve ends that serve a public purpose. Through community-engaged learning, we come to know others in new ways; we come to recognize, honor, and integrate new epistemologies, and this knowledge shapes the way we interact with the world around us. This knowledge shapes the way we participate in community. In other words,

> the act of knowing itself, if we understand it rightly, is a bond of community between us and that which we know. The act of knowing itself is

> a way of building and rebuilding community, and it is this we must reach for in our education. (Palmer, 1987, p. 25)

We close this chapter by inviting you to discuss the ways and challenges to hone your craft in promoting community in Tool Kit 4.7.

> Tool Kit 4.7— Honing Your Craft—Refer to Exercise 4.7 in your workbook to explore and discuss questions to hone your craft.

Chapter 5

INTERCULTURAL COMPETENCE, CULTURAL HUMILITY, AND CRITICAL CONSCIOUSNESS

Though this book is meant to provide you with knowledge, skills, and tools to effectively implement community-engaged teaching, we are wary of fostering overconfidence. You can be well versed in the schematics of how to build the house, but the execution of the plan is not as easy as it looks because there are so many variables that come into play and so many people with whom you must collaborate.

It's common for faculty to enter into community as the "ugly academic," which is similar to the concept of the "ugly American" tourist who travels abroad with an air of superiority and entitlement that translates into behaviors ranging from rude to exploitive. Perhaps you have witnessed the "ugly American" in your own travels. Common "ugly American" behaviors include openly criticizing unfamiliar foods; taking photos of local people without their permission; speaking in loud, slow English when trying to communicate with non-English speakers; or ignoring signs that limit where one can go during a museum tour.

In much the same way, "ugly academics" see the community as a site for their unfettered benefit and scholarly advancement. They traverse the divide between "town and gown" and descend from their ivory tower to use the community as a laboratory, pushing their own teaching or research agenda, defining the terms of engagement, and positioning themselves as the highest source of knowledge. They discount community wisdom, student voice, and cultural context. They define communities by their deficits and fancy themselves as the savior that will solve the community's problems.

In addition to exhorting you to not be the ugly academic, we offer alternative ways of doing, and thinking about, community-engaged teaching and learning. Thus, we invite you to explore with us the concepts of intercultural competence, cultural humility, and critical consciousness. When working in tandem, these concepts encompass technical skills and knowledge, dispositions, habits, and an orientation toward justice that will allow you to maximize the positive impact of your community-engaged course on students and community.

Defining *Culture*

One of the most commonly cited definitions of *culture* comes from Clyde Kluckhohn, an American anthropologist. He described culture as "a total way of life of a people" (Kluckhohn & Kelly, 1945, p. 17). This definition includes many component characteristics like beliefs, values, language, rituals, norms, and behaviors. Some aspects of culture can be very visible, and others are latent. Watch the "Cultural Iceberg" video by swiping your smartphone or tablet over the QR code in Figure 5.1 to learn more. Then, refer to Tool Kit 5.1 to help you conceptualize the multiple manifestations of culture.

Figure 5.1 Cultural iceberg.

Note. Scan the QR code to access https://www.youtube.com/watch?v=woP0v-2nJCU

> Tool Kit 5.1—Refer to Exercise 5.1 in your workbook. Watch the "Cultural Iceberg" video clip and respond to the questions.

Culture develops at the broadest level of a civilization and at a much more minute level, like within a business start-up. Culture can describe the common characteristics of an identity-based group (e.g., ethnic culture, religious culture), geographic group (e.g., Southern culture, urban culture), affinity group (e.g., foodie culture), or professional group (e.g., academic culture, corporate culture). We each belong to multiple cultural groups, and as we are immersed in particular cultures, we find that they shape our worldviews and actions (see Tool Kit 5.2).

Tool Kit 5.2—Refer to Exercise 5.2 in your workbook. Reflect on the culture of academia as it relates to your own identity and the identities of students and community partners.

Why does this matter for your work as a community-engaged faculty member? Well, your cultural affiliations have played a significant role in determining who you are, what you do, and what you care about. The same is true for everyone else with whom you engage. Being mindful of this dynamic can help you to maximize the meaning and benefit (and minimize potential harm) of your actions. Building the requisite knowledge, skills, and sensitivities for engaging people across cultures is essential to your craft.

Intercultural Competence

Let us start with a definition of *intercultural competence* that lends itself well to community-engaged learning. Spitzberg and Chagnon (2009) describe intercultural competence as "the appropriate and effective management of interaction between people who, to some degree or another, represent different or divergent affective, cognitive, and behavioral orientations to the world" (p. 7). This description resonates because it does not focus narrowly on culture as being related to ethnicity, place of origin, or race. Nor does the term imply that intercultural competence applies only in global travel contexts. Rather, this allows us to define *culture* as something that emanates from, and shapes, one's identities, experiences, and memberships in various groups.

Given your status as a faculty member, we assume you've been socialized into the culture of your department, institution, and academia as a whole. We're also guessing you have at least a basic level of intercultural competence that you've developed over the course of your life, particularly in your professional formation as you've engaged with diverse colleagues and students. Even at racially and ethnically homogeneous institutions, it is likely that you are interacting with people who claim at least some aspects of identity that are different from your own. You've developed skills, knowledge, and dispositions that allow you to work effectively with others across difference. You probably practice some level of intercultural competence daily, and yet this is an area in which there's always room to grow and improve.

Let's break down the types of knowledge, skills, and dispositions that facilitate intercultural competence and how they apply to community-engaged courses so we can assess our own level of mastery and build our capacities. Deardorff and Edwards (2013) put forth a cyclical process model of intercultural competence that situates learning in the juxtaposition of an individual and their interactions with others. At the individual level, one develops understandings, skills, and attitudes that shape, and are shaped by, the interaction level: engagement with other diverse people. This cycle leads to both internal outcomes for the individual and external outcomes that have implications for how others experience the individual.

The realm of intercultural knowledge begins with understanding one's own identity and experience, and how these contribute to the way one makes sense of, and behaves in, the world. One must develop a basic comprehension that diverse cultures and identity groups espouse different practices and perspectives that are not inherently worse (or better) than one's own. To engage effectively with a specific culture or identity group, one might learn their particular language and social customs. It is also important to educate oneself about how historical, political, economic, and social systems affect various cultural and identity groups.

Skills for interacting with diverse people relate to building our understanding and empathy. Active listening and observation allow us to gather information directly from the people we encounter (in contrast to developing a profile of a group based on popular media or scholarly publications). In regard to listening, notice not only what people say to you but also how they say it, and consider what underlying assumptions and beliefs are being communicated. Observe body language, actions, and interactions for signs of comfort, pleasure, anger, fear, and concern. Perspective-taking guides us to then analyze and synthesize this information into comprehension of worldviews that are divergent from our own.

Our attitudes inform how we use these skills and understandings. We should *respect* people and their lived realities, even if we don't agree with their worldviews. We can employ an attitude of intellectual curiosity to guide us in learning about others. This allows us to open our minds to the possibility of changing the way we understand the world in light of compelling evidence. Likewise, we are invited to practice intercultural encounters with perseverance, recognizing that they may initially foment miscommunications and misunderstandings, but that they have potential to foster mutually beneficial learning and perhaps also authentic relationships.

To build students' intercultural competence in community-engaged courses, Van Cleave and Cartwright (2017) emphasize the importance of boundary spanning, in which students move between the spaces of campus and the community beyond, and necessarily try out, reflect on, and adapt their behaviors to function appropriately in different cultural spaces. They argue that transformation happens when students experience a "disorienting dilemma" (Van Cleave & Cartwright, 2017, p. 210) for which their existing cognitive schema have no suitable explanation and they have to struggle to synthesize the experience into a more sophisticated understanding of the world.

Bringing an interculturally competent lens to your work with students means accommodating their diverse learning needs, creating space where students feel safe to share their perspectives, and introducing students to marginalized narratives. Bringing the same lens to your connection with community requires that you learn about the community's demographics, assets, and challenges; reach out to potential partners to seek ideas about how students can be of use; and build reciprocal relationships. We invite you to begin exploring ways to build your intercultural competence in Tool Kit 5.3.

> Tool Kit 5.3—Refer to Exercise 5.3 in your workbook. Brainstorm ways you can build your intercultural competence.

Cultural Humility

Intercultural competence can take you only so far. We must temper competence with cultural humility. According to Tervalon and Murray-Garcia (1998), cultural humility is a commitment to lifelong learning from, with, and about diverse others, integrating ongoing self-reflection about one's own identity in order to act in ways that address interpersonal power imbalances. We invite you to watch a short video by swiping your smartphone or tablet over the QR code in Figure 5.2 that features physicians who have incorporated the concept of cultural humility for a more comprehensive description of integral principles and practices. Then turn to Tool Kit 5.4 in your workbook to respond to the questions posed there.

Figure 5.2 Cultural humility: People, principles, and practices.

Note. Scan the QR code to access https://www.youtube.com/watch?v=_Mbu8bvKb_U

Tool Kit 5.4—Refer to Exercise 5.4 in your workbook. Watch the cultural humility video clip and respond to the questions.

Cultural humility requires us to identify, interrogate, and act to reshape unequal power dynamics in our relationships with others. Thus, we invite you to be aware of how your own identity (e.g., gender, race, socioeconomic status, ability) and positionality (e.g., faculty member, PhD, researcher) create an imbalance of power with others in the community-engaged learning relationship.

In regard to students, your identity and positionality have an effect on the extent to which they are empowered to express fears or concerns about the course, articulate divergent perspectives from you and others in the classroom, and feel a commitment to the community to which you are connecting them. Remember that all students have their own unique identity and positionalities that shape the way they experience your course. Model humble behaviors like admitting the limits of your own knowledge and expertise, asking hard questions for which there are no easy answers, describing the evolution of your own perspective on a justice issue, and inviting community members as guest lecturers to teach students the things you don't know. In response to your demonstrated humility, students might be encouraged to embrace vulnerability and humility as well.

Further, consider how your identity and positionality create power imbalances in relationships with community partners. You may find that some community partners are quick to defer to your academic expertise and faculty status when you approach them about partnership. This could manifest as the community partner telling you that they will accommodate your students in any way you like, inviting you to set the terms of engagement. Although this can seem like an attractive scenario because you can design the community engagement activity to suit the needs of your course, it can be problematic when the activity you design doesn't actually meet a community-identified need. At the other extreme, you might find that community partners immediately stonewall you when you approach them about partnering for your course. They may have had disempowering experiences with other faculty in the past and are wary of being further exploited. They may not be willing to invest time and energy in working with you and your students because they don't feel it benefits them sufficiently. In this situation, you may need to humble yourself to the task of building trust over time with these potential partners, so they can be assured that you are not just using them to fulfill your own agenda.

It can be helpful to talk explicitly and transparently with potential partner organizations about inherent power dynamics in community-campus relationships and how you are actively trying to achieve equity and reciprocity. You might also need to educate yourself about the demographics, priorities, desires, and challenges of the people with whom you want to work prior to reaching out for partnerships. You'll want to do so not only through traditional scholarly avenues like reviewing statistics and reading academic journal articles but also by talking to local residents and immersing yourself in the neighborhood (see Tool Kit 5.5).

Tool Kit 5.5—Refer to Exercise 5.5 in your workbook. Consider ways you might immerse yourself in a neighborhood or community for the purpose of learning and building relationships.

Once you identify the particular community with which you hope to work, consider whether you and your students have the capacity to be of use. It's possible that your academic expertise might not be of primary use to the community. They might be working with you and your students for a variety of other reasons, including a simple need for additional volunteers to fill essential roles at their organization. Also, if you and/or your students do not share certain aspects of identity with the community, this may have implications for not only the level of trust and/or power dynamics that manifest in relationships but also whether you are able to accomplish desired tasks. For example, if you and your students are not fluent in Cantonese, you may not be able to work effectively with a Chinese newcomer community. A disposition of humility will allow you to honor community-identified priorities and needs, embrace an appropriate role for yourself and your students in support of community change efforts, and build relationships that are not contingent on traditional notions of faculty as knowledge holders and community members and students as knowledge receivers.

Cruz (1990b) has developed *Principles of Good Practice in Combining Service and Learning* from a diversity perspective that reflects an orientation toward cultural humility. According to Cruz, a course committed to diversity

- engages constituents to notice, reflect on, and participate in dialogues about differences in defining, interpreting, and expressing concepts like responsibility, action, and common good;
- encourages a variety of ways to do and express reflection;
- respects and acknowledges cultural practices that shape how constituents define and develop goals and provides time and structure for participants to experience a process of struggle across differences in coming to consensus and/or principled disagreement in defining what is to be accomplished and what is to be learned;
- recognizes that some stakeholders may not view themselves primarily in terms of need, and that the concept of need may be contested by those who view themselves as having borne the costs of historical legacies of colonialism, slavery, patriarchy, and other forms of subjugation and oppression;
- honors varying organizational cultures, some of which may define responsibilities more formally and explicitly, whereas others may be organized in more fluid and informal ways;
- respects different cultural approaches that inform course constituents about who is to be engaged by whom, with whom, and how;
- respects varying ways by which *commitment* is culturally defined and expressed and accounts for the possibility that failure to honor commitments may unequally and negatively affect different people;
- respects culturally different ways by which training, supervision, monitoring, support, recognition, and evaluation are defined and expressed;
- makes possible the effective participation of low-income working people, single parents, and others who experience constraints defined by different realities; and
- commits necessary resources to encourage expression of voices of diverse participants who hold competing interpretations of what good practices should look like.

We now invite you reflect on how you might put these principles into practice in Tool Kit 5.6.

Tool Kit 5.6—Refer to Exercise 5.6 in your workbook. Reflect on how you might put the diversity principles into practice in your course.

Cultural humility fosters interpersonal relationships that reflect respect for the intellectual, emotional, and social capital that each person contributes to the teaching-learning relationship in community-engaged courses. It is a necessary precursor to building and applying your capacity for critical consciousness.

Critical Consciousness

As discussed in chapter 2, Paulo Freire (1970) characterized critical consciousness as a recognition of the social, political, and economic contradictions embedded in society, coupled with a commitment to act against oppressive forces and toward the humanization of all people. This concept emanates from an understanding that contemporary human relationships, institutions, and systems have been designed to benefit society's dominant identity groups (e.g., White people, cisgender men, able-bodied people) through the oppression and exploitation of other groups. Most people are socialized to be blind to this architecture of privilege and oppression, even as they experience dissonance between what they know to be true and popular discourses about the way the world works. This systematic form of domination might manifest as conquest, manipulation, or cultural invasion but serves to dehumanize all people.

Freire (1970) described the prevalence of traditional "banking models" (p. 72) of education in which students are expected to passively receive and integrate information from the teacher, who is framed as the expert, into their understanding of the world. In this model, there is little to no room for students to challenge the reliability and validity of the information they receive, unless they are invited to do so as a strictly academic exercise for the purpose of achieving a grade from the instructor. He also argued that this form of education colonizes the minds of both oppressed people and oppressors by perpetuating purportedly common sense justifications for exploitive systems and practices and maintaining dominant/submissive power relationships between teacher and student in educational spaces.

The antidote to this educational cycle is a critical pedagogy that centers reflection, dialogue, and action to leverage the intellectual and emotional capital of those whose wisdom grows out of the experience of oppression. Those who are targets of domination are uniquely qualified to lead pedagogical transformation by contributing alternative narratives to inform new understandings of how contemporary society functions to perpetuate inequity and dehumanization. Thus, according to Freire, critical consciousness cannot be developed by traditional academics in classroom spaces. Rather, it is cultivated in the context of struggle by those who intimately know the experience of systematic oppression and shared with the broader society as a means of liberating every person's consciousness from dehumanization.

Dorinda Carter Andrews, the dean of Michigan State University's School of Education, provides some direction for how to foster critical consciousness in a short video presentation in Figure 5.3. Though her primary audience is K–12 educators and her focus is on racial inequity, her insights are applicable to college educators and to myriad social justice issues addressed in community-engaged learning. Respond to the questions posed in Tool Kit 5.7.

> Tool Kit 5.7—Refer to Exercise 5.7 in your workbook. Watch "The Consciousness Gap in Education" video clip and complete the accompanying activity.

Embracing community-engaged education for liberation and social transformation has implications for your pedagogical practices, course content, and strategies for student and community engagement. It involves reshaping the way you teach to include practices like modeling how to challenge oppressive constructs, valuing the wisdom gained from life experience, illuminating community exemplars who are doing the work of social change, and inviting students to engage in a praxis of reflection and action that leads them to think about and enact equity and justice.

Figure 5.3 The consciousness gap in education.

Note. Scan the QR code to access https://www.youtube.com/watch?v=iOrgf3wTUbo#t=815

Honing Your Craft

Although the concept of intercultural competence is probably somewhat palatable to most people, we realize that cultural humility and critical consciousness are complex and controversial concepts that may spark a range of reactions from readers, including skepticism or indignation. However, we felt it essential to introduce these concepts and offer ways that they may shape community-engaged courses to reflect an agenda of positive social change. Whatever your reaction, we hope you will at least allow yourself to be open to further exploration of these topics.

You will also want to attend to these same constructs in the formation of your students. You can probably expect that most of the students who walk into your classroom demonstrate an emergent level of intercultural competence, cultural humility, and critical consciousness at best. Likewise, a combination of limited life experience, assumptions about life based on their family's own context and values, and their developmental trajectory will influence their behaviors, perceptions, and attitudes. Thus, it will be important to determine ways that you can move them to greater levels of competence and understanding, both through your classroom and through community engagement, while also ensuring that students who are struggling to enact these concepts are not inadvertently causing harm through their interactions with other students and community members. We know that this is a tall order, and it will take a great amount of risk and determination on your part to guide students through what can be uncomfortable learning experiences. We encourage you to start by integrating ideas that suit your own comfort level the first time you teach the course (see Tool Kit 5.8).

> Tool Kit 5.8—Honing Your Craft—Refer to Exercise 5.8 in your workbook to begin planning for the development of intercultural competence, cultural humility, and critical consciousness of your apprentices.

To keep with the analogy of community-engaged teaching as a craft, this chapter invites you to determine the aesthetic that will guide the composition of your course. This aesthetic will be shaped by your identity and related values, beliefs, and worldviews; as well as your aspirations for whom your course will serve and how it will function. In Part Two of this book, we will guide you through taking the abstract and theoretical foundations from this section and applying them in the process of designing your community-engaged course.

PART TWO

DRAWING THE BLUEPRINT AND USING THE TOOLS

Chapter 6

OBJECTIVES

The word *objective* means a goal—a task or purpose to accomplish. From a semantic perspective, it makes sense that professors can easily profess what they intend to teach as it is near and dear to them. Most instructors can and will rattle off the topics, key individuals, significant events, and skill sets associated with the course. That said, this approach reflects a traditional teaching paradigm euphemistically referred to as the "sage on the stage" approach that has been used in traditional classroom settings for centuries. In this model, students are passive recipients of knowledge they are expected to assimilate, memorize, and restate through written assignments, class discussions, or exams to demonstrate their understanding of the knowledge that was *taught*.

We are now shifting from a teaching paradigm to a learning paradigm that focuses on not only what we teach but also what and how students learn, as we prepare to conceptualize, design, deliver, and assess an engaged course. As discussed earlier in Part One, this pedagogical and epistemic shift also expands our understanding and expectations of who the teacher and student are. Through this approach, the instructor learns right along with the students because the students and the community partners take an active role in the teaching process. To begin this process, refer to Tool Kit 6.1 to reflect on what "teaching" and "learning" look like—how are they the same and different?

> Tool Kit 6.1—Refer to Exercise 6.1 in your workbook to reflect on "teaching" and "learning." Discuss your ideas with colleagues and/or your center director.

The fundamental shift is from what is *taught* to what is *learned* and *how* it is learned. In this way our rudimentary instructional objective or goal moves away from "getting through the content" to providing opportunities for students to apply and demonstrate what they've learned. It is one thing for a student to be taught a definition and correctly identify or repeat it on a written exam. It is possible that this type of performance may really only attest to the student's ability to recall information rather than understand and apply it. However, it is a completely different matter when students can show an instructor they understand the definition or concept by using it in real-life settings. For example, students in a marketing class can authentically demonstrate their understanding of key marketing principles by applying their new knowledge and skills through developing a marketing plan with a local nonprofit agency. Their performance is socially validated when and if the community partner actually adopts the product. This is an added feature of engaged teaching and learning as the application of that assimilated knowledge and skill is mutually beneficial—for the student earning a grade and for the community that is part of the course. Therefore, the initial step to conceptualizing an engaged course is to determine what we would like to see our students *do* with the knowledge and skills both in the classroom and *with* (not for) the community partner. In this sense, our focus is on the students' acquisition and application of specific skills to help them grow in multiple domains.

Starting with instructional objectives also minimizes the trend for instructors to begin the planning process by (a) focusing on a service project and (b) "putting in hours." Some instructors mistakenly view engaged courses as completing a project "out in" and "for" the community. Sometimes these projects resemble cocurricular service activities, such as conducting food drives or painting a school, that embody a shallow learning experience grounded in a charity model as opposed to deeper, transformative experiences that facilitate achieving specific academic and cognitive goals. To be frank, and at the risk of sounding glib, there is relatively little academic purpose to these types of projects unless, of course, the class is about food pantries or painting. Likewise, instructors sometimes begin the conceptualizing process by focusing on a "site" where students can "put in" a certain amount of clock hours. This approach contradicts the pedagogical purpose of engaged courses that reflect the tenets of community engagement as presented in Part One of this book. As explored in chapter 3, the service is a form of pedagogy, just like a reading or writing assignment, designed to help students understand and apply specific cognitive information and skills. As such, the objective is not to complete a specific number of hours but to *learn*. As is discussed in chapter 9, the learning often occurs during reflection. As we will see in chapter 8 about exploring engagement activities, an instructor must consider with a community partner a reasonable number of clock hours to interface with learning activities outside of class, as well as how those hours are distributed over an academic quarter or semester. A common question arises as to whether or not any time devoted to in-class activities "counts" as engagement hours. The key here is to focus not so much on where the activities occur but on the purpose and outcome. Similarly, the detailed discussion in chapter 4 addressed the issue of placement versus partnership.

Given that many instructors initially need a sense of what an engaged course can look like as they begin to contemplate instructional objectives, brushstroke course descriptions are provided in Table 6.1. Note these courses are not tied to professional credentialing or internships in which students are expected to demonstrate mastery of specific professional skills to obtain a practitioner license. Likewise, these are not typical "service projects." The engaged learning activities are meaningful exercises tied to academic content in which students meet instructional objectives.

You were introduced to various foci, forms, and frameworks of engaged pedagogy in chapter 3. These included exploration of what the focus of a course might entail: civic, disciplinary, project based, competency based, solidarity, or research (Heffernan, 2001). Likewise, that chapter introduced critical service-learning (Mitchell, 2008), liberation service-learning (Stoecker, 2016), and decolonizing service-learning (Yep & Mitchell, 2017). Finally, specific formats such as activism, community-based research, direct service, philanthropy, policy/politics, and social entrepreneurship were also described (Haas Center for Public Service, 2010; Schnaubelt & Schwartz-Coffey, 2016). That early passage was foundational in purpose. Now that you are actively and intentionally designing your course and establishing its academic objectives, it is time to revisit those foundational concepts in Tool Kit 6.2 to determine how they will frame and shape your course and the form of engagement it will take.

> Tool Kit 6.2—Refer to Exercise 6.2 in your workbook, where you will be invited to return to an earlier Tool Kit activity and review your initial thoughts about foci, forms, and framework for your emerging course.

Explicit and Ancillary Curricular Objectives

As instructors, we naturally tend to focus on academic objectives for our students. These are usually associated with explicit concepts and

TABLE 6.1
Examples of Engaged Courses

Course	*Description*
Nursing	Preprofessional nursing students were assigned (in pairs) to be companions of senior citizens. They made home/assisted living center visits once a week to have conversations with seniors. The students observed and commented on specific medication issues related to geriatrics in class discussions and reflection activities. Students were also able to help their senior companions by reading/writing letters or doing odd jobs around the house (e.g., changing light bulbs). Issues/topics such as cultural views of elders, Medicare rules/regulations, dementia, gait/physical movement, and medication routine/confusion were observed and discussed in terms of how preprofessionals will care for and interact with seniors in their careers.
Chemistry	College students learned and applied chemical analysis skills working with schools and community gardens while conducting soil, water, and pH analysis for toxins. Students had to articulate their results to a lay audience with recommendations for practice. The class collectively reflected on the role of chemists as professionals and citizens in policymaking, especially revolving around issues such as environmental racism in which exposure to toxins was greater for underresourced agencies/communities than for affluent areas.
English	Students in a service-learning course called Literature of Poverty tutored Title I high school students. During their interactions, students noted social, economic, cultural, and medical indicators of poverty within the school and the high school students and explored the reciprocal role these factors and conditions had on academic performance.
Marketing	Students in a marketing course applied and demonstrated their mastery of skills by working with nonprofit agencies to create marketing plans. The class collectively discussed the underlying issues for the existence of these agencies. They compared and contrasted specific concepts/skills applied in this experience with corporate settings.
Political Science	One political science course focused on the creation, administration, analysis, and reporting of a survey created on behalf of a nonprofit agency. The survey was used to assess the impact of programming and outreach to clients. Students were able to apply their survey development and analysis skills in ways that helped the community partner create a new strategic plan. A second political science course did "indirect" service by doing research to create policy briefs on best practice for agencies. The briefs were used in program development and grant writing.

Research Methods	A statistics course provided indirect service to schools and nonprofit agencies by "crunching numbers" of existing surveys and assessment measures. Students were able to apply their statistical analysis knowledge to helping agencies.
Communications	Students demonstrated mastery of video production skills by producing a 10-minute video for a nonprofit agency. Students reflected on the cultural, sociological, and economic factors related to the mission of the agency coupled with the role of popular media/video depicting accurate and/or inaccurate portraits of the clients served and/or issue being addressed.
Religious Studies	This service-learning course focused on "food and faith" issues by working with community gardens and/or local food banks. Students provided direct service through stocking shelves, delivering food, and working in gardens. They explored issues of social justice, poverty, and hunger using Christian scripture and tenets. Students critically reflected on society's role (or lack of it) in caring for the hungry as well as the intertwined issues of nutrition with other health/social needs.
Modern Language	Students in an Italian class developed their language skills and cultural understanding by meeting with elderly Italian immigrants to create/produce an oral history on a DVD given to the seniors. Students reflected on cultural values, including American views of "elders" and family.
Nutrition and Fitness	Pre-med/nursing students developed and delivered a health/nutritional literacy program for senior citizens in assisted living settings and/or families in underserved schools. Students focused on their interpersonal communication skills as well as their technical/medical skills in taking vital signs and other assessments (flexibility, strength, cardiovascular) and developed an intervention plan. Reflection included social/cultural perceptions of this population as well as social/political factors that contribute to poor health/nutrition and how this would impact their practice as care providers.
Computer Science	A computer science course created a mobile phone app for a local wildlife center in which community residents could snap photos of wildlife they observed in the area and submit them to the center to identify the animals and obtain information about them.

skills from the discipline that we want our students to understand and apply. Referring to our case study example from the nursing course on geriatrics, we can see the course objectives are directly tied to behaviors, conditions, and syndromes associated with the aging process that nurse practitioners must be able to recognize and understand to provide ethical and professional health care to senior citizens (see Figure 6.1).

You will note that the first five objectives of the course are explicitly tied to disciplinary-based content areas. The instructor also included cultural and systemic contexts for students to demonstrate their understanding in ways that will inform and enhance their practice as nurses. The remaining four objectives reflect what we are characterizing here as ancillary objectives.

As explained in previous chapters, engaged teaching and learning is a different type of experiential education in the community that presents an opportunity to expand instructional objectives to include other skill sets and domains. The interactive and applied nature of engaged teaching and learning readily lends itself to Bloom's taxonomy (Bloom et al., 1956), consisting of a hierarchy of cognitive skills: recall, comprehension, application, analysis, evaluation, and creativity. Indeed, many engagement activities students are assigned incorporate nearly all of these skills. There are similar skill sets that empower students for meaningful personal and professional lives. This "hidden curriculum" consists of effective written and oral communication, problem-solving,

Figure 6.1 Nursing course title, description, and objectives.

New or Revised Course Title and Description

Title: NUR 350: Geriatrics

Course Description

This preclinical practice course provides an overview and introduction to the developmental characteristics of aging patients. In pairs, students will become companions to elders in assisted living facilities to observe specific traits and behaviors common to aging seniors. Students will explore and reflect on how cultural, political, and economic and family ecosystem dynamics that interplay with health and the aging process will influence and impact their practice as future care providers.

OBJECTIVES: What do you want your students to experience, demonstrate, and/or accomplish at the end of this course?

1. Name, identify, and describe various characteristics, conditions, and syndromes common in human aging.
2. Name, identify, and describe possible medical and/or physical treatments for common geriatric conditions as prescribed by a physician or social worker.
3. Name, understand, and articulate current federal, state, and local health policies and programs related to the health of geriatric patients.
4. Demonstrate an understanding of available health care options for elders and possible interagency/cross-professional collaborations in serving elders.
5. Conduct basic approved health-screening procedures (e.g., blood pressure, pulse, temperature).
6. Reflect on cultural, economic, and political factors that impact the overall well-being of elders, aging patients, and their families.
7. Reflect on how cultural, economic, and political factors may impact the role and performance of caregivers as they interact with aging parents.
8. Reflect on the role of care providers given their personal and cultural contexts.
9. Collaborate with a classmate to create and deliver nonmedical activities appropriate for their elders and that interface with class topics.

time management, and teamwork. Although some instructors might dismiss this as irrelevant to the disciplinary content of the course, it is important to understand these skills will enable students to become not only knowledgeable but also more likely to succeed in their personal, professional, and civic lives.

We can endeavor to provide students a wider perspective of their learning experience and holistic development by considering civic, cultural, political, and systemic factors and contexts (Harward, 2012). Reading and writing assignments, class discussions, and reflection activities provide students a lens to explore and consider how these other contexts shape not only their learning experiences but also their roles and responsibilities as competent professionals and citizens in a just and democratic society. This holistic approach of teaching promotes transformative learning experiences that transcend merely assimilating new information and skills.

Two important things should be taken into consideration in regard to ancillary objectives. First, this type of objective, as our title suggests, is ancillary rather than a primary content-specific goal. As such, this type of objective need not take too much time that overrides the primary academic goals of the course. Second, instructors need not be "experts" to "teach" within these domains. Instead, it is an invitation for students to explore and discuss these topics and contexts during reflection exercises that will embellish the academic component of the course. Instructors can also and are encouraged to invite their community partner to explore these topics in classroom discussions as well as colleagues from other departments who might specialize in these areas. This reflects our reconceptualization of community partners as coeducators and public scholars who bring their own perspective to the engaged teaching and learning experience. Based on the realities they often face each and every day, our public scholars can help students go beyond the theory to consider various contexts and how they impact the work. Begin to consider possible ancillary objectives that transcend traditional academically focused goals in Tool Kit 6.3. Don't worry about *how* you will go about meeting any of these objectives for now—that will come later as you and your community partner explore what activities your students will engage in. Another example from a chemistry course is provided in your workbook to help you get started.

> Tool Kit 6.3—Refer to Exercise 6.3 in your workbook for examples of ancillary objectives and then consider possible ancillary objectives for your course.

Here We Go

We are nearly halfway through this book and it is now time to actively apply the concepts in the actual design of a course. Using the nursing course as an example, identify a new or revised course you are planning to teach as an engaged course. Provide the title and a brief description of the course that might be found in a course catalog in Tool Kit 6.4. This is your first opportunity to articulate what you want your students to be able to do, understand, demonstrate, apply, and master by the end of the course.

> Tool Kit 6.4—Refer to the example in Exercise 6.4 in your workbook and then list your tentative course title, description, and course objectives.

Objectives Squared

At this point, our pedagogical focus and efforts have been student centered. We have identified and articulated *what* we want our students to do and learn. We will focus on the *how* in chapter 8, exploring ways students will be engaged with the community partner. Designing and implementing effective community-engaged teaching and learning experiences has an additional layer of complexity in which the objectives and goals of the community partner are also incorporated. In this way, we might expand objectives focused primarily on instructional and ancillary objectives to "objectives-squared" to include the objectives and goals of the community partner. There is only one way to find out what their aspirations are and that is to ask them. But there is a prerequisite step to this, which is identifying potential partners in the community. The next chapter explores this process of identifying and collaborating with community partners in detail. For now, it is useful to begin the process by contemplating potential ways your course and students might be used to help community agencies meet their goals and aspirations. In this way, you enter into a dialogue exploring possible engagement activities to be mutually vetted and agreed on.

There is, however, a very important caveat to state here and now. Instructors cannot and must not presume to know the aspirations or goals of a community agency. In the past, well-intentioned and eager faculty members have assumed the role of expert and approached a community agency in what can seem a condescending, or worse, messianic manner that implicitly and sometimes explicitly connoted a charity model. As discussed in earlier chapters, instructors should enter into this endeavor as coeducators and as guests recognizing, valuing, and honoring the public scholarship and expertise of the community partner in *the partner's* setting. As such, there is a bit of a dance in which an instructor must initially visualize possible engagement activities that might interface with the course while not imposing them on a community partner. It has actually been the case that the initial ideas of an instructor took a radical detour during the initial discussions with a representative from a community agency after the community partner proposed a "better" engagement project after hearing about the course.

Now it is time to speculate on possible objectives and goals that might interest a community partner and that might be related to the instructional and ancillary objectives you have thus far considered. This is an important prerequisite step to help us determine if there is a possible match with an agency. However, it is important to note here, and this will be examined in much more detail in the next chapter, that as we anticipate or speculate on possible goals, we do not impose our assumption of "what they need" on a community partner. It is quite likely that a community partner will have different but appropriate ideas. As the next chapter, on forming partnerships with community agencies, will describe, instructors must be open to partners' goals and aspirations. Instead, we are merely preparing talking points to begin the conversation. In other words, instructors need to step back and consider "what's in it for them" rather than merely focus on what we want for our students, as explored in Tool Kit 6.5.

> Tool Kit 6.5—Refer to Exercise 6.5 in your workbook to see an example on how to begin contemplating potential partnerships and engagement activities that you can discuss and explore with a community partner.

Honing Your Craft

This chapter focused on developing explicit and ancillary objectives for your engaged course. Hopefully, the chapter provided some basic nuts and bolts for you to begin designing and constructing your engaged course. In honing your craft, we invite you to take a broader perspective and continue reflecting on this idea of "objectives" in the context of what it is we espouse to accomplish in our classroom, in our scholarship, in our community. We articulated two somewhat radical concepts that deviate from traditional notions of teaching and learning.

First, by shifting from a teaching paradigm to incorporating a learning paradigm, we reimagine the roles of teacher and student. You are, no doubt, a skilled professor with expertise who will quite literally profess your knowledge in your course. That is a given. But we are inviting you to shift from the traditional "sage on the stage" role to become the "guide on the side" whereby your students take on a great deal of responsibility for their own learning by applying what they learn in meaningful and purposeful ways beyond getting a good grade. In this way, students are constructing their own educational experience (with your guidance) in ways that they, too, become a teacher of sorts. Be advised that many students will resist this new role and responsibility imposed on them as they have been socialized in the teaching paradigm to be passive recipients of factoids rather than view learning as the developmental process depicted in Bloom's taxonomy. The effort and application that engaged teaching and learning entails is and will quickly sound like actual work to students. This, once again, flies in the face of the traditional teaching paradigm where students are often absolved from any responsibility in their learning. Instead, they expect the instructor to spoon-feed them what will be on the test by providing copies of lecture notes they can peruse right before an exam. The learning paradigm of engaged teaching and learning requires students to work and be accountable for their work as they provide service to and in the community.

Likewise, in the learning paradigm the community partner is viewed as a coeducator, bringing their own public scholarship and expertise to the experience. In some ways, you as the instructor become a student as well by becoming the beneficiary of your partner's knowledge. You, too, will gain insight and have an opportunity to test your own theory and practice out in the "real world" and not merely within the relatively controllable and benign four walls of a classroom or erudite pages of academic journals. As suggested previously, the community partner may actually be better qualified to address some of the ancillary objectives of your course. Therefore, inviting them to share their insight in your classroom is yet another radical departure from the "sage on the stage" approach of teaching.

The second nontraditional concept presented in this chapter is expanding our notion and application of instructional objectives. Again, a shift from a teaching to a learning paradigm allows us to provide opportunities where students can show us what and how they learned through the service they provide in the community. Additionally, consideration of ancillary objectives that reflect a "hidden curriculum" of skill sets to promote students' civic, cultural, professional, and personal development reflects a shift from focusing exclusively on academic and discipline-based goals. Some (perhaps yourself) would argue this is not the role or purpose of an instructor. Traditionally, an instructor's role and responsibility are to generate and disseminate new knowledge within their discipline. We would agree with this role. We also, however, suggest that is a narrowly defined role and responsibility that does not reflect the public purpose of higher education. The traditional disciplinary focus is what Harkavy (2004) described as "disciplinary guildism" (p. 12) in which faculty members' loyalty and vocation is to their discipline rather than the holistic development of students and pursuing the public purpose of higher education by serving the common good within the community. Harkavy (2004) noted that Stanley Fish (2003), former dean at the University of Illinois at Chicago, wrote a provocative white paper published in *The Chronicle of Higher Education*. Fish (2003) argued professors cannot make their students "into good people . . . and shouldn't try," suggesting that "emphasis on broader goals and especially on the therapeutic goal of personal development can make it difficult to interest students in the disciplinary training it is our job to provide" (p. C5, as cited in Harkavy, 2004). We would disagree with this premise, reminding colleagues of the foundational public purpose of higher education introduced in chapter 1 and embedded throughout this book. This, in turn, is a rejection of the commodification of higher education in which a growing number of students and their families, as well as society at large, view the primary objective of higher education as providing a pathway to a well-paying career. Likewise, we are not suggesting engaged course activities are intended or designed to be therapeutic.

A recent study revealed that political, social, and economic forces in an emerging urban, industrial, class-stratified society have reframed students' and their families' expectations of higher education's priorities to focus on preparing professionals for careers rather than citizens working toward a just and democratic society (Dorn, 2011). We believe that a college experience provides a pathway to a meaningful personal and professional life, as well as a civic life and it begins in the class—your class.

Articulating a set of specific terms, concepts, and skills on a course syllabus is a fairly straightforward task. Talking *at* (rather than to) students and providing a textbook for them to obtain information are equally perfunctory. Intentional and deep contemplation on what we hope to accomplish in our classroom coupled with what we hope our students accomplish and do is an artful, nuanced craft. Consideration of how our work can make an impact on the community as a whole transcends our disciplinary guildism. Therefore, to truly hone our craft, we must revisit and reconsider a broader perspective of what we mean and say when we use the term *objective* as engaged scholars, as explored in Tool Kit 6.6.

> Tool Kit 6.6—Honing Your Craft—Refer to Exercise 6.6 in your workbook. Have you ever considered or implemented ancillary objectives in your course? Have they ever accidentally or surreptitiously emerged in your courses? What are your thoughts about explicitly incorporating nondisciplinary-based objectives into your course? Is that appropriate or necessary?
>
> What are your reactions and thoughts to Harkavy's premise that faculty have traditionally practiced disciplinary guildism rather than considered their larger role in the public purpose of higher education? What are your thoughts and reactions to Stanley Fish's argument that it is not the role of faculty to prepare "good people"?

Chapter 7

PARTNERSHIPS

Now it's time to establish and maintain a partnership. We explored the concept of partnerships as an alternative to the traditional placement approach in chapter 2. Likewise, previous chapters in Part One of this book examined and considered the dynamics associated with "town and gown" relationships. Historically, community partners and those they serve have had reservations about working with higher education, and rightly so. In the past, forms of experiential education often viewed and used community settings as laboratories, actually exploiting them rather than working with them. Although stated before, it bears repeating. The tenets and principles of community engagement have been designed and implemented to view community partners as coeducators in ways that faculty and students work *with*—not *for*—community agencies and those they serve. In this way and incorporating cultural humility as described in chapter 5, faculty and students enter into this partnership as guests who have been invited into this setting. Aside from the philosophical notion of partnerships, what does or can a community partnership look like? Tool Kit 7.1 gives you a glimpse of what to expect.

> Tool Kit 7.1—Refer to Exercise 7.1 in your workbook. Watch the "Engaging Conversation" video clip (Figure 7.1) to learn more about community partnerships. Respond to the questions in your workbook posed about the video clip.

Figure 7.1 What community partnerships look like.

Note. Scan the QR code to access https://vimeo.com/207844893/5dca3d77d9

Partners as Coeducators and Public Scholars

A key component of community-engaged teaching and learning is viewing and collaborating with the community partner as a coeducator and public scholar. As discussed in Chapters 1 and 2, this is a significant paradigm shift from the placement model in which we look for a place where students can go and "put in hours." The partnership approach recognizes, honors, and incorporates the community partner's valuable experience and perspective (see Figure 7.2 and Tool Kit 7.2).

Figure 7.2 Role of community partners.

Note. Scan the QR code to access http://vimeo.com/207844846/eaa01a16e8

> Tool Kit 7.2—Refer to Exercise 7.2 in your workbook. Watch the video clip in Figure 7.2 and respond to the questions posed about the video.

Identifying Potential Community Partners

Now it is time to identify potential partners who can help you achieve your instructional objectives and explore if there might be a match in meeting their objectives. Going beyond a traditional transactional approach of merely "picking a partner," this process includes a prerequisite step of considering and aligning institutional goals and mission. Furthermore, as we will soon see, we align the academic and institutional goals with those of the organization or group we hope to work with. This includes

TABLE 7.1
Example: Identifying Potential Community Agency Partners

Question to Ask	*Notes/Ideas*
What *type* of community agency or organization might serve as a coeducator partner?	Local assisted living centers. Contact local county social service agency to discuss home visit programs.
Are there specific organizations you know of or have already worked with? If so, what are they?	Evergreen Park Assisted Living Center on Main Street.

considering large multiservice organizations as well as informal community collectives. Using the example from the previous chapter, the instructor for the geriatrics nursing course identified some potential partners, listed in Table 7.1.

Now it's your turn. Begin listing potential partners or consult with your CEP at your campus center for community engagement for some ideas in Tool Kit 7.3.

> Tool Kit 7.3—Refer to Exercise 7.3 in your workbook to consider and list possible community agency partners for your course.

Good! That's an important first step. However, it is easy to constrain our notion of what potential partnerships are and look like into a narrowly defined box. You are invited to think outside that box. For example, an instructor of a women's studies course typically contacted agencies such as women's shelters to serve as partners. While attending a community partner fair at her institution she met the director of a food bank. During the course of their conversation, the director noted that a significant number of the food bank's clients are homeless women and single mothers. His insight led to establishing new partnerships for the course that provided a slightly different perspective and setting for students to learn and address critical issues facing many women.

Don't worry if you don't know of or have any organizations in mind right now. Your campus center for community engagement can help you identify potential partners. Consult with your colleagues as they may have existing partnerships that might be appropriate for your class. Sometimes the community agency may find you! A representative of the organization may contact your campus center for community engagement looking for an instructor or course that could help with a project.

Nuts and Bolts

Okay, the gears are starting to turn. Some common, basic nuts and bolts questions about partnerships usually start to emerge right about now.

How Many Partner Organizations Do I Need?

There's no hard-and-fast rule. It depends on many factors. How many students will be working with the agency? Will students work individually or in teams? What times of day can students come to the agency, and can the agency accommodate that schedule? How many students can an agency realistically work with? This is one of those "less is more" situations in which coordinating and working with two or three agencies is easier than a dozen. Be strategic. For example, many organizations, like schools, provide services and programming in the morning, afternoon, evening, and sometimes even on weekends. Likewise, many agencies typically have one staff person coordinating all programs. Seek and identify efficient and experienced organizations as well as smaller, less structured agencies that may not have had experience hosting community-engaged learners. The latter will initially have a steeper learning curve whereas the experienced organizations will enter into the partnership with some background experience. It depends on the size of your class, but two to three partners seem to work best.

Do I Let My Students Identify and Choose the Agency They Will Work With?

Yes and no. For starters, do you allow your students to choose your course textbook? Probably not, because you have selected the text that best meets your instructional objectives. This same practice should apply to choosing community partners. However, you can allow your students to choose from a "menu" of partners you have carefully vetted and that provides options that may accommodate students' schedules. Furthermore, the old days of allowing or assigning students to go out and find a partner are long over. Many organizations, like K–12 schools and senior citizen assisted living centers, have legal requirements for volunteers/service-learners such as background checks and health screenings. Similarly, it's likely that your institution has risk management policies that you and your students will need to follow. In other words, it's important to make sure you're working with agencies that have existing liability and risk agreements with your institution.

How Many Hours Should My Students Work With the Agency?

This is a common question that will be addressed in more detail in chapter 8. For now, a rule of thumb for hours is based on how much time students are expected to spend outside of class on course activities, such as readings and papers. Because community engagement is a form of pedagogy, an instructor must determine a realistic amount of hours students must spend each week working with and for the community partner. *Generally*, students spend 20 to 30 hours over a 15-week semester. As we will see in the next chapter, the distribution of hours can vary over the period of a course. Be prepared for students to ask if travel time is included in the required amount of time to spend with the agency. As discussed in the previous chapter, the ancillary life skill of time management generally looms to life for students at this point as they attempt to juggle this expectation with other things on their personal and academic calendars.

Next Steps

Now it's your turn to consider some "nuts and bolts" questions regarding your potential community partnerships in Tool Kit 7.4.

> Tool Kit 7.4—Refer to Exercise 7.4 in your workbook to consider some "nuts and bolts" questions on how many partners you might need and how many hours you think your students might work with the agency.

The Courtship Process

Like any relationship, there is an exploratory or "courtship" process that allows people to get to know each other and see if this is going to work. You are encouraged to set up an appointment to visit your potential partner and have a conversation. To help you plan, here are 10 steps to take during this "first date."

1. Introduce Yourself

Briefly tell the partner who you are and what you teach. Bring your course outline and/or syllabus to share to describe your course and instructional objectives.

2. Describe the Course and Students

Explain that this is a community engagement course—not a volunteer project or an internship. Describe the skill level of the students—is this an entry-level course or an advanced capstone course? Further, describe specialized skills, like graphic design or accounting, your students may bring. Are the students undergraduates or graduate students? Also explain the time line of the course—how many weeks and hours are involved?

3. Get a History Lesson

Continue the discussion by asking the partner how long they have been doing this work and/or how long they have been with this organization. Ask about the history and mission of the organization. This serves as an effective foundation for a relationship and building trust. These questions show you have an interest in *them*—not just your class and students. It is also good background information for you to make an informed decision as to whether or not this partnership is viable.

4. Explore Their Goals

Ask about the organization's goals and aspirations. Note the asset-based language that is used—avoid deficit-based language such as *problems* or *issues*. Another way to frame this discussion is to inquire about potential projects or aspirations that have been on the back burner. Continuing with the example introduced in the previous chapter, consider the tentative goals articulated by the community partners for the geriatrics nursing course presented in Table 7.2.

5. Explore Possible Projects

Based on their projected goals and aspirations, discuss possible projects your students could complete that would help the organization build capacity.

TABLE 7.2
Examples of Possible Goals of Community Partners

What are some potential community partner goals and how do they align with the instructional objectives?

Speculating on Possible Community Partner Goals	*Match or Mismatch With Instructional Goals*
Take and monitor vital signs of residents.	Okay
Help lead recreational/social activities in the commons area.	Probably Not
Be a companion and assist with minor day-to-day tasks (e.g., letter writing, changing lightbulb, helping with computer).	Okay
Write grants.	No

6. Reach a Decision Point

This is more of a procedural decision step as you now have a very basic sense of whether there is the potential for moving forward and "getting engaged" as it were. If it seems like a potential match, indicate you'd like to explore and discuss a possible partnership that could facilitate meeting their goals—notice the emphasis here is on *their* agenda, not yours. This is also a good place to move beyond merely applying some logistical skill to practice our craft. It is important to observe the other person's verbal and physical communication. Although their words may be implying a willingness to work with you and your students, their vocal tone and body language may be saying something else. Sometimes people are just too polite to say what they are really thinking or feeling. Likewise, some community volunteer coordinators may be compelled or feel obligated to increase their volunteer count to report back to a board of directors or a grant proposal. That said, there is also the very real possibility that this organization may not be suitable because they don't have a goal or project that fits your course and instructional objectives. You and your students may not have the skills, time, or resources to offer. It is much better to discover this before the course is launched than during it. In this case, you indicate how appreciative you are that they took the time to meet with you and how impressed you are with their mission and organization, but feel you and your students would actually be doing them a disservice as this doesn't seem to be a good match. No one will be offended with this genuine assessment. As such, instead of getting engaged, you part as "good friends." Keep in mind the community partner might decide to opt out and not participate. They can and should say no if it's not going to work for them as well.

7. Create an Action Plan

Once a project(s) has been identified, begin mapping out a series of steps that articulate who does what, when, and where. This step and an action plan template are presented again and in more detail in the next chapter. Take a blank copy of the action plan template with you. This ensures that you and your partner are literally "on the same page" in terms of deliverables. This includes exploring and determining the partner's roles and responsibilities as discussed earlier in this chapter. Finally, articulate how you will assess and evaluate the entire experience. This is examined in more detail later in chapter 10, on assessment.

8. Determine Orientation and Discuss Protocol

Discuss and schedule when and where the representative of the organization will provide an overview and orientation of the agency and project to students. The orientation should explain specific policy, procedures, and protocol for behavior to the students. This might include a policy of "line of sight" in which students are always in the line of sight of a staff person. Issues such as confidentiality, safety, and check-ins/checkouts are also discussed. Complex policy and procedures such as background checks and health screenings must be identified early on to provide ample time for students to comply with and meet those requirements.

9. Discuss Communication Channels
Determine the best way and times to communicate with each other as well as how students should communicate with the organization.

10. Create and Sign a Course Agreement Form
This is not a legal contract. It is a written statement articulating what everyone has agreed to do. This includes a description of the "deliverable" that will be a product or outcome of the community-engaged course. It holds the instructor, students, and community partner accountable. It is also the basis for summative evaluation and assessment. Some instructors and institutions have students sign the agreement. A sample copy of a course agreement form is provided in chapter 8. Keep a copy on file. Save your records with your campus center for community engagement.

Next Steps
You are now ready to prepare and "script" your conversation with a potential partner using these Top 10 steps in Tool Kit 7.5.

> Tool Kit 7.5—Refer to Exercise 7.5 in your workbook. Begin to prepare and "script" your conversation with a potential partner using the Top 10 steps of the courtship process.

You and your partner are officially "engaged" once this courtship is completed. But like any budding new relationship, roles and responsibilities need to be discussed and agreed on.

Roles and Responsibilities

Let's continue to think outside the "placement box" and consider possible roles for partners as coeducators and public scholars. The following sections discuss some possible roles and responsibilities for community partners.

Coordinating/Coconstructing the Course
Sharing a course outline or a tentative course syllabus with a community partner is an opportunity for them to share ideas or activities that could be integrated into the community engagement experience, perhaps noting different reflections, discussions, topics with specific activities, or course readings.

Guest Speakers
Representatives of community agencies and organizations are "public scholars" with their own expertise and perspective. Invite them to a class session to discuss key topics from the course syllabus that they apply or can relate to their setting and work.

Conducting Reflection
Discussed later in chapter 9, reflection is the intentional consideration of an experience in light of instructional objectives (Hatcher & Bringle, 1997) that occurs before, during, and after service. Invite them to develop a reflection topic for your students or conduct a reflection discussion in class or at their location.

Assessing Student Performance
We will explore assessment in more detail later. For now, a common approach is to allocate a small percentage of the course's final grade (e.g., 10%) to student performance as assessed by the partner. This will be discussed in more detail in chapter 10.

Copresent or Coauthor
Community public scholars bring a unique perspective to scholarship. Consider inviting them to contribute to an article and/or conference presentation. Although dissemination of new knowledge is often paramount to faculty, it is less of a priority for community partners—but they often appreciate being asked and included. Their board of directors and donors are likely to be pleased and/or impressed.

Down the Road
Over time, you and your community partner may establish a very strong and enduring relationship. At some point, it may be appropriate to explore ways of expanding the partnership beyond engaged courses. Many departments and/or institutions rely on community partners for advice and input on various aspects of the institution's mission. This might be something a community partner might consider after a successful and

trusting relationship has been established over time. Likewise, many directors of agencies appreciate this type of invitation as it validates their public scholarship and expertise. This type of discussion typically ensues over time, but it is important to keep it in mind for the future. Refer to Tool Kit 7.6 to explore possible roles and responsibilities for your community agency partner.

> Tool Kit 7.6—Refer to Exercise 7.6 in your workbook to explore possible roles and responsibilities for your community agency partner.

As you can see from the exercise, community partners can take on a much more robust role than merely serving as a placement site. Sometimes these roles and responsibilities can emerge quite unexpectedly (see Tool Kit 7.7). When and if a trusting relationship exists in which the community partner is truly a coeducator, an instructor can reach out to their colleague and tap into their public scholarship and insight in class.

> Tool Kit 7.7—Refer to Exercise 7.7 in your workbook to read two case studies on working with community partners as coeducators and reflect on the discussion questions provided.

Trouble in Paradise

In any and all relationships, there are bound to be bumps along the way. This work can be messy and complex. Missteps, mistakes, and mishaps are to be expected. The key to any effective partnership, built on trust, relies on open and honest communication. Some of the best learning and outcomes emerge from these unexpected challenges, as depicted in Tool Kit 7.8.

> Tool Kit 7.8—Refer to Exercise 7.8 in your workbook and read the case study. Reflect on the discussion questions provided.

The case study presented in your workbook reveals how potentially messy community partnerships can be. More importantly, it also illustrates the necessity of establishing trust and maintaining communication with the community partner. This story also demonstrates the unexpected learning objectives that are often not formally articulated on a course syllabus as well as the unanticipated role of community partners as coeducators.

Honing Your Craft

Thus far, time, energy, and attention have been focused on the basic steps and tools to identify and establish a partnership with a community organization. Now it is time to hone your craft to integrate and promote the art of community engagement while applying the technical skills and tools. Think about any relationship or partnership you have in your personal and professional life. What does it take to sustain it? What are the challenges to maintaining a meaningful relationship? Is it worth the effort? If so, why and for whom? How does this apply to a partnership in engaged teaching and learning? Or does it apply at all? To what extent do community organizations trust faculty and students? What may have been their previous experience? What can you say or do to alleviate any hesitation they may have on their part? How can you present yourself as a partner rather than an expert? These are not abstract questions. These questions reflect the complexity of establishing and maintaining meaningful partnerships. It is relatively easy to ponder these questions as an intellectual exercise here and now. However, the underlying premise and meaning behind these questions will clearly manifest themselves as you begin to establish a partnership. Chapters in Part One of this book addressed the importance of cultural competence and cultural humility. They are critical behaviors and attitudes to embody and practice.

We close this chapter by reminding you that directors of community organizations have a day job. They have an array of priorities as well as their own purpose and mission. We need to understand, realize, and remember that our course and students do not necessarily fall within their priorities or purpose. In this sense, their willingness to form a partnership with you is a gift. Therefore, you and your students have been invited to work with them. You and your students are guests. Refer to Tool Kit 7.9 to further hone your craft as a coeducator with a community partner.

> Tool Kit 7.9—Honing Your Craft—Refer to Exercise 7.9 in your workbook for further consideration and discussion about establishing and maintaining partnerships with the community.

Chapter 8

ENGAGEMENT

We now have a list of mutually beneficial objectives for you and your partners. It is time to determine how those objectives will be achieved through meaningful engagement in and with the community. Tentative ideas for activities and projects will emerge during early conversations with your community partner during the courtship process. Previous consideration of explicit and ancillary objectives coupled with tentative ideas of focus, form, and framework articulated in your workbook will now be put into action. Much of this has been discussed during the courtship process with your partner as you mapped out an action plan as discussed in the previous chapter. Now it is time to formalize the engagement activities articulating who does what, when, and where using the course agreement form and action plan (see Figure 8.1).

Who Does What?

There are at least three key players in the engagement process: (a) instructors, (b) students, and (c) the community partner administrator and ancillary support personnel. An administrator at the community agency who agreed to the partnership may assign a staff person at the organization to do the actual coordination and supervision of students. An example of such an arrangement in the community might be a case in which a school principal has made a commitment to you and your students, but it is the school volunteer coordinator or a classroom teacher who will be working directly with your students. Similarly, some institutions provide student assistants to an instructor to serve as liaisons to the community partner.

Figure 8.1 Sample course agreement form and action plan.

Course Name, Number, and Term:	
Instructor Name:	
Instructor E-mail, Phone:	
Community Partner Organization Name:	
Address:	Website:
On-site Supervisor Name and Title:	Phone and E-mail:
Executive Director or Principal Name:	Phone and E-mail:
Term Start Date:	Term End Date:
Best Method of Communication for Partner:	

This Community Partnership Course Agreement ensures academic rigor; creates and/or sustains a reciprocal relationship between the college and community partner; and promotes best practices that lead to quality experiences for students, the instructor, and the community partner. This agreement will be reviewed, discussed, and completed by the instructor and community partner organization or agency (hereafter called "community partner"). Approval represents a commitment by the instructor and community partner to oversee the project and ensure that appropriate supervision, safety, and ethical standards are met. No provisions relating to liability, indemnity, insurance, or financial obligations may be added to this template without authorization from appropriate campus authorities.

Community partner site supervisor agrees to the following:

- Provide an orientation to the mission and goals of your organization and the issues being addressed.
- Provide a description of student community engagement responsibilities. *If direct service, a schedule will be created that outlines days and hours per week the student will serve and in what capacity. If indirect service, a time line will be created that outlines due dates for project components, to whom project components should be submitted, and how.*
- Provide sound supervision through (a) providing an on-site orientation, (b) meeting and/or speaking consistently with the student about community engagement experience and performance, and (c) involving the student in on-site training and reflection.

(*Continues*)

Figure 8.1 (*Continued*)

- Respond to student; instructor; and, if applicable, student course assistant communications in a timely manner, ideally within 48 hours.
- Review, sign, and return paperwork related to community engagement in a timely manner.
- Become familiar with the course content and time line and explore ways to be part of the teaching-learning "team."
- Participate in a formative midterm evaluation and follow-up with the campus center for community engagement support.
- Provide summative assessment/evaluation of student performance (service) and the community engagement partnership at term's end.

Faculty member agrees to the following:

- Articulate course learning objectives and community partner service objectives connected to community engagement.
- Plan an in-class orientation to community engagement opportunities, specific course-based project(s), and the community setting.
- Provide indirect support for community engagement supervision. *If direct service:* Frequently check and/or collect students' logs, schedule frequent in-class reflections, and assign frequent reflection assignments to determine what students are doing and how they are connecting it to course content. *If indirect service:* Provide academic support for project components and actively reinforce project time lines.
- With the assistance of the campus center for community engagement, keep in contact with site supervisors and respond promptly to community partner needs and concerns. Respond to community partner, campus center, and student communications in a timely manner, ideally within 48 hours.
- Participate in a formative midterm evaluation and follow-up with campus center support.
- Integrate reflection throughout the course (prior to service/research, during, and after).
- Review, sign, and return paperwork related to community engagement in a timely manner.
- Provide summative assessment/evaluation of student performance (learning) and the community engagement partnership at term's end.

(*Continues*)

Figure 8.1 (*Continued*)

Plan for Student Community Engagement:

These points should be negotiated and recorded. This template can be modified to reflect the specifics of student community engagement in the context of a particular course.

Number of students, given community partner capacity:
Number of hours per student and allocation of hours over academic term (max 30 hours):
What form will student community engagement take? Provide a detailed description of what students will do (nature of direct service, indirect service, or both). How will the community engagement experience respond to community partner priorities and contribute to the organization's mission? What is the product or deliverable for the community partner?
How will community engagement experiences be linked to course concepts? What course activities and assignments will demonstrate that students are connecting course concepts to community engagement experiences?
Roles and responsibility(ies) of community partner in class (if any):

(*Continues*)

Figure 8.1 (*Continued*)

Role(s) and responsibility(ies) of community partner in terms of assessing student performance (if any):
In-class orientation date, time, and location:
On-site orientation date(s), time(s), and location(s):
Important dates (i.e., school holidays and vacations) worth noting:
How and when a transition plan for students will be executed with vulnerable population being served (if applicable):
What special preparation will be required prior to the start of community engagement? Special training (provided by community partner), tuberculosis tests, background checks (live scan or fingerprints), other?

Signing this agreement indicates both parties' best intentions to meet these mutually agreed-on components and to complete the summative evaluation following.

Instructor: ______________________________

Date: ______________________________

Community Partner: ______________________________

Date: ______________________________

(*Continues*)

Figure 8.1 (*Continued*)

Summative Evaluation

To be completed by the community partner within two weeks of the course conclusion either using this form or by phone interview using these questions and response formats:

To what level did the instructor, students, and/or course meet your satisfaction on the following?

0 = No evidence 1 = Poor 2 = Satisfactory 3 = Good 4 = Excellent

1. Quality of product or implementation of project
   0 1 2 3 4
2. Quality of student professionalism/behavior
   0 1 2 3 4
3. Quality of students following protocol, policy, and procedures
   0 1 2 3 4
4. Quality of communication with students
   0 1 2 3 4
5. Quality of students following directions/supervision
   0 1 2 3 4
6. Quality of student timeliness and follow-through on task completion
   0 1 2 3 4
7. Quality of communication with instructor
   0 1 2 3 4
8. Quality of interaction/cooperation with instructor
   0 1 2 3 4
9. Would you work/interact with this course/instructor again?
   Yes No
10. Was the product/project/deliverable acceptable?
    Yes No
11. Have you/will you adopt/implement the product?
    Yes No

In this sense, the student assistant serves as an ancillary support to and extension of the instructor. As such, it is important to identify and articulate the roles and responsibilities of both of these individuals.

Instructor

The instructor must introduce and explain the engagement component of the class to students and emphasize it as a form of teaching and learning, similar to taking notes during lecture, completing reading assignments, and turning in written assignments. However, the way in which community engagement differs from these other learning activities is that it involves higher stakes. Namely, other people are counting on students to do the activities in good faith and be of use to the community. Avoid using the term *volunteer* for two reasons. First, students are not volunteering—they are required to engage in these activities just as they would any other assignment. This minimizes the oxymoron that students are being "required to volunteer" as well as the misperception they are paying tuition to do a charity project. Second, the concept of volunteering connotes a completely different dynamic and expectation that often suggests less of a formal commitment. Emphasize how the community partner and those they serve are relying on the students as paraprofessionals.

Remember, too, that the community engagement is not an "add-on" to the course. Instead, the instructor should be integrating key concepts and topics from the course into the experience and the reflection activities. The case study of the nursing course on geriatrics does a nice job of infusing course content into the community-engaged activities as the students serve as companions to elders. The case study is interspersed throughout this narrative and the accompanying workbook (look ahead to Tool Kit 9.2 in your workbook).

Once the course is up and running, the instructor must maintain ongoing communication with the community partner, either directly or through their student assistant, to monitor the students' activities and performance.

Community Partner

We explored potential roles and responsibilities of the community partner in the previous chapter. Now it is time to formalize that understanding and agreement in writing. Articulate how often and how you will communicate with them to monitor the progress of the class and students. Determine if and when the partner will make in-class presentations or conduct reflection activities. Finalize any assessment procedures that the community partner will conduct.

Another key step is providing an orientation to the organization and project activity. If possible, invite all of the community partners during the first week of class to provide an overview of the mission and history of the organization as well as the planned activities. This way, students can learn from and ask questions firsthand of the partner. The orientation includes important protocols such as checking in and out of the agency, policy and procedures, issues and practices related to confidentiality, and expectations regarding dress and behaviors.

Individual Students or Student Teams

Students will now be actively engaged in meeting instructional objectives as well as achieving the goals of the community partner by participating in projects and activities that often take the form of a tangible product or specific task. An instructor must now determine if students are working individually or in teams. Many traditional approaches of direct service such as tutoring have individual students working one-on-one with children in school settings. Accounting courses may have students assisting individuals with their tax returns. Similarly, students may work collectively on projects such as trail restoration, but not necessarily as teams with delegation of specific roles and responsibilities.

Enter into the use of student teams prudently and realistically. Students do not possess innate teamwork skills—like any skill, effective teamwork must be taught. Consequently, teamwork becomes part of the ancillary "hidden curriculum" as discussed in chapter 6. It will require allocating class time to teach and discuss essential team functions and dynamics such as time management, effective communication, problem-solving, and conflict management. This may involve ongoing "check-ins" for 10 to 15 minutes once a week to reflect on and assess their performance as individuals and teams. This formative assessment process can include articulating individual and team goals to address specific issues that arise (see Figure 8.2). The form is submitted by each team to the instructor for review. Finally, as instructor, you will need to determine how grades will be assigned to a team. One way to do this is to assign a team grade based on the community partner's satisfaction with the students' product and performance, which might comprise 10% of the final grade. This assessment component can be included and embedded with the overall course evaluation that is included as part of the course agreement form, action plan, and syllabus.

Figure 8.2 Sample student team assessment form.

Team Performance Assessment

Team Member Names:

0 = No Evidence 1 = Poor 2 = Okay 3 = Good 4 = Super

We were prepared for our tasks.	0 1 2 3 4
We stayed on task and accomplished what we set out to do.	0 1 2 3 4
We gave positive/constructive feedback to each other.	0 1 2 3 4
We started and ended on time.	0 1 2 3 4
We treated each other with respect.	0 1 2 3 4
We allowed each person to participate in meaningful ways.	0 1 2 3 4
We were able to monitor individual and/or the team's emotions/feelings and act accordingly.	0 1 2 3 4
We were able to use effective communication skills.	0 1 2 3 4
We were able to effectively solve problems.	0 1 2 3 4

Things we could do differently or better next time we meet:

Individual Performance Assessment

My Name:

0 = No Evidence 1 = Poor 2 = Okay 3 = Good 4 = Super

I let others know when I liked or didn't like something in an appropriate manner.	0 1 2 3 4
I did not dominate the conversation or work.	0 1 2 3 4
I was not withdrawn or disengaged.	0 1 2 3 4
I clarified/paraphrased information to check for understanding.	0 1 2 3 4
I attended and listened carefully to others.	0 1 2 3 4

(Continues)

Figure 8.2 (*Continued*)

I encouraged and affirmed others on the team.	0 1 2 3 4
I came prepared.	0 1 2 3 4
I accomplished my task/assignment for the team.	0 1 2 3 4
I tried to give constructive comments and feedback to the team.	0 1 2 3 4
Things I could/will do differently or better next time we meet:	

When

It is usually at this juncture that instructors begin to ask the inevitable questions, "How many hours of engagement are required and how are they distributed over the duration of the course?" Although important questions, they are actually somewhat peripheral and driven by the objectives. Remember it is the *learning* and the *deliverable* when working with the community that are the focus here and not the number or distribution of hours. Likewise, the actual distribution and allocation of clock hours will and do vary in every course according to the objectives and activities. The range must be reasonable to ensure a meaningful experience for both the student and community partner. Five hours over the course of a quarter or semester would be considered a "shallow" experience, whereas 40-plus hours is unrealistic and moves into the realm of capstone or preprofessional practica experiences leading to licensure or a credential. Although it is important to follow through on the time commitment to the partner, overemphasizing "putting in hours" with students negates the intentionality and meaningfulness of the learning experience. In a nutshell, there is no "right" formula. Likewise, take into account the first and last week of the course to "ramp up" and "wind down," essentially eliminating at least two, if not three, weeks from the quarter or semester. Finally, consideration of time lines must include a deadline. Determine when the engagement activities conclude and when any deliverable is to be completed.

Instructors should also consider students' schedules when identifying partners and projects. Providing an array of engagement activity schedules helps students work around their other courses, work, travel/commute, and family. As such, some partnerships might provide opportunities for students to participate early in the mornings, midday, afternoons, evenings, or weekends. Many schools have before, during, and after school program options as well as evening programs that might mesh well with your course project. The orientation provided by the partner should articulate the schedule parameters. Consider using a lottery approach of assigning students to community projects or instruct students to have a first, second, and third choice.

Based on experience, the following are some of the common ways hours can be distributed and allocated during the engagement activities: (a) weekly, (b) the bulge, (c) the roller coaster, and (d) the wave (see Figure 8.3). The allocation and distribution of hours are determined with the community partner.

Figure 8.3 Options for dispersing service hours over an academic term.

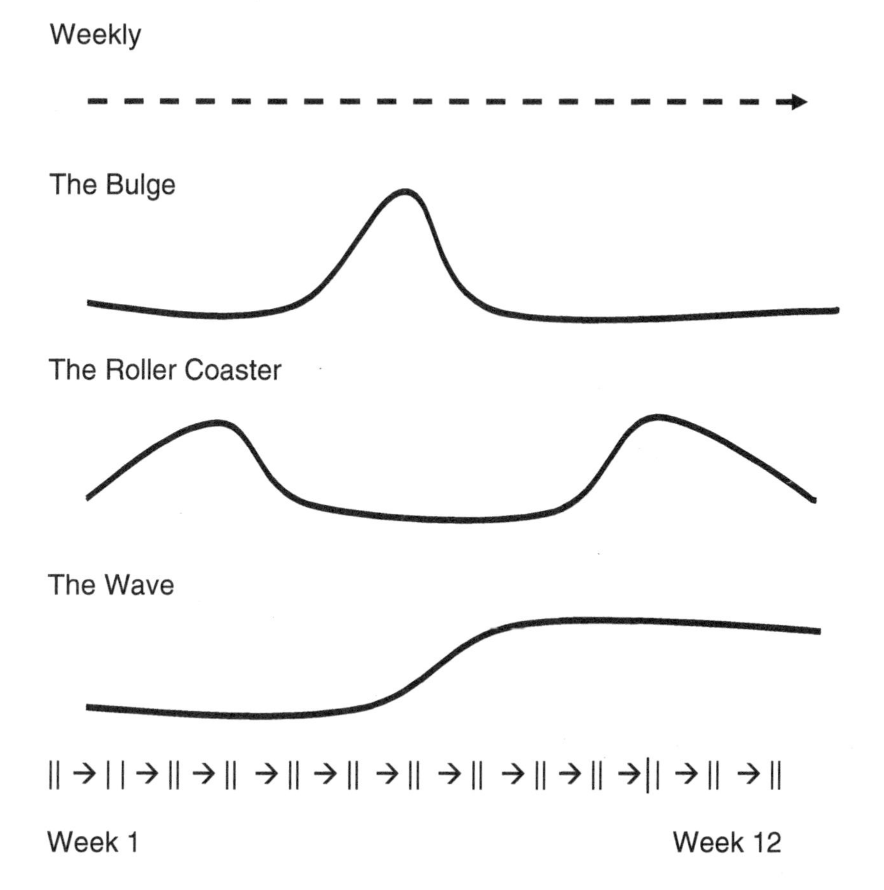

Weekly

Weekly allocation of hours reflects traditional direct service in which students work on a regular basis and at a specific location with an individual or on a specific task. The case study example of the nursing students in the geriatrics class reflects this approach. Tutoring children in an after-school program or doing trail restoration in a wildlife area are other good examples of this. However, another example might be students in a sociology or political science course constructing a survey to be conducted, collected, and analyzed, with each of these steps completed approximately every two weeks, culminating with a final report.

The Bulge

As the title aptly illustrates, a "bulge" of contact and engagement hours may occur in the middle of a course. This approach works well with short-term immersion experiences in which students spend several weeks in a classroom setting learning about and preparing for the engagement exercise in advance of going out in the community. For example, a marine biology course may focus on invasive plants along shorelines or sea life habitat in which students spend their weeklong fall or spring break working with a government agency eradicating nonnative plants or taking a census of endangered species along the beach.

The Roller Coaster

The "roller coaster" illustrates situations in which students may spend considerable time early on in the course conducting on-site observations or data intake, followed by off-site planning and design of a product before returning to the community partner. In this approach, students spend time in or out of class developing the product. After a few weeks, the students return to the community agency to implement and pilot their product or project. Examples of this approach include marketing students creating marketing plans for a nonprofit agency, a sociology class gathering data or conducting interviews that culminate in a report or policy brief, or a computer science class developing a website or application for an organization.

The Wave

Finally, the "wave" represents a gradual dispersal of hours over time. Producing a documentary film to be debuted at a local film festival showcasing a specific issue in the community or a letter-writing campaign or petition drive on a ballot issue or impending legislative bill are good examples of this approach.

Where

Community engagement occurs outside the classroom and in the community. That said, an instructor should be spending time in class discussing and reflecting on what is going on out in the community setting. As we will see in the next chapter, significant learning occurs in class time through reflection activities whereby students integrate what they are doing and experiencing with the content of the course. Similarly, the reflection activity helps students make meaning of their experience. As you will see in the next chapter, the reflection process becomes a teaching and assessment tool as well as a learning exercise.

Another question that often arises is if allocating class time for students to work on their project counts as service time. Keep in mind that all courses require a certain amount of out-of-class work, traditionally through readings and written assignments. As discussed previously and throughout this book, the community engagement is a pedagogy—not volunteering—to be completed outside of class. That *could* include students working as teams in a common study area of the library in the evening to plan and develop their product or organize their project that will take place in the community setting. Although the team is not "out in the community," members are doing work associated with the community-articulated priorities. As such, there is a degree of discretion that is necessary for determining hour allocation. We encourage instructors (and students, for that matter) to neither become too preoccupied with the "where" nor spend time counting hours and instead focus on the learning that occurs.

Transitioning

A critical and yet often overlooked aspect of engagement is transitioning. Although not always germane or necessary in certain contexts, this is especially important when working with vulnerable populations such as children, the elderly, inmates, or individuals with disabilities. Instability is often a common factor in the lives of these groups. Students entering and leaving their lives could potentially contribute to that instability. In many scenarios, college students endear themselves to the individuals with whom they are working. This requires sensitivity in preparing for and actually transitioning away from the interaction that may have evolved into friendships and trust. Discuss this in class and possibly "script" how to broach the subject and process. The importance of transitioning is such that it *may* be included as an assignment with a modest amount of points tied to their grade to help ensure students follow through on this vital activity. The transition planning should be included in the syllabus time line. Approximately one to two weeks prior to the end of the interactions, students should remind those they are working with of their impending departure, explaining their course is about to end. Students should thank their partners and express how much they have learned and gained from this experience. A simple gift, thank-you note, or "selfie" photo that can be printed and shared may be in order. Students should not exchange personal contact information or make any promise to come back and visit as this raises expectations that could lead to more instability and disappointment. You can now begin drafting a blueprint of the engagement component of your course in Tool Kit 8.1.

> Tool Kit 8.1—Refer to Exercise 8.1 in your workbook to begin drawing a blueprint of the engagement component of your course. Once this has been completed, use it to implement the course agreement form and action plan template with your community partner to formalize the partnership.

Honing Your Craft

The mechanics of creating a course syllabus with a list of readings and written assignments coupled with preparing lecture notes and a midterm and final exam are fairly straightforward. As you now see, unlike traditional didactic courses, a community-engaged course has many moving parts as well as complex dynamics. As such, teaching a community-engaged course is not merely adding hours of service for students to complete, which is what many institutions and instructors misconstrue this type of course to be. A community-engaged course is, indeed, a craft requiring a nuanced approach that takes into account the multiple facets inherent in this type of course. Students have been socialized into taking a passive role in their learning, expecting the instructor to provide the necessary information to pass the course. In this case, students have a role and responsibility that transcends their own assumptions, expectations, and goals they typically have about the courses they take. Your course may, indeed, be students' first experience with a degree of accountability that goes beyond attending class, turning in assignments, and earning a grade. Community agencies and those they serve are counting on you and your students to make good on an agreement. It is one thing for a student in a traditional course to choose not to complete an assignment, knowing their grade will go down and accept that consequence. It is entirely another thing for a student or team of students to not complete a task designed to meet community partner goals, which could have a detrimental impact on their programming and those they serve. How, then, can and does an instructor articulate this to students in a meaningful way?

Likewise, your students are simply that—students! It is understood that students have a limited life experience and set of skills. It is quite likely they will encounter situations that call into question many of their assumptions. As we will explore in more detail in the next chapter, on reflection, it is common for students to experience some cognitive dissonance. Therefore, you and your students can and should expect to be challenged in multiple ways—cognitively, emotionally, socially, politically, and perhaps even spiritually. This is often more than what you or your students "signed up for." It is also important to realize they are not professionals or consultants with years of experience. Community partners must understand this is an educational opportunity and experience in which they are coeducators with roles and responsibilities rather than clients working with accomplished professional consultants. At the same time, you and your students are providing some kind of value-added product, possibly in the form of a tangible "deliverable," that is mutually beneficial in meeting the course objectives and the partner's goals. Also keep in mind that the director or coordinator of the community agency you are working with has a "day job" with their own priorities and a mission to fulfill. It is a gift that they are making time for you and your students as well as inviting you into their setting. How, then, do we nurture a safe partnership that is mutually beneficial and honors the community partner's expertise without exploiting them?

Despite the best planning and conversations, things don't always go as planned. An instructor must understand this going into this type of course. We relinquish a certain amount of autonomy and control. Sometimes the best learning occurs when things go awry and we must take a step back and ask, "Why?" and "What can or should we have done differently?" That said, such an academic revelation cannot be at the expense of a community partner. Conversely, poorly planned or implemented engaged courses are unethical and can have a detrimental impact on the image, reputation, and public relations image of the institution.

Although there is an array of challenges associated with engaging with the community, this type of teaching and learning can have a profound transformative effect—on not only your students or potentially those in the community but also yourself. Be prepared to learn about yourself as a scholar, citizen, and person. This type of teaching, although difficult and quite frankly requiring more work, can reinvigorate instructors as they see the impact they have on their students as well as the community, as illustrated in Tool Kit 8.2.

Tool Kit 8.2—Honing Your Craft—A number of factors, issues, challenges, and rewards have surfaced at this point of your preparation and planning. Refer to Exercise 8.2 and take time now to consider some of these. What new insights come to mind?

Chapter 9

REFLECTION

Instructors new to community-engaged teaching tend to focus on the community projects or activities in which students will participate, but reflection is equally important in that it creates opportunities for students to synthesize their community experiences and academic content into new understanding in multiple ways. This process allows students to make connections from what they are doing through the engaged work to what they are learning in class. That is why it is so important to intentionally develop and integrate critical reflection questions and probes *throughout* the course. However, most instructors do not fully understand what reflection is or how to conduct it, let alone use it as a tool for teaching, learning, and assessment. This is not a criticism, but rather acknowledging the majority of faculty members have not received any instruction on pedagogy nor exposure to the practice of reflection during graduate preparation that focused primarily on disciplinary content. Therefore, many instructors have preconceived assumptions of what reflection is and isn't. Some equate reflection with traditional reports, whereas others perceive it as a "fluffy, touchy-feely" discussion that competes with valuable in-class time. There are assumptions about the format reflection takes, typically limited to written journal entries. So let's begin our exploration of this important yet often misunderstood component of engaged teaching and learning by reflecting on reflection in Tool Kit 9.1.

> Tool Kit 9.1—Refer to Exercise 9.1 in your workbook. Record your responses to each of the questions presented. Share and discuss your thoughts with your colleagues and your campus center director.

It is important to realize that reflection has a long history and is theoretically grounded (Dubinsky, Welch, & Wurr, 2012). Dewey (1933) described reflection as "active, persistent and careful consideration of any belief or supposed form of knowledge in the light of the grounds that support it, and the further conclusions to which it tends" (p. 6). He also suggested that intentional consideration of thoughts, feelings, and actions contributes to meaningful learning and growth. This is consistent with Schon's (1983) characterization of reflection as "a continual interweaving of thinking and doing" (p. 281). Kolb and Fry (1984) effectively incorporated reflection within the context of science and the scientific method with a cyclical set of steps: (a) Do it; (b) What happened?; (c) So what?—What do the results imply?; (d) Now what?—What can/should be done differently?

We operationalize reflection here by incorporating Hatcher and Bringle's (1997) succinct characterization of reflection as the intentional consideration of an experience in light of instructional objectives. More recently, Pigza (2010) coined the term *critical reflection* as it links critical thinking, critical questions, critical pedagogy, and critical participation of faculty and community partners. The essence of reflection in this context is a robust intellectual exercise to make meaning through the integration of engagement activities outside the classroom setting with what is being learned and taught in the classroom. Thus, reflection is not an "add-on" or conducted on a whim as a "fill-in" activity or even as a summative "wrap-up" report. Instead, reflection is intentionally incorporated before, during, and after service in ways that integrate course content with what is experienced outside the classroom in the community, as illustrated in Tool Kit 9.2.

> Tool Kit 9.2—Refer to Exercise 9.2 in your workbook for an extensive example of integrating the ABC rubric of reflection (which is described in detail on p. 124, this volume) throughout the course in ways that intentionally connect content discussed in class and readings with observations that occur during the service experience of preprofessional nursing students serving as companions to elders in assisted living settings.

Although intended to be an academic activity, reflection can often generate a form of cognitive dissonance or what Mezirow (1999) characterized as a disorienting dilemma when students encounter intersectionality during their community engagement experiences that call into question their preconceived assumptions about the world around them (Welch, 2010b).

Likewise, students are often emotionally impacted by their community engagement experience and articulate those feelings through the reflection process. This attests to the transformative power engaged teaching and learning can have on students. Therefore, the combination and intersection of intellectual, affective, and applied aspects of engaged learning require a comprehensive approach and a toolbox full of reflection strategies on the part of the instructor.

Given the intentional internal meaning-making process that occurs within the student, the primary audience for reflection is the student, with a secondary audience being the instructor. This is in contrast to the use and purpose of traditional reports or academic papers designed to disseminate data or information and document assimilated knowledge to an external audience, such as an instructor or an organization's board of directors. Students do not have the innate skills to engage in critical reflection (Dubinsky et al., 2012). Reflection must be taught, to minimize shallow "dear diary" recitations of events occurring during a service activity. Rubrics or frameworks help provide a structure for students to organize and articulate their thoughts. Simply pulling desks in a circle and asking students to "reflect on their experience" is likely to lead to either silence or perfunctory and shallow recaps, which is equally frustrating and confusing for students and the instructor. Furthermore, given the array of students' learning styles and instructors' teaching styles, there is a variety of configurations reflection can take—oral, written, large-group discussion, small-group discussion, discussion in dyads, to name a few. Basic rubrics can be used to intentionally link thoughts, feelings, and action, as Dewey espoused. You experienced one of these rubrics, the "ABCs of Reflection" (Welch, 1999) early on in the very first Tool Kit activity of chapter 1 when invited to reflect on Ernest Boyer's conceptualization of engaged scholarship. Reflection can be conducted in class, outside of class, or even in the community. Finally, reflection can be a teaching and assessment tool to assist instructors in making informed instructional decisions based on what students articulate or don't articulate during reflection activities.

Structural Rubrics for Reflection

Entire workshops can be devoted to critical reflection. Given the limited space here, we offer two structural rubrics that incorporate the theoretical premise of integrating thoughts, feelings, and action espoused by Dewey (1933) and the basic heuristic learning cycle described by Kolb and Fry

(1984). These are certainly not the only rubrics available to instructors. They were chosen and presented here due to their utility across various configurations of students in and out of class as well as oral and written formats. Both can be readily used for assessment and evaluation as described in the following sections and offered as examples in your workbook.

ABCs of Reflection

The "ABCs of Reflection" is based on the theoretical framework of Hondagneu-Sotelo and Rashoff (1994), who emphasized the following main components of reflection: (a) what and how students feel; (b) how students behave before, during, and after learning experiences; and (c) what students learn. Each of these components is categorized, respectively, as "A" for affect, "B" for behavior, and "C" for cognition, to create the ABC rubric. Instructors can frame a reflection assignment around each of the components as illustrated in Figure 9.1 and in the examples from the nursing course on geriatrics provided in your workbook. Students can respond either in a stream-of-consciousness format or in sections addressing each of the ABCs. Tool Kit 9.3 provides an opportunity to review and respond to the example of the ABC rubric illustrated in Figure 9.1.

Figure 9.1 A student's reflection response using the ABCs.

This is a student's reflection response in a sociology course titled Be the Change, examining social movements and community organizing. Included in the course syllabus was an in-class exercise worth 25 points in which students would make a 3-minute statement similar to what they would do at a city council hearing. To illustrate the concept of participatory democratic action, the instructor told the class to collectively develop an evaluation rubric for the exercise to earn their 25 points. Although not an out-of-class service activity, students were assigned to reflect on the experience using the following reflection prompt:

As a class we spent time collectively creating an evaluation rubric for one of our assignments.

- *Affect: What were you feeling during the process?*
- *Behavior: Can you think of a time you had to work with someone else in a similar situation? What did you do? With this new insight, how might you behave in the future?*

- *Cognitive: What concepts/terms from class readings reflect this process?*

Sample Reflection Response

We were supposed to take some task that was really easy and define a very basic rubric. Well I was very frustrated with the whole process [AFFECT]. First we were sitting there discussing and we found what I thought was a good rubric. Right? And all of the sudden one person raises his hand and says, "I don't like this, it's too much like this or that," and we spent at least half an hour trying to figure out something that was really easy. In the end, I think everyone just gave up and said, "You know what, I'm tired of talking about this, let's just do it." But as frustrated as it made me feel, I actually understood much more about our government [COGNITION]. What we practiced in our exercise was what we could call an example of participatory democracy. The book says [quoting from the textbook (Rimmerman, 2001)] *it is the idea that embraces active participation by the citizens in the community and workplace decision-making at a local level—it is rooted in the notion that whatever touches all should be judged by all. It requires much more than just voting for competing elitists. Through a process of decision, debate, and compromise, they link their concerns with the needs of the community.* It all sounds great in theory but when you actually try to and do it, it gets really frustrating. I don't even know if we had the best rubric that we could've had. I don't think anyone got what they wanted which could be bad or could be good. To contrast that with the democratic theory of elitism, I'm saying it is probably a whole lot easier if it just did what a couple of people thought was okay. [Paraphrasing from the textbook] *The democratic theory of elitism theorizes that elites in power should make all the crucial decisions facing society and citizens should be rather passive in politics, generally participating for voting and competing elites, and periodic elections. Democratic elitists argue that the role expected of the citizen in a participatory setting is unrealistic and that too much participation will contribute to the instability of the political and economic system.* This theory is normally something we look down on. And after doing this exercise and going over this, it really surprised me that I was like, "Yeah, we should do something more like that." So it really helped me see where a lot of our law makers are coming from when they don't want to listen to all these people—especially a lot of people I know in our class have a lot of views that aren't the most popular—it isn't what mainstream society is talking about. We get really upset or get really frustrated when we go to talk to these politicians and we say, "Look, what about this?" and "Who cares about this little group of people over here?" We all get really frustrated when we feel the government is not addressing our needs.

(*Continues*)

Figure 9.1 (*Continued*)

But when we did this exercise I could see how they view us. It's that one person who raises their hand and they think they have the perfect policy or the policy they think will please a lot of groups and then there's that one person who is [in] the corner saying, "I don't like it because of this" [BEHAVIOR]. I guess I'm normally that person—that one person who says, "No, no, you forgot about these people." It really surprised me that when it happened in a big group, it was so easy for me to say, "Forget the little person, let's just move on, let's just do what everyone likes." It really surprised me how quickly I switched. It helped me understand why politicians do what they do. I learned how frustrating it can be. As I go and try to do more things I hope to take that understanding with me. I hope to try and show politicians that it's not just one person bringing up a concern that only affects a minor part of the population, but try and show them the idea that these decisions benefit everyone, that helping the poor will make the whole community stronger. In addition to that, this spring I'll be doing an internship at the Capitol and I'm sure I'm going to get to see a lot of people and I'll probably get frustrated with all these people who care about this or that. I'm sure I'm going to get frustrated with all of these interest groups. But I hope to keep this exercise in mind. I want to have it help me have patience when I'm listening to these people. It just really blew my mind. I definitely think I have to take this when I go before Congress or push any issue that this will be very important to keep in mind.

Tool Kit 9.3—Refer to Exercise 9.3 in your workbook as you think about and respond to this example of reflection using the ABCs in Figure 9.1.

What? So What? Now What?

A somewhat different rubric was inspired by Kolb and Fry's (1984) learning cycle and operationalized by the Campus Outreach Opportunity League (COOL), as described in the quintessential (and unfortunately out-of-print) book on reflection *A Practitioner's Guide to Reflection in Service-Learning: Student Voices & Reflections* (Eyler, Giles, & Schmiede, 1996). Students reflect on the following components: (a) "What?"—What did they do? What did they see? What did they learn? What did they accomplish?; (b) "So what?"—What are the implications of this experience? Does it matter and, if so, why? How is what we did/saw/experienced connected to what we're learning in class?; and (c) "Now what?"—Based on what we've done/seen/experienced, what happens next? What can/

should we do differently? In many respects, the focus on the "what" is directly tied to the cognitive content from the course. That can, however, be extended to reflect on "what" happened outside the classroom in the community setting. Inviting students to reflect on the "so what" is a catalyst for making meaning of the experience and provides a portal for future application (see Figure 9.2). Likewise, consider how you might respond to the example in Tool Kit 9.4.

Figure 9.2 Example of student reflection from Chemistry 101 using What? So What? Now What?

Carla's Response

We did our test at the community garden in Bridger Heights. Our team chose to conduct the option analysis for cation exchange capacity (CEC). Ion exchange in soils is one of the most important processes influencing crop nutrition. CEC is an estimate of the capacity of soil to hold (or adsorb) positively charged (cation) nutrients. The major soil cations include: calcium (Ca2+), magnesium (Mg2+), potassium (K+), sodium (Na+), hydrogen (H+), and aluminum (Al3+). The unit of measurement used to commonly express CEC is centimoles of positive charge per kilogram of soil (cmol/kg) and is equivalent to the units formerly used to express CEC: milliequivalents per 100 grams (meq/100g). Results proved to be negligible.

What we did not expect to find was the high levels of lead in the soil. OMG! People are eating produce that comes from these garden plots and they have no idea of how toxic it is. This makes me angry and sad! I'm frustrated this has to be this way AND . . . there are some relatively easy ways to address this but these families are simply unaware. The easiest remedy would be to build and use raised beds. On top of that, we need to let gardeners know there are several methods to reduce the risk of lead poisoning from lead contaminated soils. Fruit and vegetable gardens should be located away from old painted buildings, heavy traffic, and sites where sludge with heavy metals was applied. Vegetables and fruits can accumulate lead in their leafy green tissues, although lead accumulation will be lower in fruits. In high-risk lead areas, [people should] grow crops such as tomatoes, eggplants, peppers, squash, melons, and cucumbers rather than leafy greens such as lettuce, chard, collards, or spinach. Crops such as carrots, radishes, turnips, onions, and potatoes can accumulate lead and should not be planted in heavily contaminated soils.

I think what upset me the most was discovering real-life evidence of environmental racism as we discussed in class. The other teams in class reported healthy soil sample results from affluent areas whereas the underresourced neighborhoods consistently had toxins. I don't think this is

(*Continues*)

Figure 9.2 (*Continued*)

necessarily "an accident." It seems like these places are the only geographic locations these families can afford. The expression "you get what you pay for" came through loud and clear here. It also makes me angry that our government and culture as a whole doesn't seem to care very much about this. Clearly we need some "brown-field" policy for areas that were formerly factory/industrial sites that have been converted to residential use. Why are there policies and procedures in existence and practice in SOME neighborhoods and not in others? I can see the role chemists must play in policy-making. I want us to discuss in class how government agencies and commercial chemical companies address this real life issue and what we can do about it as professionals and as citizens. As a citizen-student, I'm going to help these neighborhood gardens analyze and improve their soil . . . NOW! I'll feel much better knowing I can help.

Tool Kit 9.4—Refer to Exercise 9.4 in your workbook as you think about and respond to the example of reflection from a chemistry course, in Figure 9.2, using What? So What? Now What?

Assessment, Evaluation, and Grading

After overcoming the initial hurdle of learning what reflection is and how to conduct it comes the next daunting challenge of how to assess, evaluate, and assign a grade to something so subjective and, at times, personal. The following is merely a suggestion of one approach adapted from Dubinsky and colleagues (2012) that can be applied to the ABCs and the "What" method, as well as others. We preface this with two important caveats. First, students' feelings are not "graded," as there is no "correct" emotion. Instead, students express what they are feeling and draw on evidence to justify or explain *why* they are feeling this to earn the points. Second, and related to the previous point, students initially push back on the idea of evaluating and grading reflection based on their assumptions of what reflection is. Most students view reflection as a subjective "testimonial" of sorts, often providing somewhat emotional responses in an attempt to convince and satisfy the instructor that they did, indeed, have a transformative experience. As such, it is important to define *reflection* and explain its purpose as a learning tool.

Three points are awarded for each of the ABCs and/or each of the "Whats" for a total of nine points. An in-depth response that provides detailed accounts or even explanations that may include "whys" earns three points. This depth of reflection entails intentional consideration and rich articulation. Two points are awarded to reflective statements that provide essential information but may lack the depth, intentionality, and insight a three-point response might earn. Finally, only one point is awarded to responses with marginal articulation, as they may provide only cursory content with little or no thought. For example, a marginal or shallow journal entry might simply state the student tutored a child in an after-school program "like we talked about in class" and it was "really cool." This rather shallow "dear diary" reflection entry merely provides a fleeting reference to class discussion without actually articulating what was discussed, while describing a behavior and an affective or emotional response to the experience in a single, curt sentence. In this case, the student did, indeed, provide rudimentary information for each of the ABCs, which might warrant a minimum of three points—one for each of the ABCs. In the case of the "Whats" the student focused primarily on what they did, earning a single point, and also included a marginal articulation of "So What" indicating they enjoyed the experience, for another single point. There is, however, no mention in this case of what they will take from the experience and how they will apply it in the future.

The example from the sociology course presented in Figure 9.1 illustrates a stream-of-consciousness response in which the ABCs are intertwined rather than separated into sections delineated by headings, which is also acceptable and sometimes a useful approach for students to organize their responses. In reviewing the student's reflection response, we can readily determine (as noted and indicated in the narrative) that all three of the ABCs are addressed and with a degree of depth and insight. The affective component is addressed by clearly articulating her feelings of frustration as well as her own personal contrition when she recognized how her behavior in class contradicted her espoused political activism behaviors. In addition to describing how she behaved during the class activity, she critically reflected on her past behavior and integrated her new insights into her aspiration of how to behave in the future. Finally, she demonstrated her clear understanding of salient course content by clearly integrating those concepts into the description of her behaviors during the experience. Thus, we can clearly ascertain the student's understanding and integration of the in-class activity with a specific instructional objective. In this example, it is evident the student has assimilated not only the meaning but also the dynamics of participatory democracy and the democratic theory of elitism, both key concepts for the course, by relating it to her own experience. Her response "reflects" (pun intended) Hatcher and Bringle's (1997) definition of *reflection* as the intentional consideration of an experience in light of an instructional objective. Perhaps more importantly, her reflection response provides a glimpse into her attempt to make meaning of the experience that was, quite literally, transformative as she concluded her response by aspiring to change the way she behaves.

Beyond using reflection as a learning tool, this type of assessment procedure becomes an important teaching tool as it can assist instructors to make critical instructional decisions. A pattern of responses from an entire class may suggest that salient information or components associated with the learning objectives have not been assimilated. An instructor can return to the topic or concept for further exploration and discussion. In-class discussions on the reflection topic can overtly point to specific components of student reflections and direct students' attention to address weak, incorrect, or missing information. Similarly, student reflections may not indicate any consideration of how or why students might behave differently in the future. In this way, a teacher can invite students to think about the current experience and ponder new or better ways of applying new knowledge or skills the next time similar circumstances arise. Finally, affective responses may provide insight to an instructor regarding students' fears or inspiration. Class discussions can then be designed to explore these emotional responses in a safe and nurturing setting.

Instructors must also consider what percentage of the final grade will be composed of reflection. This, of course, is dependent upon how often reflection is assigned. Typically, 10% to 15% of the final grade could comprise reflection assignments.

Reflection Configuration

Instructors can configure reflection activities in many ways (see Table 9.1). We traditionally envision reflection as an individual exercise. This approach can be implemented during class or outside of class as an assignment. Reflection can also be effectively incorporated into dyads of students who engage in a reflective conversation. This is especially effective when attempting to engage all the students, especially shy ones who typically do not participate in large-group discussions, often with vocal students who tend to dominate the conversation. The two rubrics described previously can even be used by dyads to provide some structure to the process. Likewise, an instructor can form small groups to conduct reflection. This is even more applicable and practical when and if an instructor forms teams of students to complete the engagement activity, as discussed in the previous chapter. A team shares elements of a common experience and context that can be useful during the reflection activity. Small groups can later be reconvened as a large group for a full-class discussion. Large-group

TABLE 9.1
Configuration of Students for Reflection Activities

Configuration	*Considerations*
Large Group	• Efficient process • Everyone hears everything at the same time • Good wrap-up and/or reporting out after small-group reflection • Talkers may dominate discussion/shy students may not speak up • Takes time away from other in-class activities, but large-group reflection discussion can reinforce lecture/class content
Small Group	• Great for shy students • Divide topical areas by groups and reconvene to share out comments
Dyads	• Informal/intimate format is good for shy/reluctant students • Can cover multiple issues/topics at one time
Individual	• In-class written reflection can be done in a variety of formats • Out-of-class written reflection in a variety of formats • Private/personal opportunity to reflect on "touchy" subjects

discussions lend themselves well to revisiting specific concepts or topics that have emerged through other forms of reflection exercises and that the instructor wants to further pursue.

Reflection can take many formats. We have a tendency to think exclusively of written journal passages as the only way to conduct reflection. However, a large class makes it difficult to invest time and attention to reading and responding to a large number of journal entries. Written reflection does, however, provide ample space for deliberate consideration of an experience as well as intimate space to ponder personal and challenging revelations. It also provides room for a private exchange and conversation between the instructor and student.

Graffiti

Graffiti is a hybrid approach to written reflection and an easy and effective in-class activity that gets students up and out of their seats. Sheets of poster paper with reflection question prompts are distributed throughout the room either on tabletops or taped to the wall. Students rotate from sheet to sheet, either individually or in dyads, to respond in writing to the prompt, producing a public yet anonymous written statement analogous to graffiti. One sheet could be devoted to each of the ABCs or each of the questions in the What? So What? Now What? rubric. Another approach is to invite students to compare and contrast a concept or present the pros and cons of something, with one sheet of paper providing a list of advantages or comparisons and another sheet providing a list of disadvantages or contrasts.

Graffiti is especially useful to fully engage students who are shy and rarely participate in class discussion. An astute instructor can observe disengaged or shy students as they respond and then solicit their engagement in class discussion by noting their response and commenting, "This is an interesting response. Who can elaborate on this or help explain what they meant?" Graffiti does not, however, lend itself easily to grading student responses, due to the "anonymous" nature of the responses. Instead, it serves as a catalyst for large group class discussion immediately following the exercise or through continued written reflection out of class.

Salons

Oral discussions conducted as salons, whether in dyads, small groups, or as a large group, can be very effective and efficient. It ensures everyone is hearing the same thing at the same time. It also provides a venue and an opportunity for an instructor to respond to themes or questions that have emerged from written reflection entries. Perhaps most importantly is how oral discussions can enhance and support traditional lecture by inviting students to reflect on how what they are experiencing in the community "reflects" (or does not reflect) the content being discussed. This is precisely the approach the instructor for the nursing course on geriatrics takes in his class. It also provides an opportunity to explore some of the ancillary objectives of the course. For example, the reflection discussion may shift from a cognitive context to exploring cultural or political dimensions of the community-engaged experience, which then could be expanded further to consider "Now What?" in terms of how this new insight informs the behavior and performance of students as professionals and citizens.

Take a Stand

"Take a Stand" is another hybrid approach that Combines large-group discussion with written reflection. The instructor makes a statement—perhaps a provocative one—and asks students to stand if they agree with the statement. The instructor invites one student to explain why they "took a stand" and, following their statement, invites a student who has remained in their seat to respond to what was just said. This continues, allowing the instructor to take the role of facilitator while students actively engage in teaching and learning from each other. For example, the instructor might state, "Direct service is merely a bandage that does not address the deep, pervasive systemic issues that brought about this situation." Students are then invited to take a stand if they agree and then be prepared to defend their position. This activity models, demonstrates, and teaches civil discourse, which is an important ancillary skill and objective in this day and age.

The activity can be continued with an out-of-class written reflection or online threaded discussion by utilizing either the ABCs or the "Now What?" step to provide students an opportunity to continue their reflection and summarize their new understanding of what was discussed. A variation on this approach is to allocate one side of the room as "strongly agree" and the opposite side as "strongly disagree," creating a Likert-type of response line that students can stand on. The instructor facilitates the discussion and observes the potential shift and movement of students as their position on the topic changes.

The medium and formats of reflection briefly described here are summarized in Table 9.2. Now it is time for you to consider ways you might incorporate reflection into your course. Tool Kit 9.5 will help you with that planning.

> Tool Kit 9.5—Refer to Exercise 9.5 in your workbook. Begin planning how you might incorporate reflection in your course. Share and discuss your ideas with your learning community and/or your center director.

Honing Your Craft

This chapter and the accompanying workbook provide some nuts and bolts for you to consider using to conduct reflection. We do hope, however, that this chapter also reveals the potential transformative power

TABLE 9.2
Medium and Formats for Reflection Activities

Medium	*Formats*
Journal/Written	• Can respond to specific reflection topic • Can use a variety of rubrics such as ABCs or What? So What? Now What?
"Graffiti"	• Gets everyone engaged • Can be done by individuals, dyads, or small groups • Can incorporate ABC and/or What? So What? Now What? on separate poster paper • Provides a chance for large-group discussion/response to items listed on poster paper • Anonymous, public responses
Discussion/Oral	• Provides a public forum with a chance to teach/model civil discourse • Allows useful "Take a Stand" method
Multimedia	• Is a catalyst for discussion and/or response to various topics/issues • Allows for creativity

reflection can have for students as well as with yourself. It is an opportunity to make meaning. Because of this potential, many instructors, including your authors, initially entered into the reflection process with some trepidation and were ill prepared when student responses transcended merely spouting factoids. We may very well be left wondering, "What do I do with this?"

Engaged teaching and learning can and often does lead students into uncharted territory that challenges their assumptions and perhaps even calls into question their identity. Reflection often reveals and unveils these situations. This is referred to as the "shadow side of reflection" (Welch, 2010b, p. 1) and it is, indeed, a craft to accompany students when they enter into this dark space. We don't have to provide the answer or solutions or rescue them as they grapple with unexpected insights derived from their experience. Our students do, however, hold cultural expectations of "happy endings" found in movies coupled with commercial messages that problems can be solved with this or that new product. Similarly, because of our mantle as experts, our students often expect us to solve unsolvable problems and have answers to questions that may be unanswerable, and if we can't do this, it is very disconcerting to a young person. Thus, we must help students understand that our role is to provide a safe space and guidance for them to critically reflect on complex issues and make meaning of what they are experiencing. It is likely their initial reflection responses are centered around "I felt, I learned, I did . . . ," which is a good starting place. However, there will be times in your class when you must gently nudge your students into deeper consideration of the world around them that goes beyond "getting the right answer," as they have been socialized to do. After all, these are 19-year-olds who have limited life experience and are, developmentally speaking, somewhat egocentric. That said, community-engaged teaching and learning provide a space for students to transcend their own space and context. As engaged scholars, we can shepherd our students out of their egocentric perspective to higher levels of empathy by considering the cultural, political, and systemic contexts that frame what they're learning and doing in our class and in the community (Dubinsky et al., 2012; Welch & James, 2007).

Our community partners often have more expertise and insight as "public scholars" to shed light on the shadow side of reflection that we and our students may encounter. If this is so, might we invite them to lead and conduct reflection in their role as coeducator? And finally, we have come to learn and recognize that our students can, at times, be more adept at reflection than their instructors. Over time, we have seen and experienced students generating class reflection topics, using the rubrics described here, that have resulted in profound reflective responses and insights. To what extent can, do, or should we share the facilitation of reflection? Turn to Tool Kit 9.6 to continue reflecting on reflection.

Tool Kit 9.6—Honing Your Craft—Refer to Exercise 9.6 in your workbook to continue exploring and discussing ways to hone your craft as a reflective practitioner by reflecting on reflection.

Chapter 10

ASSESSMENT

Assessment means many different things and looks many ways. This can, and often does, create confusion and, at times, distress. Likewise, *assessment* is often confused with the similar concept and practice of *evaluation*. We begin this chapter with a quick check on your understanding of the two terms in Tool Kit 10.1.

> Tool Kit 10.1—Refer to Exercise 10.1. What is your understanding of assessment and how does that compare with evaluation?

Assessment brings us full circle to our starting point of using objectives to drive the community engagement experience. In essence, assessment is conducted to ascertain to what extent we have met our instructional, ancillary, and community objectives. We begin this chapter by quickly comparing and contrasting assessment with evaluation. The remainder of the chapter will focus on the following types of assessment: (a) summative and (b) formative. Let's get the gears turning by inviting you to reflect on what assessment is and isn't as well as how it is related to evaluation.

Assessment and Evaluation

Educators, students, and community partners alike often use the terms *assessment* and *evaluation* synonymously. Although they are related, both have specific meanings and functions. These characterizations are derived and paraphrased from Angelo and Cross (1993) and Duke University's (2018) Office of Assessment. *Assessment* is an ongoing strategic process of establishing goals coupled with obtaining, reviewing, and using information to monitor performance or operations to make necessary modifications and improvements that facilitate goal attainment. Therefore, assessment is generally formative in nature, as it takes place before and during an activity to measure efficiency of operations to "form" the experience (e.g., How much time and/or how many people are involved? Are current procedures effective? Are we meeting our goal or mission?). In many ways, assessment is a prerequisite step, a process that provides information as to the current status of a phenomenon and how to proceed in meeting a specific need or goal and a concluding step. For example, assessing one's cholesterol levels and blood pressure provides valuable metabolic information to help identify the next steps for activity, diet, and medication to achieve the goal of a healthy life. Following the implementation of those steps, the condition is reassessed to monitor progress and to determine if a targeted goal has been obtained.

Evaluation critically judges something based on a standard or criteria using a variety of observations and/or measurements. Evaluation judges and determines the quality of a product or operation and, therefore, is qualitative and often summative in nature (Dostilio & Welch, 2018). Awards, ratings, or grades are typically applied to a product or an activity as a critique to denote the level of quality during evaluation. A traditional and familiar example is assigning a grade to a student's exam or paper to indicate what standard it achieved, whereby "excellence" is denoted with a letter grade of A and an average or satisfactory performance is denoted with a letter grade of C. Grades are given in the evaluation of students' cognitive understanding and performance. In the context of community engagement, assessment is extended to determine if community partner objectives were met and to what level of quality and satisfaction. Evaluation is consideration of the quality and satisfaction of meeting those objectives and typically occurs at the conclusion of the engagement activity. For a comprehensive guide and resource on assessment, readers are referred to *Assessing Service-Learning and Civic Engagement: Principles and Techniques* (Gelmon, Holland, & Spring, 2018).

Summative Assessment

Four chapters ago, you spent time and energy identifying and articulating specific instructional and ancillary objectives for students in your class. Likewise, you and your community partner identified specific community-based goals to be met through the engagement activities your students would conduct. It is now time to determine how you will assess to what degree these objectives and goals were met at the end of the course—hence the adjective, summative, characterizing this type of assessment.

Assessing Instructional Objectives

Instructors are familiar with assessing and evaluating students' academic and cognitive development on disciplinary-based content through the use of exams, papers, and projects. Projects or tangible products lend themselves to rubrics that determine to what extent students have applied specific concepts or skill sets. For example, a marketing class may have students incorporate "10 essential building blocks" in a marketing plan. Those standards are used as "checkpoints" to assess and evaluate the degree to which students have demonstrated their understanding and application of those concepts in an authentic product intended for use by the community partner. Similarly, an instructor may apply other factors such as best practice, clarity, organization, analysis, interpretation, or recommendations to projects that culminate in a report or project. However, as explored when considering objectives in chapter 6, it is possible to have additional ancillary objectives that may not mesh well with traditional assessment and evaluation measures based on disciplinary content or contexts. For example, how does one assess students' attitudes or dispositions regarding cultural variables such as diversity, power and privilege, or civic identity? How are utilization of conflict management, effective communication, professionalism, and time management skills assessed, if at all?

These concepts and skill sets can be assessed in a variety of ways. A common quantitative approach is the use of a pre/post measure of these dimensions. Students respond to questions or items designed to measure attitudes, beliefs, or behaviors related to constructs before and after the engaged course project. Ideally, these measures are validated instruments, although that is not always possible. For example, the Civic Attitudes and Skills Questionnaire (CASQ) (Moely, Mercer, Ilustre, Miron, & McFarland, 2002) is a robust and validated instrument that assesses students' attitudes toward and application of skill in civic engagement. The Center for Service-Learning at IUPUI developed the civic-minded graduate (CMG) model and an accompanying survey (Hatcher, 2008). This model and survey identifies and assesses the specific knowledge, skills, and dispositions to describe how students develop civic-mindedness. Informal measures can also be developed and used. However, this approach rarely incorporates sophisticated content analysis or construct validity. Formal and informal assessment is based on self-report, which means students may inflate their initial responses, potentially creating a ceiling effect that does not measure true growth. Although not a standardized measure, informal pre/post probes are helpful for tracking trends that can be used to assess both cognitive/academic goals and related ancillary goals.

A common question that arises in any discussion about assessment is whether or not an instructor must obtain approval from their institutional review board (IRB). The answer to that question is it depends. If formal and/or informal instruments are being used solely to assess student growth for educational purposes, the answer is no. IRB approval is required only when an instructor intends to use the collected information for research purposes that will be disseminated through publications and/or professional conferences. Assuming that you, as an emerging engaged scholar, intend to integrate your scholarship and teaching through publications and presentations by disseminating new knowledge through your engaged teaching, you are encouraged to apply for IRB approval in advance of your course. Be sure to consult with your campus center director and/or the chair of your IRB committee on your campus to follow protocol.

A qualitative assessment approach may involve content analysis of students' reflection responses. Admittedly, this may be a new concept and practice outside the parameters of traditional assessment and evaluation procedures. The previous chapter acknowledged that critical reflection is often new to faculty, so to ponder and consider how to employ it in the assessment process is equally novel, if not unnerving. That said, research has shown that critical written reflection can effectively develop and assess critical thinking skills of preprofessional nurses (Jasper, 1999). Business courses have used written reflection to assess impact of the engagement experience on students' understanding of diversity issues (Dugal & Eriksen, 2004). Mertens (2009) assessed students' understanding and performance in an economics course through content analysis of student written reflection using the technique of writing letters to home. As examined in detail in the previous chapter, written or oral reflection responses can reveal significant evidence of growth in students' affective, behavioral, and cognitive development. Students are not assessed or graded on the "correct" feeling or emotion. However, content analysis can reveal shifts in students' comfort levels and attitudes that may be due to or attributed to their engagement experience. Likewise, reflection responses often document previous behavior patterns in contrast to aspirational behavior changes stemming from the engagement exercise. Finally, reflection can disclose students' deeper perspectives and understanding of cultural, political, and systemic factors as well as increased levels of empathy. We now provide a comprehensive description of just one example and method that can be used or adapted.

Depth of students' qualitative reflection responses can be quantitatively assessed and mapped (Dubinsky et al., 2012; Welch & James, 2007) by combining the ABC rubric (Welch, 1999) described in the previous chapter with a second theoretical foundation based on the work of Yates and Youness (1997), who characterized students' reflective awareness at three levels to create the following hybrid rubric known as the ABC123 rubric:

1. egocentric,
2. empathic, and
3. systemic/political/cultural.

It is important to note that the procedure described here is not an evaluative measure to assign a grade. Instead, it is a heuristic for instructors to use in assessing and charting the students' depth and broadened perspective.

Student reflection at level 1 is usually somewhat shallow and typically incorporates the personal pronoun "I" (e.g., I felt . . . , I did . . . , I learned . . .), which is common and to be expected at this developmental stage of young, inexperienced college students. Over time, students will often move to level 2, expressing new empathic insight or appreciation of an experience or context outside of their own experience and sense of self. Finally, at level 3, students may express an awareness of previously unknown systemic or cultural variables that came to light during the service experience.

In this approach, an instructor continues to review students' reflection passages looking for existence of affective, behavioral, and cognitive statements. However, in this case a single point is awarded for any evidence of statements in each of the three categories rather than for the number of articulations, for a possible total of three points. For example, a student may reflect on what they did (behavior) and how they felt about the experience (affect), earning two out of three points because they did not include a cognitive statement. The accumulated points for the ABCs are then multiplied by the numeral delineating the level of the statement: one for egocentric, two for empathic, and three for systemic/political/cultural. Unlike the cumulative nature of scoring the ABCs, in this model a point value per level is awarded. A reflection entry that is primarily egocentric receives a 1, an empathic statement receives a 2, and a statement regarding systemic or cultural factors receives a 3. The points attributed to the level of the reflective depth are multiplied by the accumulated points from the ABCs domain.

The example in Figure 10.1 from an introductory chemistry class demonstrates the review and scoring process just described, revisiting a student reflection entry presented in the previous chapter. The student begins by articulating her application and understanding of the cognitive content pertaining to her chemical analysis assignment. The second paragraph shifts from a cognitive focus to a level 1 affective response articulating her shock and frustration at the social and health implications of the analysis findings. She infers an empathic concern for the community growing the produce in a toxic setting, demonstrating a shift from an egocentric level 1 perspective to level 2 of empathy. Her narrative continues by articulating what she would do and say, depicting specific behaviors, to the community garden patrons to circumvent the potentially toxic conditions, which also reveals her understanding of cognitive content from the class. The third and final paragraph articulates her emotional response to her awakened awareness of complex social issues of environmental racism, depicting a level 3 response. She concludes by pondering and proposing questions for in-class discussion coupled with suggestions for public policy. In sum, this response reveals not only her academic understanding but also her depth and insight of broader, more complex social issues that transcend a technical report. Her response addresses each of the ABCs, earning one point for each. She ultimately moved to a level 3 response that is delineated by the numeral 3. Multiplying the ABCs score of three points by the level score of three provides a final score of nine out of nine points, depicting an in-depth and comprehensive reflective response (see Figure 10.1).

Figure 10.1 Reflection entry assessed using the ABC123 rubric.

We did our test at the community garden in Bridger Heights. Our team chose to conduct the option analysis for cation exchange capacity (CEC). Ion exchange in soils is one of the most important processes influencing crop nutrition. CEC is an estimate of the capacity of soil to hold (or adsorb) positively charged (cation) nutrients. The major soil cations include: calcium ($Ca2+$), magnesium ($Mg2+$), potassium ($K+$), sodium ($Na+$), hydrogen ($H+$), and aluminum ($Al3+$). The unit of measurement used to commonly express CEC is centimoles of positive charge per kilogram of soil (cmol/kg) and is equivalent to the units formerly used to express CEC: milliequivalents per 100 grams (meq/100g). Results proved to be negligible [COGNITION].

What we did not expect to find was the high levels of lead in the soil. OMG! People are eating produce that comes from these garden

(*Continues*)

Figure 10.1 (*Continued*)

plots and they have no idea of how toxic it is. This makes me angry and sad! [AFFECT—LEVEL 1/LEVEL 2]. I'm frustrated this has to be this way AND . . . there are some relatively easy ways to address this but these families are simply unaware. The easiest remedy would be to build and use raised beds [BEHAVIOR]. On top of that, we need to let gardeners know there are several methods to reduce the risk of lead poisoning from lead contaminated soils [BEHAVIOR]. Fruit and vegetable gardens should be located away from old painted buildings, heavy traffic, and sites where sludge with heavy metals was applied. Vegetables and fruits can accumulate lead in their leafy green tissues, although lead accumulation will be lower in fruits. In high-risk lead areas, [people should] grow crops such as tomatoes, eggplants, peppers, squash, melons, and cucumbers rather than leafy greens such as lettuce, chard, collards, or spinach. Crops such as carrots, radishes, turnips, onions, and potatoes can accumulate lead and should not be planted in heavily contaminated soils [COGNITION].

I think what upset me the most was discovering real life evidence of environmental racism as we discussed in class [LEVEL 3]. The other teams in class reported healthy soil sample results from affluent areas whereas the underresourced neighborhoods consistently had toxins. I don't think this is necessarily an accident. It seems like these places are the only geographic locations these families can afford. The expression "you get what you pay for" came through loud and clear here. It also makes me angry that our government and culture as a whole doesn't seem to care very much about this. Clearly we need some "brown-field" policy for areas that were formerly factory/industrial sites that have been converted to residential use. Why are there policies and procedures in existence and practice in SOME neighborhoods and not in others? I can see the role chemists must play in policy-making. I want us to discuss in class how government agencies and commercial chemical companies address this real life issue and what we can do about it as professionals and as citizens. As a citizen-student, I'm going to help these neighborhood gardens analyze and improve their soil . . . NOW! I'll feel much better knowing I can help [AFFECT + BEHAVIOR].

A – 1 or 0 LEVEL 1 OR LEVEL 2 OR LEVEL 3
B – 1 or 0
C – 1 or 0 ABC SCORE = 3 X 3 LEVEL RESPONSE = 9

This method is described here as merely one way to assess the impact the engaged experience had on the student. Naturally, there is a degree of subjectivity to any qualitative interpretation. However, one study (Welch & James, 2007) demonstrates how this approach combines a qualitative and quantitative approach that provides insight into student impact and can also be used to document or chart developmental shifts in depth of an entire class over time (see Figure 10.2). Begin considering ways you might conduct summative assessment of your instructional objectives in Tool Kit 10.2.

Figure 10.2 Trajectory of reflection responses.

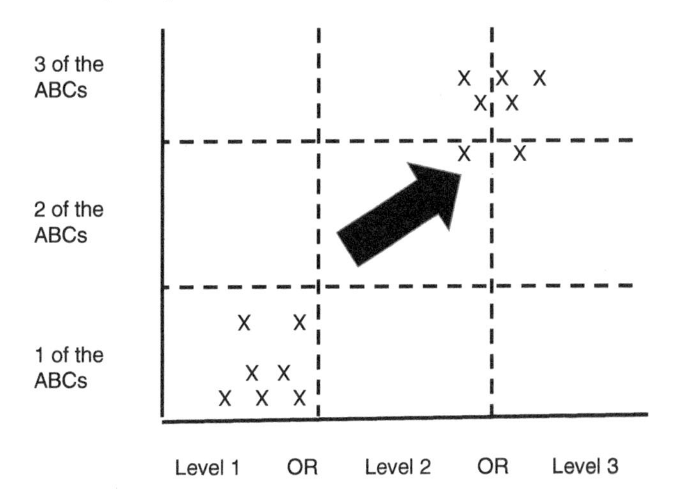

> Tool Kit 10.2—Refer to Exercise 10.2 in your workbook and begin identifying ways you might conduct summative assessment of your instructional objectives.

Assessing Community Partner Goals

In some cases, depending on the goals and objectives for the community partner, assessing goals can be a fairly straightforward dichotomous process of answering either "yes" or "no" and sometimes "partially" to questions like the following: Did the students provide adequate after-school tutoring to children? Was a marketing plan created and adopted by the nonprofit organization? Was the trail restored? Additionally, qualitative questions can be asked to assess level of acceptability (see Figure 10.3).

Figure 10.3 Community partner goal attainment assessment report.

Please indicate your level of satisfaction on the following aspects of your community engagement partnership using the following rating scale:

0 = Not Evident
1 = Very Unsatisfactory
2 = Unsatisfactory
3 = Satisfactory
4 = Very Satisfactory

1. Communication and coordination with the instructor
   0 1 2 3 4

2. Overall follow-through and cooperation with the instructor
   0 1 2 3 4

3. Development, implementation, completion of the project(s)
   0 1 2 3 4

4. Quality of service and/or projects provided by the students/class
   0 1 2 3 4

5. Completion of mutually agreed-on project objectives
   0 1 2 3 4

6. The overall quality of the project/product was:

   _____ Easy to adopt/implement

   _____ Partially adopted/implemented with slight modification

   _____ Not acceptable or applicable for adoption/implementation

7. Based on this experience I/our organization would be willing to work with the instructor and course again.

   _____ Yes _____ No _____ Undecided

Community partners can also provide assessment information on their overall experience with the students and the instructor. A fairly simple and succinct summative assessment report can be done through a written and/ or online survey or phone interview consisting of a handful of questions using a Likert-type rating response (see Figure 10.4). To ensure impartial and candid responses, staff from the campus center coordinating community engagement typically conducts this type of assessment on behalf of the instructor, who receives that information following the course.

Figure 10.4 Community partner assessment of student performance.

Please indicate your level of satisfaction regarding student performance using the following rating scale:

0 = Not Evident
1 = Very Unsatisfactory
2 = Unsatisfactory
3 = Satisfactory
4 = Very Satisfactory

1. Communication and follow-through of the students
   0 1 2 3 4
2. Professionalism and behavior of the students
   0 1 2 3 4
3. Student adherence to our organization's policy/procedure/protocol
   0 1 2 3 4
4. Responsiveness to feedback from me/my staff
   0 1 2 3 4
5. Timeliness on project/service and time management skills
   0 1 2 3 4
6. Effort and commitment to the project/service
   0 1 2 3 4
7. Overall organizational skills
   0 1 2 3 4

(*Continues*)

Figure 10.4 (*Continued*)

8. Overall conflict management skills
   0 1 2 3 4

9. Overall quality of the students' project/service/product
   0 1 2 3 4

10. Overall quality of student or team performance
   0 1 2 3 4

Assessment of student performance by the community partner can be included in the final grade. Although it is important to remember that it is the students' *learning* that is graded and not the service, community partners have a unique perspective on student performance on other important ancillary skill sets. And quite frankly, partner assessment of students' performance provides an additional incentive and sense of accountability to ensure full commitment and engagement. This level of assessment may comprise approximately 10% of the final grade, which can make a significant difference in a student's letter grade. Many times, this manifests itself as a team grade, but it can also be applied to individual student performance. As such, this type of assessment is an appropriate and authentic measure of ancillary life skills and professionalism as explored in chapter 6. Refer to Tool Kit 10.3 in your workbook to consider how you might incorporate some of these approaches.

Tool Kit 10.3—Refer to Exercise 10.3 in your workbook to consider and discuss how you might incorporate some of these approaches and/or tools with your community partner. Which, if any, already exist through your campus center for community engagement?

Formative Assessment

Formative assessment is an opportunity for instructors and community partners to step back and consider the overall format of the community engagement experience as detailed in the course agreement action plan. Formative assessment allows for adjusting logistics such as the number of students that can realistically be assigned to the agency as well as how much time can and should be allocated to the engagement experience. It is also an opportunity to review communication and coordination efforts between the instructor and community partner. This type of review minimizes the possibility of problems and increases the likelihood of a successful experience in the future. Basic questions include the following:

- What went well?
- What didn't go as planned and why?
- What could/should be done differently in the future?
- Was the number of students workable and effective?
- Did the students have the necessary skills to do the engagement activity?
- Was the amount of time and time line for the engagement activity adequate?
- How can/should the time and time line for the engagement activity change?
- Did the channels of communication work effectively?
- How (if at all) should communication and coordination be modified?
- Was there adequate oversight and supervision of the students?
- Were roles and responsibilities of the community partner clear?

Over time, a long-standing relationship can be established between the instructor and community partner that will reduce the amount of time and effort that was initially required when establishing the partnership. You have an opportunity to consider how you might approach formative assessment in Tool Kit 10.4.

> Tool Kit 10.4—Refer to Exercise 10.4 in your workbook. Discuss the examples of formative assessment questions presented here and consider additional items you might use. Consider where and when you might conduct formative assessment with your community partner.

Honing Your Craft

As we conclude this chapter and Part Two of this book, we now turn our attention to honing our craft in the context of assessment. It is time to go beyond the nuts and bolts of designing, implementing, and assessing community engagement courses to consider some ethical issues and dynamics that are inherent in this work. We begin by challenging two predominant perspectives and methods of practice to combine our focus on both objectives and assessment. Being academics, we aim to challenge traditional forms of student assessment, as might be expected. As argued earlier, despite the importance and purpose of assessing and evaluating student attainment of instructional objectives in any and all types of educational experiences within higher education, instructors continue to use traditional forms of measures such as exams and written papers, assuming these procedures do, in fact, accurately assess student growth. It is possible that these measures are really only assessing students' ability to memorize and regurgitate information in an academically acceptable manner and parlance, rather than demonstrating actual comprehension, assimilation, and application of knowledge and skills. Engaged teaching and learning provides a more authentic approach to academic assessment by allowing opportunities for students to demonstrate their mastery of key topics and skills by implementing them in an environment outside the classroom. This approach is much more robust than traditional exams and requires more work for the student and the instructor. That's the proverbial rub.

Academia has effectively socialized students to assume and accept that traditional assessment and evaluation procedures will be incorporated. Indeed, students have been socialized to master those methods, to earn a grade, preferably an A. As such, be prepared for students to push back on the expectation that they must actually take some role in and responsibility for the learning. Students are adept at academic rationalization to mentally and emotionally accept a lower grade if they don't do the work or do an adequate job. They will and do, quite literally, conduct an informal mental cost/benefit analysis as to the value and worth of doing the work in return for what they deem to be an acceptable grade. In addition to assuming more personal responsibility, engaged teaching and learning requires students to assume a degree of public accountability to follow through in meeting the goals of a community partner. When students do not adhere to the pedagogical covenant with their community partner, there is the very real risk their truncated effort and follow-through can have a detrimental impact on the organization and those they serve. In other words, the assessment and evaluation process is no longer about "getting a grade." In this context, it is a commitment to the public purpose of higher education as well as their community partner. Students must be taught this. This also means more work and accountability for the instructor.

Another predominant practice is related to the issues articulated previously. The field of engaged teaching and learning is, at long last, coming to terms with its tainted history of not assessing community impact (Reeb

& Folger, 2013). As academics, we can readily see the positive impact this work has on students in a variety of domains beyond academic and cognitive growth. That, however, often is and can be at the expense of our community partners. In fact, sometimes the "best learning" takes place when fairly spectacular failures or mishaps occur, prompting students and instructors to conclude, "Wow, that sure was a good learning experience, and I'll never make that mistake again." Although the student is the beneficiary of that insight, it is to the detriment of the community partner. Thus, as explained in chapter 6, on objectives, it is not merely pedagogically incumbent on instructors to assess to what extent our efforts met community partner objectives; it is a moral and ethical responsibility. We must essentially embrace and adhere to a tenet of "Do no harm." Research clearly shows that for nearly two decades faculty have been lax in our efforts and attempts to ensure positive impact for our community partners. Tool Kit 10.5 provides an opportunity to explore ways to hone your craft in regard to assessment.

Tool Kit 10.5—Honing Your Craft—Refer to your workbook to continue to explore and discuss ways to hone your craft in regard to assessment.

Therefore, we must transcend a technical approach of implementing the nuts and bolts of this work to hone our craft as engaged scholars. We are obligated to understand and accept the roles and responsibilities of engaged teaching and learning through the artful and nuanced approaches presented in these pages. It is no longer about "getting through the material" or "putting in hours" in the community. Any instructional technician can do that. A dedicated engaged scholar enters into this craft committed to the ethos presented in Part One of this book by integrating research, teaching, and service that has meaningful impact on our students, discipline, institution, and community at large.

PART THREE

ADVANCING THE CRAFT

Chapter 11

SCHOLARSHIP

A scholar is an individual who pursues high levels of lifelong learning and inquiry that incorporate rigorous methods to generate and disseminate new knowledge for many purposes (Diamond & Adams, 1993). Scholarly work generally requires expertise in a discipline that generates new knowledge that has impact and can be documented, disseminated, replicated, and critiqued by other scholars (Diamond & Adams, 1993, as cited in Jordan, 2010). This chapter will provide an overview of traditional perspectives and an alternative approach of community-engaged scholarship (CES). We begin by reviewing the traditional paradigm of scholarship that emerged following World War II. We continue by considering various approaches and types of scholarship as described by Boyer (1990). We then shift our attention to how to disseminate CES.

Traditional Paradigm of Scholarship

The role for faculty, and tenure-track faculty in particular, is to generate and disseminate knowledge production and dissemination through scholarly venues that are normally separated from the general public (Juergensmeyer, 2017). Rice (1996) stated the dominant paradigm and expectations largely existent today of what it means to be a faculty member in higher education are based on at least seven assumptions (as paraphrased from Bringle, Games, and Malloy, 1999):

1. The key endeavor of academic life is research.
2. Peer review ensures quality and professional autonomy.
3. Knowledge is generated and understood for its own sake.

4. Disciplinary departments frame the pursuit of knowledge.
5. Stature and prestige are determined through national and international disciplinary organizations.
6. Professional stature and promotion are accomplished through specialization.
7. A scholar pursues cognitive truth.

Outcomes and Impact

When one critically examines Rice's depiction of the seven traditional assumptions of scholarship, it becomes evident that the emphasis and focus is on outcomes, primarily for the scholar and secondarily for the discipline and institution, rather than on impact on various stakeholders such as students and the community. Moreover, the terms *outcome* and *impact* are often interchanged as synonyms (see Tool Kit 11.1).

> Tool Kit 11.1—Refer to Exercise 11.1 in your workbook. Compare and contrast the terms *outcome* and *impact*. Are there differences between the two? If so, what are those differences and how might that impact your work as an engaged scholar?

An *outcome* can be defined as a limited, predefined, and measurable goal designed to demark change, whereas *impact* can be conceptualized as the longer and broader term effect of an outcome (Harding, 2018). Traditionally, scholarship has manifested itself in the form of scholarly products such as articles, books, chapters, and presentations, in which the primary outcome or goal is documenting a scholar's efforts in generating and disseminating new knowledge. Thus, the main, if not the exclusive benefactor of the scholarly activity is the scholar by virtue of publication, regardless of whether there is an impact beyond the disciplinary field. In a somewhat simplistic sense, merely having an article or a book on a library shelf constitutes an outcome that depicts a productive scholar. In other words, by virtue of publication alone, regardless to what extent that knowledge is applied and has an impact, a faculty member is being "scholarly." Likewise, this scholarly activity is beneficial to the discipline as this new information makes a contribution to the field. As useful as this is to the scholar and field, it may have limited benefit to the community at large. It is even possible that the scholarly effort may have been detrimental to or exploitive of the community. Although Boyer (1997) acknowledged and valued this type of traditional scholarship focused on disciplinary dissemination, he also called for a scholarship of engagement and lamented,

> Increasingly the campus is being viewed as a place where students get credentialed and faculty get tenured, while the overall work of the academy does not seem particularly relevant to the nation's most pressing civic, social, economic, and moral problems. (p. 85)

Impact, in contrast, extends beyond the scope of tangible evidence in the form of a scholarly product listed on a curriculum vitae to assessing the influence or bearing the material or activity has in scope to other and additional stakeholders in an array of settings or contexts. As such, CES extends traditional academic exploration beyond research for the sake of discovery to promote impact. The National Science Foundation now includes documentation of impact in the following criteria in the review process of proposals: (a) What is the intellectual merit of the proposed activity? and (b) What are the broader impacts of the proposed activity? A series of questions within the NSF *Grant Proposal Guide* helps illustrate the concept of broader impact:

> 1. How well does the activity advance discovery and understanding while promoting teaching, training, and learning?
> 2. How well does the proposed activity broaden the participation of underrepresented groups (e.g., gender, ethnicity, disability, geographic, etc.)?
> 3. To what extent will it enhance the infrastructure for research and education, such as facilities, instrumentation, networks, and partnerships?
> 4. Will the results be disseminated broadly to enhance scientific and technological understanding?
> 5. What may be the benefits of the proposed activity to society? (March, 2007)

Boyer's Reconceptualization of Scholarship

Boyer (1990) characterized four different types of scholarship (see Table 11.1). The scholarship of discovery might be considered to reflect traditional forms and assumptions of scholarship focused on generating and disseminating new knowledge through peer-reviewed venues. The scholarship of integration has an emphasis on interpreting and integrating knowledge across disciplines. The scholarship of teaching and

TABLE 11.1.
Boyer's Model of Scholarship

Type	*Purpose*	*Examples—Measures of Performance*
Scholarship of Discovery	Generating and disseminating new knowledge through traditional research	Presenting peer-reviewed publications and presentations Producing or performing creative work Developing infrastructural models for future research
Scholarship of Integration	Interpreting and integrating knowledge across disciplines	Developing comprehensive review of the literature and policy briefs Authoring textbook for use across disciplines Collaborating in designing and implementing a cross-disciplinary course
Scholarship of Teaching and Learning	Studying and applying teaching to promote learning	Promoting learning theory in the classroom Developing new teaching and learning materials, curriculum, and methods Creating and implementing comprehensive assessment methods
Scholarship of Engagement	Addressing social and professional issues and challenges	Integrating research, teaching, and service to serve the discipline and society Serving as a consultant to nonprofit, governmental, and corporate agencies Leading in professional and community organizations Mentoring students to develop their professional skills and careers

learning studies and applies new theoretically based forms of pedagogy. The scholarship of engagement addresses social and professional challenges by integrating research, teaching, and service in the classroom and community.

SoTL and the scholarship of engagement lend themselves nicely to CES. Your incorporation of hands-on learning in the community reflects and advances the scholarship of teaching. A quantitative or qualitative analysis of your engaged teaching and courses provides new knowledge to the field. Hence, as mentioned in chapter 6, on objectives, and chapter 10, on assessment, consider how you might provide a narrative describing the design, implementation, and impact of your community-engaged course. Meanwhile, some of the activities and products derived from your CES merit recognition within the scholarship of engagement. Describing the impact of those exercises and materials in publications and presentations is a manifestation of Boyer's vision of the academy as citizen. A list of potential dissemination venues is presented later in this chapter.

CES

Bringle and Hatcher (2011) argued the broad concept of engagement as a whole must reflect the following characteristics: (a) it must be scholarly; (b) it must integrate teaching, research, and service; (c) it must be reciprocal and mutually beneficial; and (d) it must encompass and reflect civil democracy. Here we offer one comprehensive characterization of CES that is embedded within the call for nominations for the Ernest A. Lynton Faculty Award in Engaged Scholarship hosted by the Swearer Center at Brown University:

> The scholarship of engagement (also known as outreach scholarship, public scholarship, scholarship for the common good, community-based scholarship, and community engaged scholarship) represents an integrated view of the faculty role in which teaching, research, and service overlap and are mutually reinforcing, is characterized by scholarly work tied to a faculty member's expertise, is of benefit to the external community, is visible and shared with community stakeholders, and reflects the mission of the institution. Community engagement is defined by relationships between those in the university and those outside the university that are grounded in the qualities of reciprocity, mutual respect, shared authority, and co-creation of goals and outcomes. Such relationships are by their very nature trans-disciplinary (knowledge transcending the disciplines and the college or university) and asset-based (where the strengths, skills, and knowledge of those in the community are validated and legitimized. (Brown University Swearer Center, 2018)

Consequently, a key and significant difference between traditional and engaged scholarship is where and how new knowledge is disseminated. Likewise, as articulated by Bringle and Hatcher (2011) CES integrates research, teaching, and scholarship. Begin considering ways to map your engaged scholarship that integrate the academic trilogy and impact multiple stakeholders. Swipe your smartphone or tablet over the QR code in

Figure 11.1 for the "Engaged Conversation" video featuring Orin Starn from Duke University. Capture your reactions in Tool Kit 11.2.

Figure 11.1 Orin Starn video on the importance of civically engaged scholarship.

Note. Scan the QR code to access https://www.youtube.com/watch?v=vCCBmKOT2nb

> Tool Kit 11.2—Refer to Exercise 11.2 in your workbook and jot down notes, comments, and/or questions you might have after watching the video clip of Orin Starn discussing his view of and approach to engaged scholarship.

Dissemination

Once a scholar has generated new knowledge, there is a professional obligation and expectation to disseminate that information. Historically, the primary venues for this process have been peer-reviewed journals, books, chapters, and conference presentations. Likewise, teaching is actually a form of dissemination as the professor is professing knowledge to students in a classroom rather than through a form of media. However, over the recent decades and largely due to Boyer's influence, CES has expanded our traditional assumptions and practice regarding dissemination to become more inclusive and impactful. The next section of this chapter explores opportunities for both traditional and alternative dissemination methods for advancing CES. We begin by graphically comparing and contrasting traditional, positivist approaches with democratically framed CES in Table 11.2.

Traditional Dissemination

Consider publishing and presenting about your engaged teaching and research. The *Michigan Journal of Community Service-Learning* is a highly revered publication within the field. The *International Journal of Research on Service-Learning and Community Engagement* (*IJRSLCE*) is an online peer-reviewed journal reporting research focused on

TABLE 11.2
Compare and Contrast Positivist Scholarship and CES

Dimension	*Expert-Centered Positivist Scholarship*	*Democratic-Centered CES*
Community Relationships	Partnership and mutuality	Reciprocity
	Deficit-based understanding of community	Asset-based understanding of community
	Academic work done *for* the public	Academic work done *with* the public
Knowledge Production and Research	Applied	Inclusive, collaborative, problem/goal-oriented
	Unidirectional flow of knowledge	Multidirectional flow of knowledge
Epistemology	Positivist/scientific and technocratic	Relational, localized, contextual
	Distinction between knowledge producers and knowledge consumers	Cocreation of knowledge
	Primacy of academic knowledge	Shared authority for knowledge creation
	University as the center for public problem-solving	University as part of an ecosystem of knowledge production for addressing public problems
Political	Apolitical engagement	Facilitating an inclusive, collaborative, and deliberative democracy

Note. Adapted from "Changing Pedagogies," by J. Saltmarsh, 2010, in H. E. Fitzgerald, C. Burack, & S. D. Seifer (Eds.), *Handbook of Engaged Scholarship: Contemporary Landscapes, Future Directions* (Vol. 1) (pp. 331–352). East Lansing, MI: Michigan State University Press.

service-learning, campus-community engagement, and civic education. The *Journal of Community Engagement and Scholarship* (*JCES*) is a peer-reviewed international journal that integrates teaching, research, and community engagement across disciplines. Another refereed interdisciplinary publication is the *Journal of Higher Education Outreach and Engagement* (*JHEOE*), which focuses on theory and practice related to community engagement. A number of peer-reviewed disciplinary journals that include publications on community engagement exist (see Figure 11.2).

Figure 11.2 List of peer-reviewed journals for CES.

Adult Education and Development
Change: The Magazine of Higher Learning
Citizen Science: Theory and Practice
Collaborations: A Journal of Community-Based Research and Practice
Collaborative Anthropologies
Community Development
Community Development Journal
Community Works Journal
Education, Citizenship and Social Justice
eJournal of Public Affairs
Engaged Scholar Journal
Gateways: International Journal of Community Research and Engagement
Global Journal of Community Psychology Practice
Innovative Higher Education
Interdisciplinary Journal of Partnership Studies
International Journal for Service Learning in Engineering, Humanitarian Engineering, and Social Entrepreneurship
International Journal of Civic Engagement and Social Change
International Journal of Research on Service-Learning and Community Engagement
International Journal of Public Deliberation
International Undergraduate Journal for Service-Learning, Leadership, and Social Change
Journal for Civic Commitment
Journal of Community Engagement and Higher Education
Journal of Community Practice
Journal of Cooperative Education and Internships
Journal of Deliberative Mechanisms in Science
Journal of Economic Development in Higher Education
Journal of Extension
Journal of Public Scholarship in Higher Education
Journal of Service-Learning in Higher Education
Journal of STEM Outreach
Journal on Anchor Institutions and Communities
Metropolitan Universities
Michigan Journal of Community Service Learning
Partnerships: A Journal of Service-Learning & Civic Engagement
Prism: A Journal of Regional Engagement

Figure 11.2 (*Continued*)

Progress in Community Health Partnerships: Research, Education, and Action
Public: A Journal of Imagining America
Public Philosophy Journal
Reflections: A Journal of Public Rhetoric, Civic Writing, and Service-Learning
Research for All
The Review of Higher Education
Revista Conexão UEPG
Science Education and Civic Engagement: An International Journal
Transform: The Journal of Engaged Scholarship
UNBOUND: Reinventing Higher Education
Undergraduate Journal of Service Learning and Community-Based Research

Note. Adapted from Engagement Scholarship Consortium, *Journals*, 2019, https://engagementscholarship.org/publications/journals.

Campus Compact provides an annotated list of interdisciplinary community engagement journals (Doberneck, 2017a) and a journal comparison table (Doberneck, 2017b). Forchuk and Meier (2014) provided a useful tool called the "article idea chart" to help scholars conceptualize publications about their CES. Similarly, Bordeaux, Wiley, Tandon, and Horowitz (2007) provided guidelines on how to prepare manuscripts about CES for peer-reviewed journals. You are encouraged to take advantage of writing retreats offered by your campus center for community engagement or center for teaching and learning. In these centers you are offered suggestions for conceptualizing articles as well as space conducive to writing in the company of colleagues.

There are also a number of peer-reviewed professional conferences within the field of community engagement where you might make a presentation or advance this work within your specific discipline. Campus Compact alternates a national conference every other year with regional conferences. The Engaged Scholarship Consortium (ESC) hosts national and regional conferences each year. Imagining America is a professional association advancing community engagement through the humanities and arts with an annual conference. The International Association for Research on Service-Learning and Community Engagement (IARSLCE) hosts a conference focused on research each year.

Many professional conferences of specific disciplines include special interest groups (SIGs) or topical strands devoted to presentations about community engagement and service-learning. For example, the American Education Research Association (AERA) has a SIG for service-learning and experiential education (AERA, 2019). Science Education for New Civic Engagements and Responsibilities (SENCER, n.d.) is a program of the National Center for Science and Civic Engagement that provides resources and materials as well as presentation and publication opportunities. Conferences of the American Society for Engineering Education and the American Sociological Association have also included presentations on CES. Consider exploring the journals and conferences within your own discipline to identify traditional opportunities and venues for disseminating your CES in Tool Kit 11.3.

Tool Kit 11.3—Refer to Exercise 11.3 in your workbook to review and consider possible publication and/or conference venues for disseminating your CES.

An Alternative Approach to Dissemination

In addition to traditional forms of and approaches to scholarship, a new alternative approach has begun to emerge over the past two decades, largely in response to Boyer's reconceptualization of scholarship. In addition to peer-reviewed journals, conferences, books, and chapters, other types of engaged work are becoming recognized as a legitimate form of scholarship. These activities and products are considered scholarly when they (a) are theoretically grounded and/or build on existing knowledge, (b) incorporate sound and appropriate methodology that meets community aspirations and goals, (c) make a significant contribution to the community and discipline through demonstrative impact, and (d) are socially validated through adoption or incorporation by partner stakeholders. Kezar, Drivalas, and Kitchen (2018) have edited a volume that advocates for and describes public scholarship that advances equity and social justice. The chapters reframe traditional positivist approaches and expert-driven policy to offer a bottom-up approach by empowering a wide range of stakeholders from marginalized communities. Engaged scholarship projects include abstracts, advocacy materials, artistic and creative work or performances/designs/displays/exhibits, curricula, digital products (e.g., apps, videos), forums, grant proposals, guides, handbooks, policy briefs and reports, posters, studies, technical support, websites, workshops, and technical support (Able et al., 2016; Holland, 2012; O'Meara, Eatman, & Petersen, 2015).

For example, an instructor in a university's school of social work assisted the county office of family services by conducting research to create a policy brief on best practices for wrap around services for families in schools that could then be utilized in writing a seed grant for a pilot program. This same information can be adapted as an article for a peer-reviewed journal or a presentation at a professional conference. Another illustration involves an art historian who formed and conducted listening circles at local churches and schools to obtain an oral history of a neighborhood. This, in turn, became a mural celebrating the neighborhood's cultural legacy for a newly constructed civic center and library. Finally, a Spanish instructor of a community-engaged language course worked with *La Raza* to identify two engaged projects for her students. The first project involved creating a pamphlet in Spanish describing the potential risks associated with payday loans. Students conducted research on the issue and translated that information into a written document that was distributed to local churches, schools, and apartment complexes. They also developed and presented a brief workshop to orally present the materials in ways that developed their spoken language skills. The second project was to develop written materials describing organ donations that could be used at a local hospital with Spanish-speaking families. The students had to research and be aware of complex social mores on this topic. In each of these examples, the engaged scholar was (a) using theoretically grounded knowledge, (b) incorporating sound and appropriate methodology that met community goals and aspirations, (c) making a significant contribution to the community and discipline through demonstrative impact, and (d) being socially validated through adoption or incorporation by partner stakeholders. This work in and of itself constitutes CES. Taking it one step further to publish or present about the work in traditional dissemination venues further strengthens the academic contributions record of the scholar.

Many institutions, such as the University of North Carolina at Greensboro, are now explicitly describing and including CES within their promotion and tenure policy and review criteria (see Figure 11.3). These often include alternative forms of dissemination venues.

As discussed later in chapter 12, it is incumbent on you to clearly and effectively articulate the theoretical foundation for these activities, coupled with a description of sound methodology for developing and implementing them, followed by a summary of impact to your colleagues as you undergo performance review. Given these are unfamiliar forms of scholarship, be prepared for this work to be questioned at best and dismissed at worst. You will learn more in chapter 12 how to use standards of excellence to support and justify your work as a scholarly activity. For now, refer to Tool Kit 11.4 to begin identifying engaged scholarly activities and materials.

Figure 11.3 University of North Carolina at Greensboro's definitions of *scholarship* and *community-engaged research*

Scholarship is characterized by creative intellectual work based on a high level of professional expertise, the significance of which can be validated by peers and which enhances the fulfillment of the mission of the University. Scholarship is not considered to be synonymous with research, but can be demonstrated by activities in teaching, research, creative activity, service, and directed professional activity. Scholarship may be conducted by a variety of methods, across a variety of contexts, and in pursuit of a variety of purposes. Such scholarship can enhance or revise disciplinary knowledge; have an impact on various populations or organizations; or offer new theoretical insights. Because of the breadth of scholarly activity and its conduct, the path of any scholarly agenda will vary according to the nature of its questions and the means of their pursuit.

Community-Engaged Research and Creative Activities

- Writing papers for refereed journals and conference proceedings
- Creating exhibits in educational and cultural institutions
- Disseminating community-engaged research through public programs and events
- Conducting and disseminating directed or contracted research
- Conducting and reporting program evaluation research or public policy analyses for other institutions and agencies
- Developing innovating solutions that address social, economic, or environmental challenges (e.g., inventions, patents, products, services, clinical procedures and practices)

Note. From UNC Greensboro, *Leadership and Civic Engagement*, n.d., https://olsl.uncg.edu/community-scholarship/about-ces/.

Tool Kit 11.4—Refer to Exercise 11.4 in your workbook. Review and identify activities and/or materials that have emerged from your CES. Make a list of those products and begin drafting a brief narrative contextualizing this as engaged scholarship.

Honing Your Craft

This chapter focused primarily on helping you establish your engaged scholarship. However, the narrative in this chapter highlighted the institutional challenges associated with CES. Engaged scholars continue to encounter misunderstanding at best and resistance at worst as they pursue this type of scholarly work. Although there have been modest gains at some institutions to expand our understanding of scholarship, this remains a significant institutional challenge. Leaders in the field such as KerryAnn O'Meara, Timothy Eatman, and Saul Petersen (2015); Diane Doberneck (2018a, 2018b); and Lorilee Sandmann (2014) have described and conducted workshops to help institutions revisit their preconceived notion of scholarship while advancing CES. As we will explore later in chapter 14, a critical mass of engaged faculty can champion engaged scholarship by taking on the role of a tempered radical by diplomatically challenging existing assumptions and paradigms. In the meantime, many campuses have established task force working groups to begin reviewing and revising policy to promote a culture of engaged scholarship (Able et al., 2016; Saltmarsh et al., 2015).

For now, and as an important prerequisite step to later work in chapter 14, begin to discuss, identify, and articulate your institution's conceptualization of scholarship in Tool Kit 11.5. This serves as a useful preface to strategic steps to advance CES.

Tool Kit 11.5—Honing Your Craft—Refer to Exercise 11.5 in your workbook. To what extent would CES be understood or supported in your department and/or institution? If CES is a new concept, what steps might be taken to begin to educate colleagues on what it is (and isn't) in ways that will lead to institutional change as discussed in forthcoming chapters? Reflect on and discuss possible steps and mechanisms you and your learning community might consider using to revisit your institution's conceptualization of scholarship and to advance CES.

Chapter 12

PREPARING FOR PERFORMANCE REVIEW

This chapter is for faculty on the tenure track who will be reviewed for promotion and tenure as well as adjunct instructors on contract who undergo periodic performance reviews, including those teaching at community colleges. This is a critically important process that ensures quality scholarship within the academy. We begin with the good news. Nearly 75% of faculty on the tenure track are awarded tenure (Chait, 2002; O'Meara, 2010). Now the not-so-good news. Most nontenured faculty feel the promotion and tenure review process is "ambiguous and difficult to navigate in terms of standards and expectations" (O'Meara, 2010, p. 275). A recent study of 410 full-time pretenured and tenured faculty at 3 universities in the northeastern part of the United States reported that respondents generally found a lack of clarity in promotion and tenure criteria (Prottas, Shea-Van Fossen, Cleaver, & Andreassi, 2017).

To complicate things further, the review process varies widely from one institution to another. Some institutions are highly centralized with a single promotion and tenure process. Others are very decentralized, and every academic department on campus has its own criteria and procedures. Some criteria provide useful descriptions and benchmarks of performance expectations. Others can be vague, which presents challenges for the instructor who is trying to meet those performance expectations. Therefore, it is incumbent on you to be aware of the process as well as the cultural and political factors that shape this exercise at your institution. The promotion and tenure process continues to be a challenge, especially for engaged faculty (Bialek, 2000; Gelmon & Agre-Kippenhan, 2002; Huber, 2002; Nyden, 2003; Saltmarsh & Hartley, 2011; Seifer, Wong, Gelmon, & Lederer, 2009; Welch, 2016), as many promotion and tenure systems do not reflect institutional priorities nor the changes in the dynamic nature of what constitutes scholarship or the aspirations of the new engaged professoriate (O'Meara et al., 2015).

One reason for these challenges is that review committees at any type of institution of higher education don't fully understand what CES is, and they tend to focus on the location of the work in the community as a form of service rather than as a scholarly activity. Another factor is that CES does not readily align with traditional standards for evaluating the quality and productivity of scholarship. Consequently, there is no accepted method of peer-reviewing the various dissemination methods that are common in CES, as described previously in chapter 11 (Hafler & Lovejoy, 2000; Popovich & Abel, 2002). Swipe your smartphone or tablet over the QR code in Figure 12.1 to hear KerryAnn O'Meara discuss some of the challenges associated with promotion and tenure review for engaged scholars. Jot down your thoughts, reactions, and questions that arise from watching the video in the space provided in Tool Kit 12.1.

Figure 12.1 Video of KerryAnn O'Meara discussing promotion and tenure challenges for engaged scholarship.

Note. Scan the QR code to access https://www.youtube.com/watch?v=2y9hE9xe9Qc

> Tool Kit 12.1—Refer to Exercise 12.1 in your workbook. Record your thoughts, reactions, and questions that arise from watching the video clip regarding some of the challenges associated with the review process for engaged scholars.

The Community-Campus Partnership for Health (CCPH) established a working group to examine issues pertaining to promotion and tenure review in the context of engaged scholarship and to develop mechanisms to fairly and accurately review scholarly performance (Jordan et al., 2009). The working group reported that (a) promotion and tenure criteria generally did not have clear language to describe community engagement nor did they have key competencies that could be used by a review committee, (b) existing definitions did not adequately characterize the purpose or spirit of community engagement as a valid form of scholarship, and (c) the review process lacked adequate tools and standards to assess engaged scholarship. As a result, the working group developed a resource package for assessing engaged scholarship (described further on p. 169, this volume).

O'Meara and colleagues (2015) argue that "the promotion and tenure process reflects institutional values, aspirations, privileges, and power structures" (p. 52). At the same time, Diamond (1995) stated that

> the promotion and tenure review has basically three components: 1) the documentation that the candidate provides, 2) the materials that the committee collects, and 3) the process by which the committee reviews these materials and conducts its deliberations. A well-prepared faculty member can go a long way in making his or her "case" by providing strong context and solid documentation for the committee to consider. (p. 14)

As such, it is in your best interest to proactively prepare for the review process as well as articulate what it means to be an engaged scholar (see Tool Kit 12.2).

> Tool Kit 12.2—Refer to Exercise 12.2 in your workbook. Obtain a copy of the promotion and tenure criteria and procedures and/or the evaluation rubric for non-tenure-track instructors that will be used for your review. Examine the nature of the expectations and benchmarks for assessing faculty.

The key to a successful performance review is to clearly articulate the rigor of engaged teaching and scholarship (O'Meara, 2010).

Frameworks for Assessing Engaged Scholarship

We present here three models that frame CES as well as provide suggested standards to assess the quality of the work. An engaged scholar may wish to use one of these as a framework to describe their engaged work. Likewise, an engaged scholar may consider offering it to their review committee as a tool to help them assess the quality of the engaged work that may be unfamiliar to them. However, it is critically important to also follow and address existing review criteria.

Standards for Assessing Engaged Scholarship

Boyer's (1990) landmark report *Scholarship Reconsidered* examined a full range of scholarly activity within the academy that moved beyond the traditional paradigm of research. Boyer characterized scholarship of engagement as that which manifests itself through scholarly activity beyond the campus to address social issues in the community. The Carnegie Foundation for the Advancement of Teaching proposed establishing criteria to help assess this new type of scholarship. As a result, Glassick and colleagues (1997) developed assessment criteria for engaged scholarship consisting of the following standards: (a) clear goals, (b) adequate preparation, (c) appropriate methodology, (d) outstanding results, (e) effective communication, and (f) reflective critique of the work. As discussed earlier in chapter 1 (p. 27, this volume) and later in this chapter, these standards have been slightly modified and expanded by two more standards to be more inclusive of the community and are presented in Figure 12.2.

Figure 12.2 Assessment standards for engaged scholarship.

1. Clearly articulated academic and community goals.
2. Adequate preparation in disciplinary content area and grounding in engaged public scholarship.
3. Appropriate methods that reflect and include rigor and tenets of community engagement.
4. Significant results that impact the field and the community.
5. Effective presentation and dissemination to both scholarly and community audiences.
6. Reflective critique to identify and articulate insight to improve scholarship and community engagement.
7. Demonstration and promotion of leadership and scholarly contributions coupled with agency and parity by all participants and stakeholders.
8. Consistent ethical behavior coupled with cultural competence and socially responsible conduct.

CES Review, Promotion, and Tenure Package

In 2005 the CCPH convened a working group known as the Community-Engaged Scholarship for Health Collaborative, composed of engaged scholars representing various health fields at several universities from across the country (Seifer et al., 2009).The group identified a number of issues related to promotion and tenure review and created a very useful and comprehensive online "package" to assist faculty in preparing their review portfolio (Jordan, 2007). The package incorporates a slightly modified version of the standards developed by Glassick and colleagues (1997), consisting of eight standards that were presented in the "Honing Your Craft" section of chapter 1 of this book as a framework for becoming an engaged scholar. Examples of how to address and articulate each of the standards in a professional statement using a table of accomplishments are provided in sample materials (see Appendix 12A).

The CCPH online package also provides a step-by-step guide to creating a narrative for the professional statement in the review portfolio that begins by defining *community engagement* and *engaged scholarship* and a list of materials to include in the review portfolio, such as (a) a career statement, (b) a curriculum vitae, (c) a statement of assigned responsibilities, (d) a teaching portfolio, (e) letters of support and appreciation from community partners and community leaders, (f) media reports, and (g) a list of peer-reviewed publications and presentations. Likewise, the preparation materials include extensive tables that describe enhancement of scientific rigor in research and community-engaged teaching. Each table is composed of (a) a list and description of incremental steps of the research and curriculum development activities, (b) examples of benefits of the community-engaged methods, and (c) examples of documenting evidence of impact and outcomes. The full package can be accessed from the Community-Engaged Scholarship for Health Collaborative website (https://www.ccphealth.org/wp-content/uploads/2017/10/CES_RPT_Package.pdf). A truncated example consisting of excerpts from the comprehensive package is provided in Appendix 12B.

Points of Distinction

Grounded in its long history of outreach as a land-grant institution, Michigan State University developed a framework to assess community outreach consisting of four domains known as *Points of Distinction* (Michigan State University, 2009), which may also be appropriate in the context of CES. The domains include (a) significance, (b) context, (c) scholarship, and (d) impact. The document provides an assessment matrix made up of the following features characterizing and describing excellence in each of the four domains: (a) components, (b) sample assessment questions, (c) examples of qualitative indicators, and (d) examples of quantitative indicators. The matrix provides a comprehensive list of indicators, far too extensive to describe here. As with the other examples of assessment standards presented previously, engaged scholars may choose to use this matrix to frame their engaged scholarship and/or provide the matrix to their promotion and tenure review committee to assist them in assessing engaged scholarship that may be unfamiliar to them. Given the volume of indicators incorporated in the matrix, a truncated example is presented in Appendix 12C. Readers may visit https://engage.msu.edu/upload/documents-reports/pod_2009ed.pdf to access the full document.

Preparing Your Professional Statement as an Engaged Scholar

Many institutions, including community colleges, require faculty to provide a professional statement in their review portfolio. This provides a background and rationale for the focus of their work. It is here that one must clearly define and describe *engaged scholarship*. This, however, can be daunting given that review committees are generally unfamiliar with CES (Calleson, Jordan, & Seifer, 2005). As such, you must advocate for yourself and clearly articulate the public purpose and theoretical foundations of your work as an engaged scholar. Using your workbook as a guide, you will be invited, beginning with Tool Kit 12.3, to identify and incorporate language from earlier chapters to define CES as well as present a theoretical framework that informs your engaged teaching and scholarship you previously identified in earlier Tool Kit exercises.

> Tool Kit 12.3—Refer to Exercise 12.3 in your workbook to begin to incrementally draft a professional statement that can be included in your review portfolio. As a preface, prepare your professional statement by reviewing and including narrative from your institutional mission that reflects engaged teaching and learning.

Defining *CES*

It is safe to assume that members of the review community will be unfamiliar with the concept of CES. It is likely they will have preconceived notions of what it is and what it is not. Therefore, it is essential to provide a definition and description early in your statement. Using Tool Kit 12.4, you should peruse and review the first chapters of this book and Tool Kit passages to identify narratives that you feel would serve you and resonate with the culture of your campus.

> Tool Kit 12.4—Refer to Exercise 12.4 in your workbook. This exercise will provide additional definitions of *engaged scholarship*. Using these definitions provided throughout this chapter and book, begin drafting a narrative that introduces and describes CES that you can incorporate into your professional statement.

Academic Trilogy

Tenure-track faculty are evaluated on their performance and productivity in a triadic structure of activities that includes research and scholarship, teaching, and service. The evaluation process should determine the degree and impact of (a) developing and disseminating new knowledge, (b) peer review, and (c) effective communication (Register & King, 2017).

Research and Scholarship

Publication of one's research or creative work is the key to obtaining tenure (Miller & Harris, 2009). As discussed in chapter 11 at great length, you should consider ways to write articles for peer-reviewed journals and/or make presentations at refereed professional conferences that disseminate new knowledge about what transpired through your engaged teaching. Publications and presentations about your engaged teaching reflect an integrated approach of engaged scholarship as well as showcase excellence in your teaching.

In addition to reporting at traditional dissemination venues, and as discussed in chapter 11, present and describe other forms of engaged products derived from your work. Products include policy briefs, reports, products, and programs grounded in theory and incorporating sound methodology for their creation and implementation. Likewise, be sure to articulate the impact or outcomes of each of the products. This may include adoption by community partners, media reports, or letters from representatives of community partners documenting the impact of your scholarly efforts. The frameworks presented earlier in the chapter may serve as useful models on how to articulate this in narrative form as well as in summary tables.

Teaching

The review process is also looking for evidence of excellence in teaching. There are two essential challenges associated with this task. The first is the limited and somewhat myopic evaluation methods that have traditionally been used to evaluate teaching excellence. Historically, evaluating teaching has been limited to the following methods: (a) student evaluation ratings, (b) peer review of teaching, and (c) self-report (De Courcy, 2015; Paulsen, 2002). The difficulty with the first two approaches is the assumption that both students and faculty are able to identify and articulate what constitutes excellence in this context as opposed to articulating teaching methods they like or prefer. A related difficulty is characterizing excellence for review committees (De Courcy, 2015; Fitzmaurice, 2010), which leads to the second challenge: many promotion and tenure criteria or adjunct instructor review procedures do not clearly characterize what constitutes excellence and those characteristics vary across departments and disciplines. Furthermore, there is no "one size fits all" definition for *teaching excellence* (Pratt, 2002, p. 9).

However, some institutional policies and procedures do, in fact, articulate what constitutes excellence in teaching. When this is the case, you must carefully address each of those defining characteristics with examples from your course. For example, Concordia College, a faith-based liberal arts college in Moorhead, Minnesota, devotes more than an entire page in its faculty handbook to articulate and describe teaching effectiveness and explicitly includes examples of engaged pedagogy such as service-learning (Concordia College, 2018):

> Teaching Performance—Faculty teaching is not limited to the classroom. Teaching occurs in the laboratory, the studio, the rehearsal hall and on study abroad experiences. It occurs one-on-one in research, independent study, cooperative education, internships and practica. Teaching also includes the coaching of athletic or speech and debate teams, theater productions, media productions, or musical ensemble groups. Teaching performance includes an array of activities related to the interaction of faculty and students in the teaching-learning process:
>
> 1. Knowledge of and enthusiasm for the subject matter;
> 2. Thorough course preparation, including statements of goals and objectives;
> 3. Course organization, including written syllabi and careful preparation for daily classroom activities;

4. Appropriate assignments and prompt evaluation and return of student work;
5. Interest in and availability to students;
6. Encouragement of critical thinking, effective communication and problem-solving skills through active student learning such as discussion, service-learning, group projects, etc.; and
7. Familiarity with, and use of, a variety of teaching techniques appropriate to the classroom audience.

This particular example essentially outlines a narrative for the instructor to describe their engaged teaching by providing a brief statement for each of the seven benchmarks. Likewise, these benchmarks include key engaged pedagogical components such as instructional objectives, critical thinking, effective communication, and problem-solving, all of which are embedded within community-based engaged courses. Consider incorporating some of these characteristics into your professional statement if your departmental or institutional criteria of teaching excellence appear ambiguous.

When the criteria for teaching are nebulous, you must proactively take it on yourself to provide evidence that your engaged teaching does, in fact, embody best practice to connote academic excellence. Therefore, you are encouraged to frame your teaching in a review process that reflects academic excellence in at least six ways. First, as examined in chapter 1, describe engaged pedagogy. Consider including the characterization of engaged pedagogy provided by Colby and colleagues (2003) in chapter 2 as (a) active learning, (b) learning as social process, (c) knowledge shaped by contexts, (d) reflective practice, and (e) an ability to represent an idea in more than one modality. Second, provide a theoretical foundation that grounds your teaching and course. You'll recall that a number of theoretical frameworks were presented in chapter 2. Such a discussion readily reveals and incorporates scholarly attention to academic excellence that is often included as part of the criteria in evaluating an instructor's teaching. Tool Kit 12.5 will help you begin this process.

> Tool Kit 12.5—Review Tool Kit 2.2 from chapter 2 to identify and select a theoretical framework to include in your professional statement. Spend time either by yourself or with your colleagues or center director drafting a narrative of that theoretical framework.

Third, enumerate the objectives of the course. This includes both the instructional goals for students and the goals for the community partner as a means of documenting impact the course had on both students and the community.

Fourth, explain the course preparation of establishing community partnerships as well as assignments, activities, and products you have incorporated. Describe whether you are participating in a learning community to prepare you to develop and teach your engaged course. Include the number of hours you committed to individual and group study. Share when, where, and how often you met with your community partner(s) in developing objectives, assignments, and partnerships. Your course description also includes a list of readings as well as the engaged activities conducted in the community that were designed to achieve the course objectives. Be sure to provide a brief definition and theoretical basis of *reflection* as well as how it was conducted throughout the course. With students' permission, consider providing anonymous reflection passages from students' written reflection entries to illustrate and highlight features of the engaged experience.

Fifth, report the impact of the course. You will recall that chapter 10 explored various ways to assess the impact of engaged courses based on instructional objectives and objectives of community partners. Briefly describe how you assessed achieving those goals and the results. This may include students' pre/post scores on various cognitive or attitudinal measures, reflection statements, and the production and adoption of a tangible product by a community partner. Such an approach provides more evidence of effective teaching than merely sharing course evaluations that often serve as the only vehicle for assessing teaching.

Finally, include the results from community partner summative evaluations. This provides social validation that you and your students effectively applied important knowledge and skills as well as documents cultural competency and effective partnership attributes as described in chapters 3 and 4. Social validity is commonly used in educational and therapeutic contexts in which practitioners in authentic settings (e.g., classrooms, clinics) assess and attest to the effectiveness of a theoretically based approach or program that has been developed and implemented (Baer & Schwartz, 1991; Schwartz & Baer, 1991; Welch et al., 2005). This validation process in real-life settings also serves as a bridge to discussing your service record. That said, you must also remember to clearly articulate that the engagement activities of your course are a form of pedagogy designed to meet instructional objectives. *Therefore, it is imperative that you address and describe your course in the context of teaching rather than service in your professional statement.* Use Tool Kit 12.6 to begin drafting a description of your engaged course.

> Tool Kit 12.6—Refer to Exercise 12.6 in your workbook. Begin to draft a description of your engaged course. Use the OPERA (objectives, partnerships, engagement, reflection, assessment) rubric as an outline. Be sure to articulate and demonstrate how the course and the engaged activities demonstrate teaching excellence either by addressing specific benchmarks or criteria your institution stipulates or by using the basic framework of excellence presented in this chapter.

Service

Traditionally, service within the academic trilogy has fallen under two, or sometimes three, formats (Welch, 2010b). The first is governance by serving on various committees at the departmental, college, or institutional level. This often includes curriculum or admissions committees as well as institutional task forces. The second form of service is as a citizen in your discipline by serving as a reviewer on the editorial review board of a scholarly journal or the governing body of a professional association. You will want to list these on your curriculum vitae. A third, and somewhat less common, form of service that may be recognized at some institutions is service to the community. In this context, some institutions recognize and reward faculty who serve as consultants or members of local boards or organizations within the city or region that hosts the institution. Eby (2010) points out that this type of outreach to the community is common in faith-based institutions. So even if your department or institution does not necessarily include service to the community under the traditional academic umbrella for this aspect of the academic trilogy, you can demonstrate how you have effectively integrated the triadic academic roles and responsibilities as an engaged scholar.

It is important, however, to anecdotally acknowledge the proverbial 300-pound gorilla in the room by noting that service is sometimes viewed as less significant than research and teaching during the review process (Bringle, Games, & Malloy, 1999; Holland, 1999). In Tool Kit 12.7, you are encouraged to consult with a trusted colleague to assess your institution's cultural perception of the value under service. As such, engaged faculty should not exclusively or solely frame their engaged teaching and scholarship under the service category, as the engaged dimension of this work.

Tool Kit 12.7—Refer to Exercise 12.7 in your workbook. Identify a trusted colleague and invite them to lunch or coffee. Ask them about and discuss the cultural and political aspects of the review process. Inquire how service within the academic trilogy is viewed. If they have taught engaged courses, ask to see their promotion and tenure portfolio and how they articulated this work. Share and discuss this with your learning community and/or center director.

Putting It All Together

You are now ready to put together each of the points from this chapter to generate your portfolio. Table 12.4 provides a suggested list and sequence

TABLE 12.4
Suggested List and Sequence for a Review Portfolio

Component	*Description*
Personal and Professional Statement	Your narrative provides an overview of your research, teaching, and service record that reflects tenets of CES. This includes definitions of *CES*. The section on teaching should include a theoretical framework that informs your courses.
Curriculum Vitae	A formal list of your research, teaching, and service activities. This includes lists of publications and presentations under research. Some departments and institutions require instructors to follow a specific outline and format.
Teaching Portfolio	This section may include a description of your courses. This includes a compilation of your course syllabi and course evaluation ratings. Many departments consider serving as an academic adviser and/or a chair of graduate committees a form of teaching. Refer to the theoretical framework articulated in your introductory personal and professional statement.
Letters of Support and Appreciation From Community Partners	Consider soliciting and including letters of support from community partners. These should include the impact of your engaged scholarship.
Media Reports	Consider including any press releases, articles, or reports from local, regional, or national media outlets.
Copies of Peer-Reviewed Articles	Provide hard copies of your peer-reviewed articles.

of components to include in your personal statement and portfolio. Keep in mind your department and institution may have a very formal and official format to use. If this is the case, consider how to incorporate important concepts presented in this chapter and accompanying Tool Kit exercises into that framework. You are also encouraged to refer to the website sources cited in this chapter. Additionally, the Campus Compact website provides useful information on how to prepare for your performance review (https://compact.org/resource-posts/trucen-section-b/). Discuss and share your draft statement and portfolio with your learning community, a mentor, and your center director or campus coordinator of community engagement for input and feedback.

Honing Your Craft

As an engaged scholar, you must approach the promotion and tenure review process professionally and philosophically, and, until there is substantial policy and cultural change within the institution, engaged scholars must also approach this process pragmatically. Later, in chapter 14, we explore ways to advance policy change regarding promotion and tenure at the institutional level, incorporating strategies articulated by O'Meara and colleagues (2015). That discussion will be at a larger, macro-level context. For now, the context in which you find yourself is and can be very challenging, but not inherently impossible. You must be strategic in this process. *Let us be frank: Creating educational experiences that address social challenges and promote capacity building in the community alone will not get you tenure.* You must effectively integrate research, teaching, and service in ways that impact multiple stakeholders: students, your discipline, your institution, and the community at large, as depicted in Figure 1.2 in chapter 1. In Tool Kir 12.8 you can identify scholarly activities and determine which of the four types of scholarship described by Boyer each reflects. Then, you can literally plot the scholarly activity on a map that displays the domain and context. This allows you an opportunity to visually identify and plot your engaged scholarship. Use Tool Kit 12.8 to help with this process.

> Tool Kit 12.8—Refer to Exercise 12.8 in your workbook. Look at the example illustrating how to document the dissemination of engaged scholarship and then draft your own dissemination statement.

Liese (2009) tells his compelling story of how he identified himself as an engaged scholar during his promotion and tenure review process at a large public research university. Wisely, he had to literally educate his peers as to what engaged scholarship was and was not. Likewise, although not part of the official review criteria, he framed his work around the benchmarks and standards of engaged scholarship as depicted by Glassick and colleagues (1997), which he learned about as part of a faculty learning community (Welch, 2002), in tandem with the departmental and institutional standards. As a result, he was awarded tenure. We have provided a link to a video in which Liese discusses this process in the first 20 minutes of a panel discussion. We invite you to scan your smartphone or tablet over the QR code in Figure 12.3 to hear him tell his story. We also encourage you to listen to the entire panel discussion about the evolving promotion and tenure challenges at a public research institution when time allows. With this new insight in mind, we invite you to hone your craft as an engaged scholar—use these standards as benchmarks to guide and inform your work as well as possibly frame your work in your professional statement in your review portfolio in Tool Kit 12.9.

Figure 12.3 Video of a panel discussion with Hank Liese discussing how to articulate engaged scholarship during promotion and tenure review.

Note. Scan the QR code to access https://www.youtube.com/watch?v=HJk129Niu4

Tool Kit 12.9—Honing Your Craft—Refer to Tool Kit Exercise 12.9 in your workbook. Use the standards of evaluation for engaged scholarship developed by Glassick and colleagues (1997) to draft a personal statement that describes you as an engaged scholar.

APPENDIX 12A

Example Of Table Of Accomplishments as Defined by The Characteristics of Quality CES

Characteristics	*Supporting Evidence*
1. Clear Goals	See career goals under the narrative heading "Focus of Scholarship and History" and project goals stated for *Comunidades de la Salud* and Promoting the Occupational Health of Indigenous Farmworkers in my narrative statement and under "Grants" in my CV.
2. Adequate Preparation	See descriptions of my investment in building community relationships, described under "Research" in my narrative statement. Also relevant is my W.K. Kellogg postdoctoral fellowship, which prepared me to undertake partnership work with rural communities and to mentor students in this work. Literature reviews and other background research on community-based research (CBR) and substantive topics conducted during preparation of book chapters and articles have allowed me to maintain and grow my foundation of knowledge in collaborative research methods as well as public health issues such as asthma, air quality, pesticides and other toxins, and other environmental health concerns; community planning; environmental justice; and disaster preparedness.
3. Appropriate Methods: Enhancing Rigor Through Community Engagement	See "Promoting the Occupational Health of Indigenous Farmworkers" in my narrative statement for an example of how the community-based public research (CPBR) model strengthened the research design.
4. Significant Results/Impact	See narrative statement for *Comunidades de la Salud* findings of improved health and decreased depression as well as increased civic participation. See letters from community partners concerning community empowerment.
5. Effective Presentation/ Dissemination	I have disseminated my work through high-quality peer-reviewed journals and peer-reviewed and invited presentations at national conferences and in graduate courses. I have given equal attention to dissemination of findings and systemic and policy implications at local workshops and community meetings. Coauthoring papers and copresenting with community research partners have been particularly effective modes of dissemination for both professional and public audiences.

Characteristics	*Supporting Evidence*
6. Reflective Critique	I have written many articles and presentations about the CBPR model, using my work with communities of color as an illustration. Undertaking these pieces of work allows me to reflect on what worked and didn't work in the projects, consider the feedback provided by community members, and offer my students and audiences suggestions for improving on the model. My willingness to alter the recruitment design of "Promoting the Occupational Health of Indigenous Farmworkers" illustrates my ability to reflect and change my plan based on feedback from the community.
7. Leadership and Personal Contribution	My leadership potential was recognized during my training years—I have held training positions of prestige including my National Institute of Health (NIH) predoctoral training fellowship and my W.K. Kellogg postdoctoral fellowship. I serve as the principal investigator (PI) on a number of grants and projects and I have demonstrated my ability to manage a large, complex project and sizable budget. At the university level, I serve on a number of committees including faculty senate, curriculum committee, search committees, and so on. At the national level, I serve on a number of workgroups, boards of directors, and advisory boards. I have served as a reviewer for journals and Centers for Disease Control and NIH grants. I have won several awards, including two since joining the faculty at UMA.
8. Consistently Ethical Behavior	Letters from community partners document my consistently ethical behavior, trustworthiness, and integrity. I have also studied and demonstrated my understanding of ethics (e.g., my book chapter "Methodological and Ethical Considerations of Community-Driven Environmental Justice Research.")

Note. Adapted from Community-Engaged Scholarship Review, Promotion, and Tenure Package, by C. Jordan (Ed.), *The Community-Engaged Scholarship for Health Collaborative 20*(2), 66–86, 2009. Used with permission.

APPENDIX 12B

Truncated Examples of the Enhancement of Scientific Rigor in Research and Curriculum Development Through Community Engagement

Research Phase	*Benefits of Community Engagement*	*Evidence*
Identify Key Issues and Research Questions	With behavioral and community health issues, it can be difficult to identify the research question. Community involvement can help define the research question or confirm its validity. When community members feel involved and perceive equity in power and decision-making, they are invested in seeing the right questions be addressed.	Ways to document the activity in dossier: Include statements in personal narrative about situations in which community input helped define or changed the research question. Include statement in personal narrative that illustrates how relevance was improved as opposed to similar types of work conducted in alternative settings. Explain in personal narrative why your research questions can be addressed with greater validity than in alternative research settings—include findings obtained from alternative settings (if available and relevant).
Study Design and Methodology	Deeper understanding of a community's unique circumstances can result in a more accurate conceptual framework and understanding of important independent, moderating, and dependent variables. Community input can help create a design and methods that are most acceptable to the community, most valid given the unique circumstances of the community, and most culturally appropriate and respectful.	Ways to document the activity in dossier: Include statements in personal narrative describing the involvement of community partners in development of research design and how their participation contributed to improved research design and methods. Document in personal narrative situations in which better understanding of the community resulted in a more refined conceptual framework. Meeting rosters and minutes that document community participation in discussions about proposal. Highlight community coprincipal investigators on grants listed in CV.

Design of Measurement Instruments and Data Collection	Community input fosters development of more culturally appropriate measurement instruments, making projects more effective and efficient and data collection more accurate. Using local staff to administer surveys and conduct interviews and as survey helpers fluent in the languages of the target group increases authenticity of responses and accuracy of data collected. Mutual trust enhances both the quantity and the quality of data collected. Increased opportunity for field-testing instruments improves reliability.	Ways to document the activity in dossier: Within the personal narrative discuss how community participation increased cultural appropriateness, validity, and reliability of instruments that were developed. How were instruments improved as a result of community input? Within personal narrative include statements from community participants about their perceptions of cultural responsiveness, their willingness to share personal information, and so on.
Translation of Findings Into Recommendations for Policy Change or Intervention, Design of Intervention Based on Recommendations	Community members can provide information about what will work, what is culturally appropriate. Increased appropriateness of interventions can result in more positive/successful application. Productive and ongoing partnerships between researchers and community members increase the likelihood that research findings will be incorporated into ongoing community programs, providing the greatest possible benefit to the community from research. Community members are more effective advocates for public policy change.	Ways to document the activity in dossier: Describe through personal narrative, annotations in your CV, acknowledgment sections, and so on, how members in the community were involved in interpretation of findings and their application to community problems/issues being investigated. Within the personal narrative cite policy changes or program development resulting from the research. If the community exhibits signs of empowerment/increased civic engagement (e.g., community problem-solving, volunteerism).

(*Continues*)

APPENDIX 12B (*Continued*)

Research Phase	*Benefits of Community Engagement*	*Evidence*
Dissemination	Community involvement provides opportunity for broader relevance and impact beyond academic arena. Community environment more accurately depicted in publications and presentations.	Ways to document the activity in dossier: Highlight community coauthors or copresenters in CV. Include examples of community dissemination products such as newspaper articles. Discuss in personal narrative evidence of reach or impact on the community. In the personal narrative discuss how dissemination through nonacademic channels has contributed to application of the findings obtained to the betterment of the communities involved. Note newspaper articles. Discuss in personal narrative evidence of reach or impact on the community, if known.
Ethics	Greater ethical credibility for research because it works *with* people to address their health concerns versus experimenting *on* them.	Ways to document the activity in dossier: Include community letters that speak to the integrity of the researcher, the ethical conduct of the research, and so on.

Curriculum Development	*Benefits of Community Engagement*	*Evidence*	*Ways to Document the Activity*
Identifying Theoretical Framing and Practical Integration for Curriculum Development	Faculty and community partners working on connecting course content with service-related activities can ensure reciprocity of benefit and deepening of the learning experience.	Activities that would create benefit: Conduct focus/training sessions with community partners to share course content, objectives, and outcomes.	Name a community partner teaching advisory committee. Report this committee formulation. Keep log of joint planning meetings with outcomes reported.
Curriculum Development and Potential Funding Support	Cultural, community-specific, socioeconomic questions/ information that might inform students regarding theoretical underpinnings of course content can be provided by community partners for information that may be unknown to the teacher.	Activities that would create benefit: Include community members on curriculum development committees and engage them in specific course planning.	Meeting rosters and minutes that document community participation.
Implementation: Teaching of the Course	Final syllabus and class schedule Identification of community-based learning activities Identification of theoretical-applied learning procedures	Activities that would create benefit: Work with community partner(s) to connect course content and theoretical underpinning with community-base learning.	Present syllabus, reading lists, and all course support materials.

(Continues)

APPENDIX 12B (*Continued*)

Curriculum Development	*Benefits of Community Engagement*	*Evidence*	*Ways to Document the Activity*
Outcomes: Student Learning	Course products created by the students (e.g., reflection journals, course assignments, exams). Community partner field assessment.	Activities that would create benefit: Community partner assessment through field observation over the course of the semester.	Meeting report of assessment of professor/community partner observations of student overall learning outcomes
Teaching Effectiveness	Course evaluations by students. Class observation by peer faculty. Class observation by community partner.	Activities that would create benefit: Community partner could give clear feedback on teaching effectiveness as observed in an appropriate teaching lesson that relates to community engagement assignment.	Report of student evaluation scores. Community partner assessment report. Peer faculty observation report.

Note. Adapted excerpts from Community-Engaged Scholarship Review, Promotion, and Tenure Package, by C. Jordan (Ed.), *The Community-Engaged Scholarship for Health Collaborative 20*(2), 66–86, 2009. Used with permission.

APPENDIX 12C

Truncated Example of Points of Distinction Matrix for Planning and Evaluating Quality Outreach and Public Scholarship

Dimension	*Components*	*Sample Questions*	*Examples of Qualitative Indicators*	*Examples of Quantitative Indicators*
Significance	Importance of issue and opportunity to be addressed	How serious are the issues to the scholarly community, specific stakeholders, and the public?	Documentation of issues and opportunities based on concrete information Magnitude of the issue	Indicators of demand or need Number of citations and issues addressed in the literature Calculations of opportunity costs in terms of resources
Context	Consistency with university and unit values and stakeholder interests	To what extent is the project consistent with the university's or unit's mission? To what extent is the project a high priority among external stakeholders?	Comparison with explicit mission statement and goals Evidence of ability to work sensitively with external audiences and key groups	Number of contracts and planning meetings of stakeholders Resources and methods used to promote program Profile and demographics of audience and participants

(*Continues*)

APPENDIX 12C (*Continued*)

Dimension	*Components*	*Sample Questions*	*Examples of Qualitative Indicators*	*Examples of Quantitative Indicators*
Scholarship	Knowledge resources	To what extent is the project shaped by knowledge that is up-to-date, cross-disciplinary, and appropriate to the issue? Is knowledge in the community or among the stakeholders utilized?	Annotated narrative showing what sources of knowledge are used Quality and fit of the citations, outside experts, or consultants Assessment of experience and accomplishments of major project participants external to the university	Number of cross-disciplinary resources utilized Number of years in positions Dates of citations Number of experts cited and participating
Impact	Impact on issues, institutions, and individuals	To what extent were the project goals and objectives met? Did the products or deliverables meet the planning expectations?	Description of impacts Documentation such as program evaluations, surveys, testimonials, and media coverage Result of changes in policy and/or change in practice	Changes from benchmark or baseline measurements Number of appropriate products generated for practitioners and the public Number of products, contracts, patents, and copyrights generated

Note. Adapted from *Points of Distinction: A Guidebook for Planning and Evaluating Quality Outreach*, University Outreach and Engagement, Kellogg Center, 2009. East Lansing, MI: Michigan State University. Used with permission.

Chapter 13

MENTORING AND COACHING COLLEAGUES

In the context of learning any craft, novices or apprentices generally benefit from having a skilled teacher who can accompany them on their journey as they hone their craft by artfully using tools and skills to create something that has elegance over mere function. However, within higher education we are typically ensconced in a siloed setting and an autonomous culture in which opportunities for continued collaborative professional development with a colleague or group of colleagues are rare. In fact, we traditionally approach teaching and learning as a private, almost secretive, activity. As Parker Palmer (1998) suggested, "Unlike many professions, teaching is always done at the dangerous intersection of personal and public life" (p. 17). He goes on, however, to say,

> When we walk into our workplace, the classroom, we close the door on our colleagues. When we emerge, we rarely talk about what happened or what needs to happen next, for we have no shared experience to talk about. Then, instead of calling this the isolationism it is and trying to overcome it, we claim it as a virtue called academic freedom: my classroom is my castle, and the sovereigns of other fiefdoms are not welcome here. (p. 142)

It is, indeed, countercultural within higher education to offer or request assistance and advice when it comes to our teaching because the cultural norm and assumption of obtaining "terminal degrees" suggests we have "arrived" at becoming experts. However, as discussed in chapter 2, although academics are experts in their disciplines, they are rarely exposed to theoretical principles and pedagogical practices to enhance their teaching. Furthermore, the complex dynamics associated with engaged teaching and learning create and impose additional challenges unknown to novice instructors that they are typically ill prepared to meet.

As you may have surmised reading these pages, we propose and depict engaged teaching and learning as inherently countercultural to traditional academic assumptions and practice. We therefore continue by proposing and encouraging that you break from the cultural isolation that dominates the academy and offer your guidance to colleagues who are exploring a similar path. This includes engaging in dialogue with others to not only promote a sense of community but also attain new insight and ideas from like-minded colleagues for oneself. By virtue of this being a later chapter in the third part of this book designed to advance engaged scholarship, you have ventured far enough into your engaged scholarship to have some experience and insight that novice colleagues neither have nor appreciate. This, of course, by no means implies that you are an expert. You are, however, experienced, which brings and provides insight. In essence, you've "been there, done that" and have something to offer and share with colleagues just beginning to explore CES. As the title of this portion of the book implies, you are quite literally advancing the field by assisting colleagues interested in exploring and practicing engaged teaching, learning, and scholarship.

This may and could potentially appear as a hierarchical relationship in which there is an inherent structure of wielding expertise and power over another (Savage, Karp, & Logue, 2004). However, as presented in this chapter, we espouse an egalitarian approach through conversation with colleagues and/or learning communities to accompany each other along the way. We intentionally employ the verb *accompany* as opposed to *guide* to embody a collegial and equitable discovery process. You may recall your own combined anticipation and trepidation as you embarked on this pathway. Consider this process as accompanying your colleagues rather than presenting as an expert who wields expertise and power over another. In many ways, the professional guidance we are describing and proposing in this chapter reflects traditional images and perceptions of mentoring. Refer to Tool Kit 13.1 to reflect on the meaning and process of mentoring.

> Tool Kit 13.1—Refer to Exercise 13.1 in your workbook. Reflect on the word and process of *mentoring*. What does it mean or look like to you? Recall when and if you have ever had a mentor or have been one to someone else. What was that experience like?

Mentoring, Comentoring, and Coaching

We begin this portion of the chapter by exploring the meaning and affective dimensions of various terms that are often used when describing the process of accompanying or assisting a colleague in their professional development.

Mentoring

The term *mentor* comes from the Ancient Greek story of Odysseus, who, when departing for war, asked his friend Mentor to care for his son. Thus, Mentor's reputation as a wise and caring teacher is the origin of this role and title (Bandura, 2002). As Parker Palmer (1998) suggested, the power of a mentor is not in their prowess of teaching as much as it is "their capacity to awaken a truth within us, a truth we can reclaim years later by recalling their impact on our lives" (p. 21). He goes on to argue that mentoring is a "mutuality in which the right teacher must meet and work with the right student" (p. 21). This characterization resonates with us as it captures the essence of the collaborative aspect of mentoring in becoming a civically engaged professional. Mentoring provides professional development, social-emotional support, an intellectual community, role models, safe space, accountability, access to opportunities and/or resources, and feedback (Rockquemore, 2013).

Cullingford (2006b) succinctly characterizes mentoring as an attempt "to enable learning in others by showing an interest in their needs" (p. 9). In traditional mentoring, a person with more experience serves as the mentor to offer and provide support to a less experienced individual (Holmes, Danley, & Hinton-Hudson, 2007). Budge (2006) suggested the traditional pairing of mentors with protégés is generally an informal and improvised process followed by a series of unstructured meetings. There is a comprehensive list of purposes for mentoring and coaching but they all have one thing in common, which is change and transition (Garvey, Stokes, & Megginson, 2018). In this context, the process is designed to help colleagues transition from traditional, didactic forms of pedagogy to engaged teaching, learning, and scholarship within a cultural setting that is typically entrenched in traditional paradigms. Cullingford (2006a, 2006b) noted that mentoring in educational contexts ranges from formal and highly structured programs to informal conversations.

We draw from the work of Davis, Boyer, and Russell (2011), who incorporated a case study approach for theory building that provides a useful perspective and framework for understanding mentoring. Their observations of what works and what doesn't provide insight and a helpful guide.

As might be expected, they found that the degree and frequency of mentoring is influenced by workloads, schedules, and cultural climate within the institution that promote collaboration. Likewise, they noted that multiple mentors, coupled with allies from various settings and contexts, have the potential to promote collegiality. Therefore, successful mentoring is based on the degree of collegiality, exchange of information, and campus climate and culture (see Figure 13.1).

Tenure-track faculty do not always consult with their assigned mentors on specific questions or issues and prefer to seek advice and insight on matters concerning the academic culture and setting (June, 2008). Lack of time, poor scheduling, haphazard pairing processes, and inadequate understanding of the mentoring process can have a detrimental impact on the protégé, mentor, or both (Ewing et al., 2008). Therefore, simply providing opportunities for new instructors to work with experienced faculty does not guarantee effective outcomes for the protégé (Davis et al., 2011).

Figure 13.1 Influences and outcomes of professional interaction in mentoring.

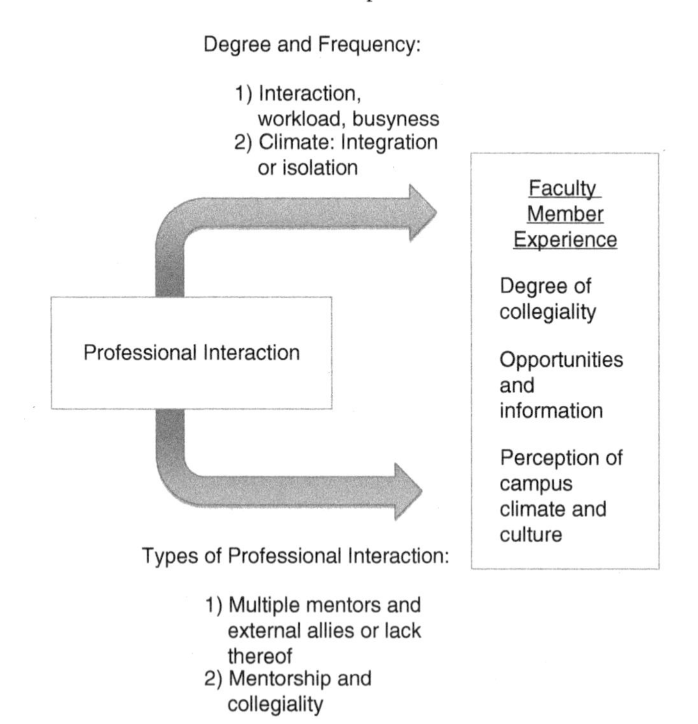

Note. Adapted from "Mentoring Postsecondary Tenure-Track Faculty: A Theory-Building Case Study and Implications for Institutional Policy," by D. J. Davis, P. Boyer, & I. Russell, 2011. *Administrative Issues Journal, 1*(1), article 6. Used with permission. Retrieved from www.dc.swosu.edu/aij/vol1/iss1/6

Further complicating this process is the challenge of poor cultural awareness and/or dynamics associated with diversity of participants. Chan (2008) reported that poor cultural awareness often resulted in reduced professional and emotional support for protégés, whereas mentoring in which both parties had similar backgrounds and cultures was more productive. Therefore, mentoring that recognizes the significance of race, ethnicity, and gender may help retain novice faculty members (Stanley & Lincoln, 2005).

We also acknowledge that the word and concept *mentoring* may connote or conjure other images, thoughts, and feelings. We take into account various dynamics that often are or can be evident through mentoring. Therefore, we embrace and advocate for a broader, more collaborative approach and lexicon. Cullingford (2006a, 2006b) acknowledged the issues and tensions associated with power when approaching the process as an expert working with a protégé. Over time, semantic alternatives and revised formats have emerged.

Comentoring

Influenced by CRT as well as Black and transnational feminism, Baldwin and Johnson (2017) describe and advocate comentoring by way of authentic conversations through nonhierarchical partnerships. Holmes and colleagues (2007) encourage comentoring in which the mentor and protégé equally contribute to and participate in each other's professional development. Peer or comentoring affords faculty from marginalized groups with similar cultural contexts as well as equal experience and rank an opportunity to share interests based on shared experiences and appears to provide greater psychosocial benefits, particularly personal support and friendship, than a hierarchical model (Angelique, Kyle, & Taylor, 2002).

Although the mentor may have more experience and expertise than the protégé, each equally contributes to the nonhierarchical learning process. In fact, we assert that such an approach allows experienced faculty an opportunity to reflect on and make meaning for themselves and, if shared, for their novice partner. We embrace this approach and expand it as a form of storytelling. Truth be told, storytelling is what essentially happens in the hallway between presentations or at the bar during professional conferences as colleagues seek safe and intimate spaces to exchange personal experiences. Any and all stories include peaks and valleys of crisis and success. By virtue of being teachers ourselves, we know that learning from mistakes can often be as, if not more, beneficial than easy success. In this way, one learns what *not* to do. This pedagogical revelation is especially compelling when the dynamics and potential outcomes of the experience involve and impact organizations and individuals in the community. In an authentic partnership, the teacher demonstrates humility by sharing failures as well as successes. Cullingford's (2006a) preferred approach and characterization of "buddying" (p. 6) also resonates with us and captures the essence and spirit of colleagues working together. Along these lines, MacLennan (2017) sees and characterizes a mentor as someone to learn *from* whereas a coach is someone to learn *with*.

Coaching

Coaching is often incorrectly viewed as a synonym for mentoring, consultation, or counseling (DiGirolamo, 2015). A mentor provides advice based on wisdom or experience, a consultant is a paid expert who diagnoses problems and designs solutions to address those problems, and a counselor addresses psychoemotional conditions of another individual (DiGirolamo, 2015). Although not truly a form of psychotherapy, Noe (2006) suggested coaches actually serve two functions by providing both professional and psychosocial support. Gold (1992) argued an effective coach recognizes the emotional needs of the protégé during stressful situations. The affective and relational dynamic embedded within coaching is based on the work of Carl Rogers (1957), who recognized the need to fully understand and reflect back the emotional context and situation of another individual to process what is occurring and develop goals that will motivate and guide the individual's behavior (DiGirolamo, 2015). Although we are not suggesting or proposing that you assume the role of a counselor or therapist, we recognize and embrace the affective dimensions and supportive nature embedded within coaching as opposed to other approaches. The Rogerian approach to focusing on the needs and goals of another resonates with us as a viable form of professional development. The word itself evokes images from sports in which a coach provides feedback and support to individual athletes who must incorporate that input and insight themselves to sometimes literally achieve a goal. Likewise, the example of birthing coaches elicits an image of accompanying a mother in delivery. In both cases, a coach is in the background playing an important supportive technical and emotional role. A meta-analysis of 18 studies of organizational coaching by Theeboom, Beersma, and van Vianen (2013) revealed it effectively promotes individuals' performance, skills, well-being, coping, attitudes, and self-regulation (see Table 13.1).

TABLE 13.1
Core Components and Steps of Effective Coaching

Core Components	*Description*
Ethics	• Maintain confidentiality. • Provide honest and sound information. • Make necessary referrals to appropriate units (e.g., community engagement center, human resources).
Coaching Agreement	• Determine and articulate meeting dates, times, and locations.
Relationship	• Seek background and personal information on the colleague. • Attend to and acknowledge expressed emotions. • Refrain from making or articulating judgment. • Respond and adjust to colleague's needs and commitment.
Effective Communication	• Identify preferred forms of communication (e.g., text, e-mail). • Engage in active listening. • Provide clear and appropriate verbal communication.
Goals	• Articulate specific goals and time lines for meetings.
Information	• Provide/share resources and information. • Promote networking with other colleagues and community partners.
Action	• Be timely and prepared for coaching sessions. • Respond to colleague's needs and requests.

Note. Adapted from *Coaching for Professional Development*, by J. DiGirolamo, 2015. Alexandria, VA: Society for Human Resource Management.

Cross-sectional studies, longitudinal studies, and literature reviews of experimental and quasiexperimental studies by Desimone and Pak (2016) revealed the following salient features of coaching: (a) content focus, (b) active learning, (c) sustained duration, (d) coherence, and (e) collective participation. Mladenovic (2012) reviewed the professional literature and characterized an effective coach as being authentic, nurturing, approachable, competent, inspirational, conscientious, and hardworking. Characteristics of effective relationships in professional development coaching include reciprocity, mutual respect, clear expectations, personal connections, and shared values (Steele, 2017; Straus, Johnson, Marquez, & Feldman, 2013). Swipe your smartphone or tablet over the QR code in Figure 13.2 to watch a short video of Bill Gates discussing the role and importance of coaching.

Figure 13.2 Video of Bill Gates discussing the importance and role of coaches.

Note. Scan the QR code to access https://www.youtube.com/watch?v=ar2VNgRDGJ0

Your Role as a Coach

We recognize that essential features and functions of mentoring, comentoring, and coaching overlap. We also acknowledge and appreciate the dynamics associated with specific terms. For the purposes of this chapter, we combine the salient features of each of the types of professional development described previously and refer to them as *coaching* to reflect and connote a spirit of mutuality and collegiality. In her review of university faculty mentoring programs, Lumpkin (2011) proposed the process must include mutually defined purposes, goals, and strategies and be conducted at regularly scheduled meetings that are evaluated on a regular basis. A report by Hanover Research (2014) indicates mentors and coaches must know, understand, and apply effective principles to promote adult learning through effective teaching strategies/techniques, as well as stages of developing meaningful relationships with their protégé. This requires an ability to plan and conduct conversations. Coaches should also be familiar with the institutional culture and available resources. A review of the literature conducted by Hanover Research (2014) identified the following general topical areas for coaching in higher education: (a) getting to know the institution, (b) excelling at teaching and research, (c) understanding tenure and evaluation, (d) creating work/life balance, and (e) developing professional networks. This list resonates with us and reflects our own experiences. A list of suggested and common activities derived from the Hanover Research report is provided in Figure 13.3.

Reaching Out and Reaching In

You have now had the benefit of developing, implementing, and assessing a community-engaged course. As a result, you have some insight that will assist you in not only making revisions for delivering the course again

Figure 13.3 Common mentoring and coaching activities.

11 Activities

1. Discuss and determine expectations, goals, and schedule for the mentorship relationship.
2. Explore and identify short- and long-term career goals and professional interests that include a research agenda and publication schedule and critique manuscripts or proposals.
3. Attend professional development workshops or events sponsored by the institution or professional associations.
4. Visit community partner agencies and have a conversation with a public scholar from that organization and/or those the agency serves.
5. Conduct observations of the protégé and provide opportunities for observing the mentor's classroom coupled with exploration and implementation of effective instructional techniques, course/syllabus development, and teaching strategies.
6. Explore and identify scholarships and funding opportunities as well as opportunities for collaborative research or evaluating applications.
7. Discuss institutional policies, guidelines, and university governance as well as identify institutional resources and support systems (e.g., psychological services and learning support services).
8. Share and describe experiences on stress management to promotes life/work balance and effectively manage time.
9. Discuss and assist in preparation for tenure and promotion and career advancement.
10. Address special needs, issues, concerns, or questions and offer suggestions.
11. Facilitate networking with other faculty with shared interests.

in the future but also sharing that insight with colleagues who are just now beginning to consider and develop their own courses. Your institution may have a center for teaching excellence that coordinates formal mentoring programs. If so, consider approaching that office and indicate your interest and willingness to serve as a coach to other faculty. However, it is more likely that your center for community engagement is working directly with other instructors either through one-on-one consultation or as an incoming cohort to a learning community like the one you may be a part of. Regardless of the context and setting, you are encouraged to reach out to these colleagues and accompany them as they develop their craft as engaged scholars. A prerequisite step to reaching out is to reach within to reflect on your own experiences and insights gained from this chapter. Tool Kit 13.1 provided an opportunity to recall your own mentoring experiences. Consider the rewarding as well as the challenging aspects of that process. The next step is to prepare for your initial conversation and interaction with a colleague in Tool Kit 13.2. In doing so, we invite you to reach within and recall your own reasons for becoming an engaged scholar. Likewise, remember what excited you about this work as well as factors that created some anxiety or apprehension. Think about the questions you had going in to your first engaged teaching and learning experience. Finally, identify the areas where you sought help. With your own experience and insights in mind, enter into your new partnership with your colleague by inviting them to ponder these same things.

> Tool Kit 13.2—Refer to Exercise 13.2 in your workbook. Palmer (1998) suggested mentoring provides an opportunity to find the truth within ourselves and those we mentor. In keeping with that spirit, we invite you to reflect on the mutuality and reciprocal nature of mentoring and coaching by reaching in and reaching out.

You may have been sought out and contacted by your colleague or you may have been assigned to work with them. We suggest your first interaction take place in a comfortable, informal setting such as a coffee shop or someplace for lunch, either on or off campus. This provides "neutral turf" as well as connotes a more collegial approach than a formal meeting in an office or a conference room. In addition to engaging in the conversation suggested in the Tool Kit exercise, consider other ways you are willing to accompany them in their professional journey. This may include inviting them to your class to observe reflection activities. You might also consider sharing your course syllabus. It could entail making a visit to a community partner and having a conversation about their experience. Later, you might discuss your engaged scholarship by sharing your publication and presentation record as well as how you articulated this work in your promotion and tenure review portfolio. As such, you must be comfortable and willing to offer or respond to a request for these activities. Keep in mind, your colleague may not ask for or seek out any of these.

Honing Your Craft

We conclude this chapter by returning to three important ideas and topics briefly addressed previously. First, although aware of and sensitive to the array of dynamics associated with the term and traditional approaches of *mentoring*, we are reminded of and intrigued by Parker Palmer's (1998) evocative invitation to reflect not on the question, "What made your mentor great?" but rather "What was it about *you* that allowed great mentoring to happen?" (p. 21). This interesting and curious juxtaposition of assumptions allows us to consider the process from a whole new perspective that may help us as we enter into the role of mentor or coach. It also provides an opportunity to consider and ponder the desires and needs of a colleague we may accompany as they become an engaged scholar in the next three Tool Kit exercises beginning with Tool Kit 13.3.

Tool Kit 13.3—Honing Your Craft—Refer to Exercise 13.3 in your workbook. Reflect on the question posed by Parker Palmer.

Second, although we recognize the potential value and benefit of this professional development process, we are cognizant of the challenges that are inherent in actual implementation. This includes not only basic logistical challenges of finding the time but also the more nuanced dynamics associated with cultural and gender differences. The challenges of finding a time and location for working together is, in the larger scheme of things, relatively easy to address. However, the issues of positionality and identity differences pose a greater challenge. How does one enter into a meaningful and mutually respectful relationship such as this? We suggest adapting the same approach as described and proposed by Mitchell, Donahue, and Young-Law (2012) when working with students from backgrounds and experiences different from our own. In this way, we minimize, although do not thoroughly extinguish, the potential of positionality that is inherent in the dynamics of an expert and protégé context as well as cultural/racial context. Here, we borrow and adapt the first of Mitchell and colleagues' three strategies in which you are invited to check your assumptions and take a reflective approach as you begin your role as coach with a colleague. We invite you to ponder these questions prior to reaching out and meeting. Tool Kit 13.4 is designed to help you prepare for your role as a mentor as well as consider cultural variables that influence the mentoring process.

Tool Kit 13.4—Honing Your Craft—Refer to Exercise 13.4 in your workbook. Review and respond to the questions that are provided. Reflect on your responses. Share and discuss this with your colleagues and/or community engagement center director.

Third, Tool Kit 13.5 invites you to consider that in a culture and setting of autonomy and isolation, how do we or can we promote a collaborative approach of continued professional development in any context? How do we challenge the assumption that earning a terminal degree suggests a professional needs no further professional development? What structures exist (or do not exist) that promote professional development in general and collegial coaching in particular?

Tool Kit 13.5—Honing Your Craft—Refer to Exercise 13.5 in your workbook. Consider and reflect on cultural and systemic factors within your institution that promote and/or impede professional development through mentoring and coaching. What approaches or strategies have been incorporated or might be incorporated?

Chapter 14

INFLUENCING INSTITUTIONAL CHANGE

Since the inception of the service-learning movement, several community-engaged scholars and practitioners have called for transformation of higher education institutions as a necessary condition for sustaining forms of community-engaged teaching and scholarship that truly serve the common good (Cruz, 1990a; Fitzgerald, Bruns, Sonka, Furco, & Swanson, 2012; Saltmarsh, Hartley, & Clayton, 2009; Zlotkowski, 2015). What we seek is an engaged institution, described by Votruba (2011) as a place where public voice permeates all aspects of the institution's functions; leadership, staff, and faculty are recruited, selected, and evaluated (in part) on their ability to contribute to civic and public goals; faculty rewards and incentives support commitments to engaged scholarship; the curriculum is infused with content that fosters students' civic learning and contributes positively to the community; budget and planning prioritize the civic aspects of the institutional mission; and conversations about public concerns and civic issues are inclusive, plentiful, and robust. In essence, we need to transform the structures and culture of higher education to achieve the vision of the engaged institution.

Furco and Holland (2013) describe various theories of change suited to higher education institutions that convey grassroots mobilizing among faculty as a necessary driver of change. Thus, you have the opportunity to function as a change agent by

- *initiating* your community-engaged teaching and research;
- *investigating* the norms, policies, and practices that shape your engaged work;
- *influencing* decision-making spaces to inform and motivate more justice-oriented ways of doing community engagement; and
- *integrating* norms, policies, and practices that center, value, and support authentic community engagement for social change.

The change process will be slow and nonlinear and will require persistence and vigilance. You will likely have to move through this cycle multiple times to catalyze needed changes, but we hope your vision of the engaged institution will sustain your spirit. Reflect on what the role of grassroots organizer means or looks like in Tool Kit 14.1.

> Tool Kit 14.1—Refer to Exercise 14.1 in your workbook to elucidate your understanding of the role of grassroots organizers in making change.

Initiation

Your journey as a community organizer starts with your role as a community-engaged faculty member. Through the process of conceptualizing and implementing your course, you'll learn about the campus context for engagement. You'll learn how community-engaged teaching fits into your professional workload and reflect on both the benefits and challenges. You'll see examples of how other faculty do this work and borrow from their promising practices to enhance your own. You'll get a feel for how students enter into, and move through, your community-engaged courses. You'll also find that community partnerships will emerge, thrive, or fizzle with each community-engaged course that you teach. You'll learn whether institutional support structures and incentives exist. At some point, you'll probably start to think, "Community-engaged teaching (or scholarship) would be so much easier/more impactful/more accessible if only . . ." And that will prompt you to start investigating why community engagement looks the way it does at your institution.

Investigation

As a community-engaged faculty member, you will come to learn how your institution functions to support or impede your efforts. If some of the

Figure 14.1 Lynton Colloquium: Tania Mitchell discusses structures of inclusion and exclusion.

Note. Scan the QR code to https://www.youtube.com/watch?v=tCFKZvf8nFI

structures and systems are not readily visible to you based on your direct experience, we invite you to learn about common structures of exclusion as described by Tania Mitchell in the video embedded in Figure 14.1 and to reflect on the questions posed in Tool Kit 14.2.

> Tool Kit 14.2—Refer to Exercise 14.2 in your workbook. Watch the video clip about structures of inclusion and exclusion and respond to the questions.

You may wonder *why* particular practices, policies, and norms exist; *what else* the institution is doing to support campus-community engagement; and *how* it compares with other higher education institutions. The investigation part of the cycle of institutional change requires you to act as a detective and uncover the untold or unheard stories behind why and how your institution supports engagement.

Starting with *why* can lead initially to some very mundane answers. For example, institutional constituents might point to how community engagement is an enactment of an institution's vision and mission. It's also typical for faith-based or land-grant institutions to tie engagement to their origin and ideology. The provost and other academic officers may describe the benefits of community-engaged learning as a high-impact practice that facilitates a number of positive outcomes for students ranging from critical thinking to retention. Community-engaged faculty may describe how they are personally fulfilled by this particular type of work. Although these justifications are genuine and valuable, we encourage you to dig a little deeper.

In regard to barriers and impediments, community engagement staff, faculty peers, and administrators will likely cite funding limitations and understaffing as reasons why particular logistical and administrative processes and policies exist. They may also share stories of past incidents to explain restrictive risk management, community partner vetting, and transportation coordination practices. Further, you might hear the phrase "That's how it's always been done" to describe how the curriculum, academic affairs hierarchy, and faculty governance confine engaged teaching and scholarship. Again, uncovering these reasons and/or assumptions for resistance is helpful because you can begin to understand the nature of the challenges and how to address them on a practical level through revisions to policies, procedures, and practices.

The next level to investigate is the framework of systems and structures that indirectly govern community engagement. The community engagement field has produced a number of rubrics and other tools that assess the extent to which an institution supports engagement. Furco (2010) articulated five dimensions (faculty support, student support, community partnerships, philosophy of engagement, and institutional support), each with multiple indicators, including some that we've already mentioned previously, like connection to mission statement, faculty incentives and rewards, and allocation of funds and staff. Advocates of community engagement have used Furco's rubrics to conduct institutional self-assessments and identify areas of success and weakness, moving beyond anecdotal descriptions of why and how community engagement happens to aggregate multiple data sources. Although this is an important step in the investigation process, there's still another layer to peel back. You are invited to reflect on Furco's dimensions in Tool Kit 14.3.

> Tool Kit 14.3—Refer to Exercise 14.3 in your workbook to reflect on Furco's five dimensions of institutional engagement with colleagues.

If you are aspiring to enact deeper cultural transformation, it will require critical analysis of underlying ideologies that shape the institution and higher education. Saltmarsh (2010) explicitly calls out the dominance of neoliberal and positivist ideologies in academia as fundamental barriers to achieving the aspiration of the engaged institution. A neoliberal orientation toward education emphasizes the private economic benefits of a college degree for students and necessitates subservience to the demands of students and their potential employers in order for institutions to compete with each other for enrollment and external funding. Evidence of a neoliberal orientation can be found in an institution's promotional materials and external communications (e.g., touting the percentage of alumni working in Fortune 500 companies or boasting high-profile guest speakers). Evidence also comes in the form of how funding is allocated.

Additionally, Saltmarsh (2010) synthesizes and extends scholarly critiques of the dominance of positivist epistemology in academia as a barrier to meaningful and pervasive campus-wide community engagement. Positivism encompasses research, teaching, and related scholarly activities that are rooted in traditional scientific inquiry models and technical rationality. This ideology frames the researcher as a dispassionate objective expert, conducting studies that apply disciplinary expertise in the discovery or application of knowledge (often through quantitative methodologies) and disseminating findings to other academics for peer review and further study. The positivist framework also positions faculty as the sole knowledge holders in the classroom by virtue of their advanced studies and terminal degrees, suggesting that student learning is best achieved when faculty impart expertise via lectures and readings. The positivist epistemological paradigm shapes higher education at every level, from how physical classroom spaces are organized to the guidelines for promotion and tenure. By privileging this particular way of knowing, higher education institutions are implicitly devaluing other epistemologies, including ways of knowing that emanate from lived experience and informal education. To be clear, we are not arguing against positivism as a framework for scholarship. Rather, we are arguing against positivism as the *dominant* ideology and *only* (legitimate) framework for research, teaching, and other scholarly activities. Through your investigation process, we invite you to peel back the layers that begin with identifying existing practices and policies, move to surfacing the overarching structures that guide practice, and then finally to examining the ideological and cultural undercurrents. Tool Kit 14.4 provides an opportunity to investigate how your institution communicates neoliberalism and positivism.

> Tool Kit 14.4—Refer to Exercise 14.4 in your workbook to guide you in investigating your institution's external communications for indicators of neoliberal and positivist influences.

What you uncover about policies, practices, structures, and dominant ideologies is not entirely unique to your institution, so it can be extremely helpful to research how other institutions do community engagement to benchmark your efforts against other examples. You may discover exemplars that you aspire to emulate, or cautionary tales that you can proactively avoid. The process of broad internal and external inquiry, employing a critical lens, will help you to locate potential sites of influence where you and your colleagues can use your voices to advocate for integration of more just, inclusive, and equitable community engagement.

Influence

As an informed practitioner and scholar you have the power to influence collective perceptions and practices of community engagement. Just as Dostilio and Welch (2018) invite CEPs to take up the role of "tempered radical" (p. 40), further characterized by Meyerson and Scully (1995), we encourage you to try it on as well. A tempered radical in the context of higher education is a person who organizes with colleagues to facilitate incremental changes in response to the inconsistencies and challenges they have experienced while trying to advance the work of community engagement from within the institution. Working with other community-engaged faculty and staff as coorganizers, begin by identifying a discrete opportunity or challenge to prioritize and organize around. Be sure to consider the perspectives and priorities of other community engagement constituents (faculty, community partners, students, and staff) in your decision-making, as they represent the "base" that will be affected by the change. Next, it's helpful to conduct a power-mapping analysis to identify those who have the power to make decisions (targets), those who will actively support your change efforts (allies), and those who may resist (opponents). Begin power mapping your institution in Tool Kit 14.5.

> Tool Kit 14.5—Refer to Exercise 14.5 in your workbook to conduct a power-mapping analysis of your institution.

You'll want to hold these power dynamics in mind as you move forward with influence tactics. As you read through the following tactical approaches, consider how you might adapt and scale them for appropriate application to the goal you have chosen. Recognize that you will likely need to use many or all of these tactics in tandem or in progression to achieve your goals.

Illumination

Because of the decentralized nature of higher education institutions, there are many community-engaged activities happening under the radar. Drawing these endeavors out and shining light on them can help expand the collective understanding of what community engagement looks like and how it is implemented in diverse ways across the institution. Work with colleagues to collect and organize information so you can easily see the defining elements of each program or course. You may also want to map your institution's endeavors by college/school, department, and cocurricular division. Determine ways you might share this information with targets, allies, and even opponents that you want to win over.

In addition to highlighting projects, find ways to illuminate the exemplary work of individual faculty, community partners, and students. Recognition serves as a reward (especially in the absence of formal reward structures) and might take the form of an event, an award, or a published acknowledgment. It's a good idea to invite administrators to nominate faculty for these recognitions and invite faculty to nominate community partners.

Alignment

Incremental change can also grow out of alignment between community engagement offerings and other institutional priorities like student retention, diversity and equity, and faculty recruitment. In this way, you build a coalition of support across diverse interest groups and raise the status of community engagement as a mechanism for fostering cultural and structural change. To determine current priorities, reference strategic planning and accreditation documents, institutional climate surveys, recruitment and retention reports, or national survey data. If your institution is focused on recruiting and retaining diverse students, reference literature on community-engaged learning as a high-impact practice that yields significant positive outcomes for students of color (Finley & McNair, 2013; Kuh, 2008). Further, whether you are able to conduct direct assessment of student work products or draw on indirect assessment measures, you should also be able to link student participation in community engagement to development of critical thinking, open-mindedness, and acceptance of diversity, all of which are desirable outcomes. In addition, institutions focused on recruiting and retaining diverse faculty will want to strengthen their institutional support for community-engaged teaching and research, because studies show that community-engaged work is primarily undertaken by faculty of color and women (Aguirre, 2000; Vogelgesang, Denson, & Jayakumar, 2010; Welch, 2016).

If your institutional leadership is motivated by national recognitions and designations, then leverage this to make change. In particular, an increasing number of institutions apply for the Community Engagement Classification bestowed by the Carnegie Commission on Higher Education, which requires an extensive application that illuminates how institutions measure up to several dimensions of community engagement and the quality of their requisite support structures.

Education

We can educate others about community engagement, and the related opportunities and barriers, in both formal and informal ways. If you are reading this book as part of a faculty fellowship program, then you are participating in formal education. If your prior knowledge of community engagement was formed through hallway conversations with engaged faculty in your department, this is an example of informal education. Consider how you can be an informal educator of peers, administrators, and community partners. As discussed in chapter 12, you might do this simply by providing a comprehensive narrative of your community-engaged teaching and scholarship in your tenure portfolio. Further, you may identify particular colleagues (especially those with tenure) who might be powerful allies if they had a basic knowledge of the principles and practices of community engagement and seek them out for conversations over coffee or lunch. Mentoring new faculty is another opportunity to educate toward developing a critical mass of informed and passionate community-engaged educators. Similarly, you can educate your community partners about the principles, practices, and policies of community engagement so they can be empowered to advocate for changes that support them as coeducators. For each of these potential "converts," you should tailor your message to appeal to their motivations and interests, which means you need to have enough of a relationship with them to know what these are. Relationships are an integral foundation for grassroots organizing.

In terms of formal education, consider creating a learning community with peers from across your institution and focusing on a topic that relates to your specific goal for community engagement. If it's helpful to bring in external experts and scholars to persuade your targets and potential allies, find ways to do so. Again, be mindful of your audience and make sure the content not only meets them where they are but also pushes them a bit outside their comfort zone to develop new understandings.

You can also capitalize on your institution's efforts to treat students as customers by educating students to be informed consumers of community engagement. If you teach students what authentic and transformative community engagement should look like, they can demand more robust and authentic learning experiences at the institution. Reach out to your admissions office with stories and examples to showcase community experience that reflect the institution's mission and will appeal to prospective students.

Representation

In addition to educating people in positions of power, get yourself, your coorganizers, and your allies onto decision-making bodies at the institution. At a micro level, focus on advancing allies into departmental leadership positions and ad hoc working groups that relate to community engagement. Participating in faculty search committees might be a way to influence hiring to include attention to community-engaged teaching and scholarship. Determine ways to join and influence strategic planning committees for centers or divisions that do community engagement. At a macro level, target institution-wide standing councils and committees that play a role in developing policies and procedures. Taken one step further, representation should also apply to intentional and strategic inclusion of community voice in decision-making processes. Continue to consider this in Tool Kit 14.6.

> Tool Kit 14.6—Refer to Exercise 14.6 in your workbook to think about which committees, working groups, and so on might be influenced by advocates for community engagement.

Influencing institutional change can seem overwhelming if you think of yourself as an individual actor within the institution, but if you imagine yourself as a tempered radical who is working in coalition with others, then you should feel empowered to enact incremental changes that will ultimately lead to integration of new policies, practices, systems, structures, and cultural norms that support community engagement.

Integration

With sustained strategic effort, your institution will manifest positive changes that strengthen its capacity to support community engagement. Collectively, these changes should demonstrate a new level of permeability in the "walls" of the ivory tower, meaning students, faculty, and staff leave campus to interact purposefully and positively with the surrounding community, and community members visit campus for social activities, educational events, guest lectures, and participation on committees. Relatedly, the binary of teacher/learner is dismantled and reimagined to recognize that every person functions as both a teacher and learner, regardless of role or title. Further, institutional leadership and other university constituents feel a sense of accountability for contributing to positive social change and are empowered and supported in their related endeavors to function as community change agents.

Community Partners as Coeducators and Committee Members

If an institution truly values the role of community partners in educating students and faculty, then community partners should be compensated for their time and expertise, including any labor that seems to go above and beyond basic support for your community-engaged course. Additionally, institutional change can manifest as community partners having a seat at the table on decision-making bodies and committees. Community partners should participate to some extent in institutional strategic planning processes, search committees, public event planning, and so on. Ultimately, community partner representation should be inclusive of multiple community stakeholders from a variety of organization types and neighborhoods.

Engaged Departments

Kecskes (2006) proposed the model of "engaged departments" as an organizing strategy that can ultimately lead to institutional transformation. He argues that community engagement should be mapped out and integrated at the departmental level so students and faculty understand how it supports the broader disciplinary learning goals. Further, this structure allows for the creation of a developmental progression of community engagement experiences, which might include community field trips and community partner visits for first-year students, then progress to ongoing direct engagement activities at partner organizations, and culminate with a collaborative community-engaged research project for the department's capstone requirement. Within an engaged department, faculty have agency to adapt community-engaged principles and pedagogies to their specific discipline and determine how to evaluate community-engaged research and teaching within their particular context. Ultimately, proliferation of engaged departments can lead to broad institutional transformation that supports student learning and faculty retention.

Tenure and Promotion Guidelines

Many community engagement scholars name tenure and promotion guidelines as the most important indicator of the extent to which community engagement is institutionalized (O'Meara, 2010; Sturm, Eatman, Saltmarsh, & Bush, 2011; Welch, 2016). This is primarily because the faculty triumvirate of teaching, research, and service governs several aspects of how the university functions, including allocation of funds, hiring and retention, program and course offerings, and so on. O'Meara and colleagues (2015) describe the following steps for creating change in tenure and promotion guidelines: (a) define and describe *community-engaged teaching and scholarship* in a way that illuminates its value to the institution, (b) identify and articulate benchmarks and criteria for evaluating community-engaged scholarship, (c) develop specific criteria for evaluating community engagement practices, (d) determine what types of artifacts and evidence appropriately convey the quality of community-engaged teaching and research, and (e) design inclusive peer-review processes that draw on community expertise as well as traditional academic expertise and value community impact equitably with other outcomes. As you can imagine, it's best to move through this process with a diverse working group of faculty, where diversity encompasses disciplines and career stages as well as race, gender, and other demographic characteristics.

Community Engagement Council

Weaving connections between community engagement endeavors and the constituents involved in them might ultimately lead to a formalized campus-wide community engagement council. This body should be composed of faculty, staff, students, and community partners who are experienced in community engagement; it should meet regularly to maintain ongoing relationships and dialogues, as well as catalyze institutional change efforts. At the most basic level, members of the council can keep each other apprised of community engagement initiatives happening in various institutional silos. The council may also be responsible for reviewing and proposing revisions to policies and procedures that support community engagement. Further, this body may be charged with recognizing and rewarding exemplary efforts and identifying and addressing problematic practices.

Place-Based Initiatives

Place-based initiatives (PBIs) entail a campus-wide commitment to collaborating on the achievement of positive outcomes in a defined issue area for a particular population in a defined geographic area (Welch, 2016; Yamamura & Koth, 2018). The motivating idea is that campuses can create measurable impact if they more narrowly focus labor and resources than if they take a "scattershot" approach to doing community engagement. This approach recognizes that each community context is unique and thus requires interventions that are place-specific. In practice, this often looks like several community-engaged courses working with community partners in the defined geographic area, faculty collaborating on community-engaged research projects, cocurricular service activities designed to support outcomes, grant funding for events and activities in and with community, and place-specific resource drives and donations.

We invite you to invoke the principles developed by Siemers, Harrison, Clayton, and Stanley (2015) when advocating for (or contributing to) PBIs: (a) use an ecological lens to examine the relationships between people and place, including the natural world; (b) create opportunities for inviting diverse epistemologies and ontologies to shape the initiative and its outcomes; (c) value storytelling as a catalyst for building understanding and community; and (d) engage the tensions and dilemmas that are rooted in historical and contemporary power dynamics between campus and community as well as individuals. A PBI that embodies these principles will, indeed, be transformative for the institution. Refer to Tool Kit 14.7 to consider how a PBI exists or could exist at your institution.

> Tool Kit 14.7—Refer to Exercise 14.7 in your workbook to guide you in analyzing a PBI at your own institution or a peer institution.

Anchor Institutions

Anchor institutions take community engagement and investment to the next level (Dostilio & Welch, 2018; Welch, 2016). Dubb, McKinley, and Howard (2013) define *anchor institutions* as

> place-based entities such as universities and hospitals that are tied to their surroundings by mission, invested capital, or relationships to customers, employees, and vendors. These local human and economic relationships link institution well-being to that of the community in which it is anchored. (p. v)

In addition to developing connections between the community and academic and cocurricular programs, the anchor institution model fosters other forms of community capacity-building through business practices like staffing, real estate acquisitions, environmental sustainability initiatives, and vendor relations. As with PBIs, the anchor institution model can be a powerful engine for positive community transformation or an insidious mode of exploitation, depending on the principles and motives that guide the effort and the capacity for follow-through. As a tempered radical, you have a responsibility to contribute to an authentically community-oriented vision for these institution-wide endeavors.

Honing Your Craft

Facilitating institutional change will be a big challenge, but one that can be accomplished through an ongoing cycle of initiation, investigation, influence, and integration. Leading this transformation means working with colleagues to achieve collective action that ultimately challenges and reshapes both structural and cultural barriers to achieving the ideal of the engaged institution. In this chapter, we suggest practical ways of making change at the micro level of policy, practice, and procedure and describe how structural changes might manifest. The hardest part will be reshaping the culture because the ideological undercurrents that drive education run broad and deep. Imagine your role as a grassroots organizer in forming your vision for change in Tool Kit 14.8.

> Tool Kit 14.8—Honing Your Craft—Refer to Exercise 14.8 to reflect on your potential role as a grassroots organizer and your vision for change.

Chapter 15

THE CITIZEN SCHOLAR

The nature of being an educator is such that the profession itself is meant to contribute to the public good (Dewey, 1927). There is an expectation that your teaching and research are meant to add value to civil society. Further, your training and experience as an educator have guided you to develop skills that are transferable to participation in the public sphere. Thus, this chapter is meant to encourage your reflection on the ways you are a civic participant in the context of your educator role and your role as a citizen. To be clear, when we use the term *citizen* in this chapter, we do not mean a person who is officially recognized and accepted by a government as a member of a country, state, or city. Rather, we borrow from Choi's (2016) notion of the "active citizen": one who practices ongoing engagement in multiple civic activities. As a citizen scholar, you'll explore the mutuality among the identity, values, dispositions, skills, and knowledge that guide your professional work and those that shape your civic life. Tool Kit 15.1 invites you to examine your professional motivations to become a citizen scholar.

> Tool Kit 15.1—Refer to Exercise 15.1 in your workbook to examine your professional motivations.

The Case for Being Civically Engaged

You have been invited to consider how your identity, values, dispositions, skills, and knowledge guide your professional work throughout this book.

We now build on that initial exploration and extend it to reflect on the interface between your professional and disciplinary profile and your role as a citizen scholar.

Your propensity to be a participant in civic life is shaped by your values, as explored in Tool Kit 15.2. You are likely drawn to community-engaged teaching and scholarship because they allow you to enact your values. Perhaps you are motivated by a desire to promote equity, inclusion, intellectual curiosity, humanity, or social justice. As you engage in meaningful professional work and reflect on the impact and implications of your work, your values may be reinforced or challenged. The longer you do this work, the more clarity you'll gain about what your values are and how best to enact them. Your professional praxis will necessarily influence the way you engage in civic and public life beyond the confines of your institution and its community partnerships.

> Tool Kit 15.2—Refer to Exercise 15.2 in your workbook to reflect on your values.

Beyond the essential public purpose of your profession, you should see yourself as a necessary contributor to civic life. What you do and learn as a community-engaged faculty member is particularly valuable in deepening and extending your capacity and agency as an informed and active civic participant. Just as you organize your students to collaborate on community-engaged projects, design curricula to examine justice issues, and disseminate information to diverse audiences as a faculty member, you can use the same skills to organize, educate, and empower your own communities. Further, the knowledge gained through community engagement is transferable, including a thorough understanding of a particular policy issue, familiarity with community-organizing tactics, and awareness of the stories and perspectives of the most marginalized people in your community. In sum, we are inviting you to be a participant in the life and vitality of your *community*, however you define it, beyond the scope of activities that are measured by the teaching, research, service triumvirate. You can begin this process by completing the activity in Tool Kit 15.3.

> Tool Kit 15.3—Refer to Exercise 15.3 in your workbook to assess your current level of civic involvement.

Intersections Between Civic and Professional Practice

In the past 15 years, scholars have put forth theoretical frames to help us consider the reciprocity between our profession as academics and our responsibilities as citizens (Boyte & Fretz, 2010; Dzur, 2004; Hatcher, 2008; Peters, 2003; Sullivan, 2004). This body of scholarship offers descriptions of what it looks like to be a citizen scholar and also embeds a call to action. Contemporary scholars on this subject build on the visions of scholars and philosophers, including Alexis de Tocqueville and John Dewey, who argued for the importance of broad participation and communal efforts to sustain democracy.

Civic/Democratic Professionalism: The Professional as Purveyor of Public Good

If we buy into the belief that higher education institutions serve a public purpose, then we must also believe that the faculty who work in these institutions have a responsibility to contribute to the common good. Civic professionalism provides a description of what this might look like. According to Peters (2003), *civic professionalism* is the

> tradition of professional practice that casts professionals' identities, roles, and expertise around a public mission. Civic professionalism places scholars inside civic life, rather than apart from, or above it, working along their fellow citizens on questions and issues of public importance. (p. 185)

To be sure, there is some disagreement among scholars about how civic professionalism should be enacted. Peters (2003) argues for the following action steps: (a) reshaping our scholarly identities and work to prioritize a commitment to the public, (b) directly engaging with the public to inform scholarly endeavors that are relevant and useful, and (c) embracing a democratic political view that is reciprocal, iterative, and interactive while rejecting a stance focused on technocracy, advocacy, and ideology. This model is situated in the notion that scholars' value to the public is defined by their capacity to teach and do research. It also seems rooted in values of positivism and objectivism in that Peters calls faculty to create space for democratic discussions and practices, and to inform policies and services with research, but not to tip toward any sort of ideological or advocacy orientation that could be seen as advancing one's own political agenda.

In contrast, Wood (2003) very much calls for faculty to orient their scholarly goals toward a politics of solidarity and social transformation, explicitly using teaching to advocate for a more just redistribution of wealth and resources, and more equitable access to public services. He provides an example of a course in which students work with a coalition advocating for a living wage, organize rallies and fund-raisers, and read about economic justice. Though Wood focuses on creating solidarity learning opportunities for students, we can extrapolate his call to action to undertake civic participation that addresses inequity as something that can also be done in one's research and scholarship. The focus of this scholarship would be addressing injustice, and the method of conducting research would likely be participatory, involving underserved communities. Peters (2003) dismisses Wood's model as too rooted in the faculty member's political ideology and too oriented toward cultivating activism, protest, and oppositional politics, which in his view undermines democratic ideals and limits the scope of how faculty teach students to participate in civic life.

Boyte and Fretz (2010) argue for a civic professionalism that aligns somewhat with Wood's vision of a radical civic professional. They invoke a civic populist tradition reminiscent of the work of the Highlander School and emanating from the values of diversity, equity, and justice. Their call to action is for faculty to "recover methods of practicing their crafts in public life and in public ways, using their academic skills to create powerful public relationships, and becoming culture-workers and facilitators of meaning-making in the public sphere" (p. 78). They situate this type of work in the particularity of individuals and communities, and their essential knowledge of contextualized public issues and resources, as a starting point for organizing diverse coalitions that transform unjust structures in society. Faculty, as civic professionals, should facilitate the participation of community members in generating lines of inquiry and knowledge that can effectively address public problems.

Although there are disagreements among scholars about how civic professionalism should manifest in one's identity and role within the academy, the point of agreement is that faculty are called to function as civic professionals, and there is a need for them to bring their professional capacities to bear to facilitate the common good. We invite you to do your own discernment in Tool Kit 15.4 about how you currently live your role as a civic professional and how you might strengthen your commitment to doing so.

Tool Kit 15.4—Refer to Exercise 15.4 in your workbook to help you determine what type of civic professional you are.

Civic-Minded Professional Framework and Scale

Hatcher (2008) provides a framework that builds on the concept of civic professionalism to articulate specific knowledge, skills, and dispositions that describe a civic-minded professional. Her dissertation includes a synthesis of how civic professionalism is conceptualized across diverse disciplines, including philosophy, political science, and philanthropic studies (e.g., Daloz, Keen, Keen, & Parks, 1996; Dzur, 2004; Peters, 2003; Sullivan, 2005). The resulting table of 31 characteristics derived from the literature review can be used as a starting point for self-assessment and reflection (see Table 15.1). You can begin to assess your own civic-mindedness in Tool Kit 15.5.

TABLE 15.1
Knowledge, Skills, and Dispositions of a Civic-Minded Professional: A Multidisciplinary Perspective

Knowledge: Volunteer and pro bono opportunities	Is aware of volunteer opportunities Is aware of pro bono service opportunities Is knowledgeable about non-profit organizations
Knowledge: Contemporary social issues and community issues	Is knowledgeable about community goals Is aware of social challenges Is knowledgeable about public policy
Skills: Competency with diversity	Has the ability to interact with others from diverse backgrounds Listens to understand the perspective of others
Skills: Consensus building across diverse opinions	Builds consensus across diverse opinions Engages in dialogue with others Has strong connections with others
Skills: Participatory civic skills	Organizes others to address community challenges Has the ability to inspire others to take action(s) Works with others to achieve the public good Participates in voluntary associations Has the ability to navigate political processes
Dispositions: Values voluntary and pro bono service	Values voluntary and pro bono service

TABLE 15.1 (*Continued*)

Dispositions: Motivated to serve others	Is motivated to serve others
Dispositions: Sense of gratitude	Has a sense of gratitude for life in general and for work more specifically
Dispositions: Social trustee of knowledge	Sees oneself as a social trustee of knowledge Has a sense of social responsibility to be actively involved in the community Has a sense of social responsibility and commitment to the good of society Supports the public role of professionals in society
Dispositions: Passionate about work	Enjoys an intrinsic satisfaction from work Integrates personal values with professional life
Dispositions: Sense of calling in work for larger purposes – either religious or civic	Has a sense of calling, either religious or civic, in one's professional work Embraces religious values, faith, or transcendent ideals Has a sense of obligation to give back to society
Dispositions: Democratic values	Values democratic ideals (e.g., reciprocity, justice, equality) when working with others Values democratic ideals of citizen participation Values reciprocity and mutual respect between professionals and client

Note. Adapted from Hatcher, J. A. (2008). The public role of professionals: Developing and evaluating the Civic-Minded Professional scale (Doctoral dissertation). Available from ProQuest Dissertations and Theses Database, AAT 3331248 (https://scholarworks .iupui.edu/handle/1805/17469)

Tool Kit 15.5—Refer to Exercise 15.5 in your workbook to complete the civic-mindedness self-assessment.

Hatcher (2008) conducted a study focused on developing and evaluating the Civic-Minded Professional Scale. Through a survey administered to a national sample of 373 faculty (with a response rate of 39.7%), an exploratory factor analysis yielded the following factors that comprise civic-mindedness, including (a) voluntary action, (b) identity and calling, (c) citizenship, (d) social trusteeship, and (e) consensus building. These five factors have remained consistent in subsequent research (Richard, Keen, Hatcher, & Pease, 2016), using the 23-item Civic-Minded Professional Scale (Hatcher, 2008).

Hatcher's findings indicate important links between the practices of community-engaged teaching and research and measures of civic-mindedness. Based on statistical analysis, faculty who had taught service-learning courses at least once in the past three years scored higher on the Civic-Minded Professional Scale than those who had not. Further, faculty members who had collaborated with a community partner on a research project in the previous three years also scored higher on the scale than those who had not. The study does not establish causality between community-engaged teaching and scholarship, on the one hand, and civic-mindedness, on the other, yet it is valuable to reflect on the potentially reciprocal nature of these two variables. In other words, how might faculty members' civic values and commitments drive them to practice particular forms of community engagement in their profession, and how might that practice challenge, enhance, and reshape those values and commitments in new ways? Further, what new action and strategies can be integrated into faculty development programming and professional education to cultivate civic-mindedness?

Citizen Scholars in Action

Although initially the notion of the citizen scholar may seem foreign to our preconceived notion of academic work, our field is ripe with faculty who embody the role of citizen scholar. Most of these folks do their thing quietly, without pursuing recognition. They aren't in this for the glory. They do this because they are driven by a sense of responsibility to their community, a passion for justice, and a commitment to civic participation. However, there are a number of awards that spotlight community-engaged faculty and help bring attention and appreciation for their work.

The Ernest A. Lynton Award was established in 1996 to recognize the work of community-engaged faculty. The award criteria highlight the engagement work of early career faculty who are exemplary in the following dimensions: (a) sustained effort in community outreach and professional service; (b) use of innovative and imaginative approaches; (c) evidence of institutional impact through teaching, program development, and student/faculty participation; and (d) external success through scholarly output, community impact, and student learning (Brown University Swearer Center, 2018). Cumulatively, stories of Lynton honorees paint a hopeful picture of what is possible when one embraces a calling as a citizen scholar. Scan your smartphone or tablet over the QR code in Figure 15.1 to hear some of those stories.

The Thomas Ehrlich Award recognizes faculty who perform "exemplary engaged scholarship, including . . . advancing students' civic learning,

Figure 15.1 Lynton Award recipient biographies.

Note. Scan the QR code to access https://www.brown.edu/swearer/lynton/past-lynton-award-recipients

Figure 15.2 Ehrlich Award past recipient list.

Note. Scan the QR code to access https://compact.org/thomas-ehrlich-civically-engaged-faculty-award/recipients/

conducting community-based research, fostering reciprocal community partnerships, building institutional commitments to . . . civic engagement, and other means of enhancing higher education's contributions to the public good" (Campus Compact, 2018). Campus Compact has bestowed this award annually to faculty at its member institutions since 1995. We encourage you to review the bios of Ehrlich Award recipients in the videos found in Figure 15.2 and find inspiration in their work.

The American Association of State Colleges and Universities offers two awards for community-engaged faculty at public institutions: the Barbara Burch Award for Faculty Leadership in Civic Engagement (see Figure 15.3) and the John Saltmarsh Award for Emerging Leadership in Civic Engagement (see Figure 15.4). The former is given in recognition of "exemplary *faculty leadership* in advancing the civic learning and engagement of undergraduate students and advancing the work of AASCU's American Democracy Project on campus and/or nationally" (American Association of State Colleges and Universities, n.d.a), and the latter is given in recognition of "exemplary *early-career leaders* who are advancing the wider civic engagement movement through higher education to build a broader public culture of democracy" (American Association of State Colleges and Universities, n.d.b).

We urge you to consider pursuing these awards or other relevant honors so your citizen scholar work can be celebrated and shared as an

Figure 15.3 Burch Award recipient list.

Note. Scan the QR code to access https://www.aascu.org/programs/adp/awards/BarbaraBurch/

Figure 15.4 Saltmarsh Award recipient list.

Note. Scan the QR code to access http://www.aascu.org/programs/adp/awards/JohnSaltmarsh

inspiration to peers. We also look forward to increasingly diverse representation of faculty across race, gender identity, and disciplines among the honorees. Begin this process by referring to Tool Kit 15.6 in your workbook.

> Tool Kit 15.6—Refer to Exercise 15.6 in your workbook to reflect on how peers inspire your work.

Over the years, we have had the privilege of working with some amazing colleagues whose citizen scholar contributions are recognized institutionally and locally. These faculty have generously allowed us to share their stories to highlight what's possible when professional and personal commitments converge into a holistic civic purpose.

Belinda Hernandez-Arriaga

Belinda Hernandez-Arriaga is assistant professor of marriage and family therapy (MFT) and faculty coordinator of the master's in counseling Psychology program with a concentration in marriage and family therapy (MFT) at the University of San Francisco (USF). She came into academia with experience as a licensed clinical social worker, specializing in childhood trauma and mental health in Latinx communities (B. Hernandez-Arriagga, personal interview, September 17, 2018). Hernandez-Arriaga teaches courses including Counseling Across Cultures and Community Mental Health: Concepts of Recovery, Wellness, Systems of Care, and Advocacy. She has published on trauma and the power of cultural arts as a therapeutic intervention for undocumented and mixed-status Latinx youth and children, the use of *testimonio* in counseling as a practice of resistance to injustice, and the effectiveness of indigenous clinical interventions in communities of color. In addition, Hernandez-Arriaga cofounded and remains active on Half Moon Bay's Latino Advisory Council and launched her own nonprofit, Ayudando Latinos a Soñar (ALAS), which provides cultural arts, education, and social justice programming for Latinx youth and wraparound social services, legal support, and mental health interventions for their families.

Hernandez-Arriaga is celebrated at USF for the learning and community-building she facilitates in the spaces between community and academia's rigid categories of teaching, research, and service. Hernandez-Arriaga has mobilized her students and colleagues to meet the most urgent needs of communities, responding to wildfires in Santa Rosa, California; Hurricane Harvey in Houston, Texas; and the 2017 earthquake in Puebla, Mexico. Over the summer of 2018, she was called to respond to family separations and detentions at the Texas/Mexico border. She worked with local philanthropists to bring a group of MFT students to the border to engage with children and families as they were being released from detention. The story of what they observed and learned is summarized in a local news interview with Hernandez-Arriaga (see the video embedded within Figure 15.5).

Indeed, she sees this work as her activism in response to persistent global injustice and describes this particular project as an act of resistance against racist immigration policies that marginalize, criminalize,

Figure 15.5 Interview with Hernandez-Arriaga on work with separated immigrant families in Texas.

Note. Scan the QR code to access https://vimeo.com/284241797

dehumanize, and devalue. Though these crisis response efforts have not been in the context of credit-bearing courses or research projects, they demonstrate the synthesis of Hernandez-Arriaga's professional expertise as an educator, a scholar, and a social worker for the purpose of building a more just and equitable world.

Luke Garrott

Luke Garrott is an associate professor and lecturer in the Department of Political Science at the University of Utah. The first community engagement course he designed, Neighborhood Democracy, incorporated service-learning to foster a sense of authentic citizenship. In 2002, the university launched University Neighborhood Partners (UNP) in the culturally diverse Glendale neighborhood of Salt Lake City. Over the course of 4 years, Garrott's students completed 10 projects with 5 different community partners. He states, "Over the years I have learned the difference between full community partners and pseudo-partners. For a project to have staying power and meaning for students and community members, it must be conceived in a true partnership of mutual interest" (Garrott, 2009a, p. 125). Projects and activities have been wide-ranging, including attending and speaking at city council meetings, recruiting participants and teaching a financial literacy course, helping to start a community festival, and engaging after-schoolers in urban planning. In hindsight, he realizes he probably would not have embarked on this journey had he been on the tenure track. "For the faculty in my department, civically-engaged work is a tightrope walk above manifest dis-incentives, unless, of course, one can meet publishing schedules within civically-engaged work" (Garrott, 2009a, p. 122). He realized his role as a lecturer "allowed" him to do this work that, coincidentally, served to draw potential majors and encourage and develop potential graduate students. As such, his experience reflects much of the tension explored in previous chapters regarding legitimate scholarship coupled with the review process. Gradually, Garrott's attention and energy shifted from the academic setting to the city government. He was twice elected to the city council and launched a bid (albeit unsuccessful) for city mayor, literally embodying the role of citizen scholar. In a campaign video for city council (see the video embedded in Figure 15.6), Garrott's academic qualifications and civic commitments are enumerated by his friends and local residents.

Though he wasn't elected as mayor, Garrott returned to the university with an increased knowledge of practical politics. He currently teaches

Figure 15.6 Luke Garrott, Salt Lake City Council video.

Note. Scan the QR code to access https://www.youtube.com/watch?v=YNQNGRP4fmc

classes like Neighborhood Democracy, Urban Politics, and Politics and the City in the political science department while engaging in local issues and formulating his next community-based course. He has chronicled his journey as a citizen scholar (Garrott, 2009a, 2009b).

Ron Ahnen

Ron Ahnen is a professor in the politics department at Saint Mary's College of California. Ahnen's scholarship is focused on comparative politics and international relations. He researches and has an interest in Latin American politics with a special concentration in Brazilian politics, having lived in Brazil for six years. He has conducted research on police violence against minors in Brazil and is currently working on the politics of microcredit policies and outcomes in Argentina, Brazil, and Costa Rica. His focus on human rights led him to offer a course and work in the area of prisoners' rights for seven years with the Oakland-based nonprofit California Prison Focus, for which he served as board president for eight years. During a recent hunger strike conducted by inmates protesting the policy and practice of solitary confinement, Ahnen was asked to serve on the prisoners' mediation team meeting with state government officials. In this role, he conducted dozens of direct interviews with prisoners who were locked in solitary confinement at Pelican Bay and Corcoran State Prisons (see the video embedded within Figure 15.7). His other courses explore the ethics of warfare (Just and Unjust Wars) and American politics (Politics of Incarceration). His community engagement course, Political Polling and Survey Research, has students develop, distribute, collect, and analyze surveys, culminating in a full report for nonprofit organizations in the Bay Area. He has served on several committees within the college, including the Community Engagement and Common Good Subcommittee and the Diversity and Global Perspective Subcommittee, as part of the campus

Figure 15.7 QR code: Ron Ahnen news clip video.

Note. Scan the QR code to access https://www.youtube.com/watch?v=MIGAvdinOyk

Core Curriculum Oversight Committee. This citizen scholar successfully approached the Social Justice Coordinating Committee of the college to choose an alternative venue when the alumni association contracted with a local country club for a social event when its food service workers were on strike. He was recognized for his engaged citizen scholarship by the campus center for community engagement with its annual Award to Outstanding Engaged Faculty.

The work of each citizen scholar highlighted in this chapter represents civic professionalism in action. These faculty have figured out how to synthesize their professional skills, subject matter expertise, and moral and spiritual values into a comprehensive commitment to creating a more inclusive, equitable, and just world.

Honing Your Craft

We hope you're inspired by stories of colleagues who embody forms of civic professionalism and citizen scholarship in their work and other aspects of their lives. Taken together, these examples give us hope that we can move toward more equitable, informed, and justice-oriented participation by all members of our society. As you educate students for democratic participation, collaborate on community-driven research that informs public policy, foster opportunities for civic discourse with peers in and out of the academy, and contribute to the transformation of your institution to be more accessible and accountable to community, you become part of a movement to actively work toward achievement of the common good. Begin by drafting your vision of the common good in Tool Kit 15.7.

> Tool Kit 15.7—Honing Your Craft—Refer to Exercise 15.7 in your workbook to draft your vision of the common good.

Chapter 16

THE REFLECTIVE PRACTITIONER

This closing chapter invites you to be a reflective practitioner. In many respects, you have already begun this process throughout these pages, Tool Kit exercises, and conversations in your learning community and/or with the CEP coordinating your campus center for community engagement. Likewise, this chapter serves a cumulative and summative role by revisiting and incorporating many of the key concepts presented in earlier chapters. We also explored the purpose and specific strategies for reflection with students in chapter 9. We now invite you as an engaged scholar to integrate and continue the reflective process to guide and enhance your work.

Theoretical Foundations of Reflective Practice

Earlier chapters presented theoretical principles on how reflection can have an impact on student learning. Here we argue that many of those same concepts can be applied to our own professional practice and development. Using our theme of craft-making, constructivism's conceptualization of using tools to construct knowledge through iteration, analysis, critique, reiteration, and reanalysis is an apt analogy for reflecting on our own professional growth (Guba & Lincoln, 1994; Schwandt, 1994). Theoretical frameworks such as Freire's conscientization (1970, 1998) and feminist consciousness-raising (hooks, 2003; Seethaler, 2015) go beyond assimilating knowledge and skill to inspire critical examination of ourselves and the world around us to help us discern how to build a more just world as part of our practice as engaged citizen scholars. *Practice* is both a noun and a verb (Welch & Koth, 2013). In the former, the word *practice* is used in the context of certain professions such as law or medicine. In the latter, *practice* is an action. As in the case of a profession, the arts or sports, an individual or a "practitioner" must devote attention and effort to nurture this craft or skill. One may call on a series of behaviors sometimes referred to as exercises to maintain and sustain the internalization of values and principles.

Donald Schon coined the phrase "reflective practitioner" in two landmark publications, *The Reflective Practitioner* (1983) and *Educating the Reflective Practitioner* (1987). As briefly discussed in chapter 2, both of Schon's works call for an epistemology of reflective practice that incorporates knowing-in-action, reflection-in-action, and reflection on reflection-in-action. The context for his approach was describing how educators (you the reader) can prepare preprofessionals (your students) to be artists in their professional practice. Here he draws on the influence of John Dewey in viewing professional practice as a "calling" (Schon, 1987, p. 32) to be part of a "community of practitioners" (p. 32) with shared conventions, language, and tools. In keeping with the premise and theme of this book's attempt to advance engaged teaching and learning as a craft, Schon advocated "teaching artistry" through reflection-in-action (p. 22). This resonates with us, drawing us to incorporate his term as the title of this chapter. Although his intent was to imbue this approach with his students, we maintain that we can and should adapt and apply the same premise to our own work as engaged scholars. As you continue to develop your craft as an engaged scholar, the artful application of the work will become more and more familiar over time. Schon (1987) suggested:

> When we have learned how to do something, we can execute smooth sequences of activity, recognition, decision, and adjustment without having, as we say, to "think about it." Our spontaneous knowing-in-action usually gets us through the day. On occasion, however, it doesn't. . . . All such experiences, pleasant and unpleasant, contain an element of surprise. . . . We may reflect on action, thinking back on what we have done in order to discover how our knowing-in-action may have contributed to an unexpected outcome. (p. 26)

He continues, illustrating this process with the analogy of jazz musicians who, as skilled artists, know specific skills and are therefore able to adjust their performance moment by moment by being present and responsive to what is occurring as they improvise and play together. The these concepts are elaborated in his two comprehensive volumes of work, using examples and illustrations from architecture, design, music, and even psychotherapy and are far too complex to replicate here. That said, and at the risk of oversimplification, we summarize and present his concept of the "ladder of reflection" (1987, p. 114) as a basic template for our own reflective practice.

This "ladder" consists of "rungs" that include intentional consideration and dialogue (Schon, 1987, pp. 115–116): (a) design/designing, (b) description of design/designing, (c) reflection on description of design/designing, and (d) reflection on reflection on description of designing. Here we use some analogies to illustrate the steps or rungs in this process. A composer composes a musical piece. The score of the composition must be articulated in a musical score so musicians can perform it. A football coach designs a specific play that must be diagrammed and described to be understood by both the coach and the team in order to execute the play in a game. After rehearsing or performing the musical composition, the composer and performers reflect on the overall performance. After executing the football play, either on the sidelines or after the game the coach (and perhaps the team) reflects on the overall design and execution of the play—Did it work? Why or why not? What should be done differently? Finally, the composer and the coach reflect on this description of the redesign to make a decision on how or whether to proceed. An engaged scholar essentially does the same thing with their course and/or research.

The astute reader might observe or recognize a similar parallel of this process to Kolb and Fry's (1984) experiential learning model presented in chapter 2 and the "What? So What? Now What?" model of reflection (Eyler et al., 1996) described in chapter 9. Both begin with a concrete experience followed by observing and reflecting on what occurred during the experience. Speculation on alternative actions is applied and then tested. In essence, we reflect on What we've done, accomplished, experienced to consider So What to determine impact and then move forward by contemplating Now What? The same degree of consideration from each of these frameworks can be applied to our own practice and craft of engaged teaching and learning. This can occur as an individual or in community with colleagues. Over time, like a skilled jazz musician, an engaged scholar is able to make what seems almost like an instant and intuitive adjustment to the engaged teaching and learning experience. Until that level of mastery is achieved, it is incumbent upon the instructor to intentionally pause and reflect on their own practice as an engaged scholar to make necessary adjustments.

Four Frames of Reciprocal Reflective Practice

We offer four frames of a holistic perspective to assist your reflective practice (see Figure 16.1). Each of these is based on key contexts presented throughout this book and the theoretical foundations presented previously. The reflection is reciprocal by incorporating a two-way process to intentionally consider the outward impact of our work as well as the inward impact the work has on us as engaged scholars. This holistic framework (Welch & Plaxton-Moore, 2018) includes (a) the personal, (b) our students, (c) professional and disciplinary, and (d) the community. We can then employ the basic premise and structure of Schon's ladder of reflection to explore and consider our current practice and possible next steps.

Personal

The first frame is your personal experience. This includes an array of possible considerations such as (a) why you have chosen to do this kind of work and the impact it has had on you, (b) your strengths and weaknesses, and (c) recognizing your identity as an engaged scholar. We call on and borrow from Parker Palmer's work (1998) to discover the potential

Figure 16.1 Reflection cube.

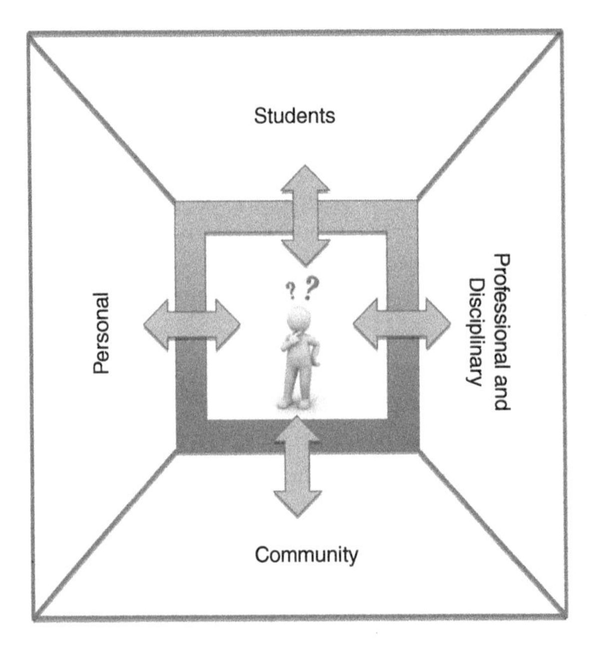

and limits of our true self. He invites us to examine our vocation or calling to do this challenging and rewarding work. How or why does this work reflect Frederick Buechner's (1993) notion of vocation as "the place where your deep gladness and the world's deep hunger meet" (p. 119)? Likewise, Palmer encourages us to identify two moments from our teaching experience—one a glorious moment in which we felt we were born to teach and the other a time when we utterly failed and questioned our value and purpose as teachers. This exercise is not so much intended to identify deficits or problems to be fixed as much as it is to remind us of the continuum of the teaching experience as a whole and to be mindful of our gifts as well as our liabilities. Similarly, our personal reflection provides yet another opportunity to employ our critical consciousness as we did in chapter 5 to identify our own power and privilege. Next, as you did in chapters 1 and 11, you are encouraged to reflect on and articulate your identity as an engaged scholar—what does that look like and mean to you? Consider your own experience in the performance review process. Was it successful? What do you anticipate as you prepare for it? Finally, to what extent has, does, or could your work manifest a citizen scholar role as described in chapter 15? In this way, we reflect on not only who we are but also *whose* we are (Palmer, 2000). Begin this reflective process by referring to Tool Kit 16.1.

> Tool Kit 16.1—Refer to Exercise 16.1 in your workbook to reflect on the personal impact your work has had.

Students

Here you are invited to reflect on the possible impact you have had on your students as well as ways they have impacted you. Naturally, as instructors, our goal is to provide opportunities for students to assimilate and apply new knowledge and skills. But as discussed in chapter 3 on engaged pedagogy and the discussion regarding learning objectives in chapter 6, a major aspect of engaged teaching and learning is to provide a holistic and transformative educational experience. We can readily "measure" students' academic or cognitive growth through traditional means such as exams and assignments. Above and beyond that, we can reflect on our efforts to enhance their civic behaviors coupled with their professional prowess. It is also important to discern to what extent the design and implementation of the course accounted for the hierarchy of cognitive skills enumerated in Bloom's taxonomy. In what ways are or were we the proverbial "sage on the stage" as opposed to being the "guide on the side" as students constructed their own learning experience? This helps minimize the traditional transactional model and banking model of depositing information into students' heads and providing opportunities for students to coconstruct their learning through engaged activities and partnerships. Likewise, we should consider to what extent we acknowledged students' multiple identities and diverse experiences, and how those informed our decisions about pedagogy and content. Finally, as discussed in chapter 6, the reflection process should consider the impact of including ancillary objectives derived from the "hidden curriculum," such as time management, problem-solving, and teamwork.

Conversely, it is incumbent on you to also consider the impact your students have had on you as a person and teacher. In many ways, this part of the reflection process found in Tool Kit 16.2 incorporates a critical consciousness as discussed in chapter 5 as it allows you a space to step back from your assumptions and initial experience and take a wider perspective of your students as people and teachers. What did your interactions with them reveal about yourself? What insights did you gain about their experience and sense of place? What is and/or was important to them? What or where were the shadows they entered during their engaged learning experience? What were your assumptions of "Who are they?" and how accurate were they? What gifts did they bring to you? To each other? What assumptions might they have of you and your course? In what ways were those assumptions accurate?

> Tool Kit 16.2—Refer to Exercise 16.2 in your workbook. Reflect on the ways you and your course may have had or hoped to have an impact on your students. Conversely, reflect on the impact your students have had on you as a person and professional.

Professional and Disciplinary

This is a broad context that frames the academic aspects of our work encompassing the institution, discipline, and profession. In this way, we reflect on the impact our engaged teaching and scholarship has had on our respective departments, institution, and discipline. This allows us to consider how our work reflects the mission of the institution as well as its culture and values. Likewise, our reflection should include consideration of our ability to navigate that same culture as well as policy and procedures. Aspects of this were explored earlier in chapter 11 as we considered the meaning of engaged scholarship and also how to advance it with colleagues through coaching in chapter 13 and institutionally in chapter 14. To what extent have we educated colleagues and administrators as to what this work is and its value? Is engaged scholarship as described in chapter 11 understood and valued? Why or why not? What could be done to enlighten others? Have we been effective tempered radicals as described by Meyerson and Scully (1995) in our attempts to advance this work and to derive the credibility it deserves? In what ways were we able to initiate, interrogate, infiltrate, and integrate practices and policies to advance community engagement at the institution? Has our work had any effect on dismantling the primacy of neoliberalism and/or positivist ideologies?

Outside the walls of your institution, consider your impact on the discipline. Have you been successful in disseminating new knowledge to shape your field? To what extent has your discipline embraced engaged scholarship? In what ways have you advanced this work in your own discipline? Reflect on these questions in Tool Kit 16.3.

Conversely, this process provides an opportunity to consider the impact the academy has had on our engaged teaching and scholarship. There are bound to be challenges and obstacles to your engaged scholarship. Additionally, take time to identify and celebrate the people and resources on your campus who support you and your work. Similarly, there are others outside your institution within your discipline or the field of community engagement who have inspired or supported you. In this way, you are identifying and establishing a community of like-minded, kindred spirits.

> Tool Kit 16.3—Refer to Exercise 16.3 in your workbook. Reflect on the ways you have had an impact on your department, institution, discipline, and field of community engagement. Conversely, identify examples of how each of these settings impacted you as an engaged scholar.

The Community

The fourth frame for reflection is consideration of the community. As discussed in chapter 4, we recognize the *community* is not a monolithic structure. Instead, the term represents a broad spectrum of settings, experiences, and people. In Tool Kit 16.4 we are encouraged to ponder and identify the assets and resources of the community as well as how these were used to meet goals and aspirations embedded within our engaged teaching and learning. In one respect, it is relatively easy to reflect on and determine whether or not our collaborative work with a community partner successfully achieved our mutual goals. However, a reflective practitioner goes beyond this cursory and somewhat superficial objective. The reflection process also provides an opportunity to recognize and celebrate the history and sense of place that were gifted to us and our students. We can reflect on the degree that community partners were truly coeducators and public scholars. We can consider the level of impact and involvement the community has had on internal departmental and institutional policy and programs. The reflection process also invites us to consider our own assumptions about the community at large and our community partners. This allows us to determine the accuracy of our preconceived notions and ponder ways to address inaccuracies.

> Tool Kit 16.4—Refer to Exercise 16.4 in your workbook. Reflect on your possible impact on the community and the impact it has had on you and your students.

Personal Journeys and Personal Experiences

In many ways, a reflective practitioner is cognizant of their personal journey and experience as an engaged scholar. The reflective process proposed and described here is essentially a travelogue. It allows us to see where we've been and hope to go. Over the years, we have had the pleasure and honor of working with colleagues like yourself as they honed their craft as engaged scholars. We have been inspired by their stories and accomplishments. We have seen firsthand the impact this work has had on their students, the community, and themselves. In many ways, their stories are a gift. Diener and Liese (2009) edited an inspiring volume of essays from engaged scholars at a public university describing how they formed a community-engaged scholar learning community. The individual stories within that volume provide a model for this type of personal and professional reflection. And although we have come to the end of this chapter and book, it is not necessarily the end of the reflective process. We invite and encourage you to embrace the role and identity of a reflective practitioner to periodically pause, at least at the end of each semester, and reflect on your practice and craft as an engaged scholar.

Honing Your Craft

We have come to the end of this book. That said, we hope this is the beginning of your continued effort to hone your craft as an engaged educator, citizen scholar, community organizer, and reflective practitioner. An array of ideas and practice, some challenging and provocative, was presented on these pages. We can safely assume you are at a different place than where you were when you opened the cover of this book. It is our hope that at this juncture you have had at least one experience developing, teaching, and assessing a community-engaged course. Likewise, it has always been our goal and hope that you read this book with a community of colleagues. If that is the case, we can also assume (and hope) that a new cohort of faculty will follow. As such, you are at the professional level of "been there—done that" and can serve as a valuable resource and mentor to your colleagues just now exploring this work. Does that imply you are now a master teacher? Not necessarily, but it has been our experience that novice engaged scholars often turn to their more experienced colleagues and ask, "If you knew then what you know now . . . what would you say?" We invite you to reflect and respond to that very question as the final Tool Kit exercise (Tool Kit 16.5) as a way of "putting a bow on the package."

> Tool Kit 16.5—Honing Your Craft—Refer to Exercise 16.5 in your workbook. Reflect on the question, "If you knew then, what you know now . . . what would you say?" Consider sharing your response with colleagues in your learning community and/or an incoming cohort.

Conclusion

We began this book by stating that it was different from other academic books. We conclude by assuming you have come to recognize that being an engaged scholar is a different kind of role and work. When you opened the cover, you were essentially a novice or perhaps an apprentice in the art and craft of engaged teaching and learning. We would argue that one never truly masters any particular craft because there are always new innovations to be forged, smoothing out the rough edges as we go and, with experience, learning from what works and what doesn't work. The same can be said for the craft of engaged teaching and learning. We believe this work is important and transformative—not only for our students, the field, and the community but also for ourselves. We sincerely believe and trust this work has transformed and inspired you to embrace your identity as an engaged scholar with the commitment, capacities, and competencies necessary to enact positive change in your classroom, institution, discipline, and community.

REFERENCES

Able, H., Blanchard, L. W., Corbie-Smith, G. M., Friedman, B. G., Muller, E. L., & Rhodes, T. E. (2016). *Provost's task force on engaged scholarship in promotion and tenure.* Unpublished report. Chapel Hill, NC: University of North Carolina.

Aguirre, A. (2000). *Women and minority faculty in the academic workplace* (ASHE-ERIC Higher Education Report, Vol. 27, No. 6). San Francisco, CA: Jossey-Bass.

Altman, I., & Low, S. M. (2012). *Place attachment.* New York, NY: Routledge.

American Association of State Colleges and Universities. (n.d.a). *The Barbara Burch Award for Faculty Leadership in Civic Engagement.* Retrieved from http://www.aascu.org/programs/adp/awards/BarbaraBurch/

American Association of State Colleges and Universities. (n.d.b). *The John Saltmarsh Award for Emerging Leaders in Civic Engagement.* Retrieved from http://www.aascu.org/programs/adp/awards/JohnSaltmarsh/

American Education Research Association (AERA). (2019). *Service-learning and experiential education.* Retrieved from http://www.aera.net/SIG041/Service-Learning-and-Experiential-Education

Angelique, H., Kyle, K., & Taylor, E. (2002, Spring). Mentors and muses: New strategies for academic success. *Innovative Higher Education, 26*(3), 195–209.

Angelo, T., & Cross, K. P. (1993). *Classroom assessment techniques: A handbook for college teachers.* San Francisco, CA: Jossey-Bass/Wiley.

Axtell, S. (2012). *Creating a community-engaged scholarship (CES) faculty development program—Phase one: Program and skill mapping.* Retrieved from http://www.engagement.umn.edu/faculty/tools

Baer, D. M., & Schwartz, I. S. (1991). If reliance on epidemiology were to become epidemic, we would need to assess its social validity. *Journal of Applied Behavioral Analysis, 24,* 231–234.

Baldwin, A. N., & Johnson, R. (2017). Black women's co-mentoring relationship as resistance to marginalization at a predominantly white institution. In O. Perlow, D. Wheeler, S. Bethea, & B. Scott (Eds.), *Black women's liberatory pedagogies* (pp. 125–140). New York, NY: Palgrave Macmillan.

Bandura, A. (2002). Social foundations of thought and action. In D. F. Marks (Ed.), *The health psychology reader* (pp. 94–106). Thousand Oaks, CA: SAGE.

Battistoni, R. M. (2002). *Civic engagement across the curriculum: A resource book for service-learning faculty in all disciplines.* Providence, RI: Campus Compact.

Beere, C. (2009). Understanding and enhancing the opportunities of community-campus partnerships. In L. R. Sandmann, C. H. Thornton, & A. J. Jaeger (Eds.),

Institutionalizing community engagement in higher education: The first wave of Carnegie Classified institutions (pp. 55–64). San Francisco, CA: Jossey-Bass.

Bell, D. A., Jr. (1980). Brown v. Board of Education and the interest-convergence dilemma. *Harvard Law Review, 93*(3), 518–533.

Benson, L., & Harkavy, I. (2000). Integrating the American systems of higher, secondary, and primary education to develop civic responsibility. In T. Ehrlich (Ed.), *Civic responsibility and higher education* (pp. 174–196). Phoenix, AZ: Oryx Press.

Benson, L., Harkavy, I., & Hartley, M. (2005). Integrating a commitment to the public good into the institutional fabric. In J. Burhardt, T. Chambers, & A. Kezar (Eds.), *Higher education for the public good: Emerging voices from a national movement* (pp. 185–216). San Francisco, CA: Jossey-Bass.

Benson, L., Harkavy, I., & Puckett, J. (2007). *Dewey's dream: Universities and democracies in an age of education reform—Civil society, public schools, and democratic citizenship.* Philadelphia, PA: Temple University Press.

Benson, L., Harkavy, I., & Puckett, J. (2011). Democratic transformation through university-assisted community schools. In J. Saltmarsh & M. Hartley (Eds.), *To serve a larger purpose: Engagement for democracy and the transformation of higher education* (pp. 49–81). Philadelphia, PA: Temple University Press.

Benson, L., Harkavy, I., Puckett, J., Hartley, M., Hodges, R. A., Johnston, F. E., & Weeks, J. (2017). *Knowledge for social change: Bacon, Dewey, and the revolutionary transformation of research universities in the 21st century.* Philadelphia, PA: Temple University Press.

Bhattacharyya, J. (2004). Theorizing community development. *Community Development, 34*(2), 5–34.

Bialek, R. (2000). A decade of progress in academic/practice linkages. *Journal of Public Health Management and Practice, 6*(1), 25–31.

Blanchard, L. W., Hanssmann, C., Strauss, R. P., Belliard, J. C., Krichbaum, K., Waters, E., & Seifer, S. D. (2009). Models for faculty development: What does it take to be a community-engaged scholar? *Metropolitan Universities, 20*(2), 47–65.

Bloom, B. S., Engelhart, M. D., Furst, E. J., Hill, W. H., & Krathwohl, D. R. (1956). *Taxonomy of educational objectives: The classification of educational goals—Handbook I: Cognitive domain.* New York, NY: David McKay.

Bordeaux, B. C., Wiley, C., Tandon, S. D., & Horowitz, C. R. (2007). Guidelines for writing manuscripts about community-based participatory research for peer-reviewed journals. *Progress in Community Health Partnerships: Research, Education, and Action, 1*(3), 281–288.

Boyer, E. L. (1990). *Scholarship reconsidered: Priorities of the professoriate.* Princeton, NJ: Carnegie Foundation for the Advancement of Teaching.

Boyer, E. L. (1997). *Ernest L. Boyer—Selected speeches: 1979–1995.* Princeton, NJ: Carnegie Foundation for the Advancement of Teaching.

Boyte, H. C., & Fretz, E. (2010). Civic professionalism. *Journal of Higher Education Outreach and Engagement, 14*(2), 67–90.

Bradshaw, T. K. (2008). The post-place community: Contributions to the debate about the definition of community. *Community Development, 39*(1), 5–16.

Bransford, J. D., Brown, A. L., & Cocking, R. R. (2000). *How people learn: Brain, mind, experience, and school.* Washington DC: National Academies Press.

Bringle, R. G., Games, R., & Malloy, E. A. (1999). Colleges and universities as citizens: Issues and perspectives. In R. G. Bringle, R. Games, & E. A. Malloy (Eds.), *Colleges and universities as citizens* (pp. 1–16). Needham Heights, MA: Allyn & Bacon.

Bringle, R. G., & Hatcher, J. A. (2011). Student engagement trends over time. In H. E. Fitzgerald, C. Burack, & S. D. Seifer (Eds.), *Handbook of engaged scholarship: Contemporary landscapes, future directions. Vol. 2: Community-campus partnerships* (pp. 411–430). East Lansing: Michigan State University Press.

Brown University Swearer Center. (2018). *Earnest A. Lynton Faculty Award in Engaged Scholarship*. Retrieved from https://www.brown.edu/swearer/lynton

Budge, S. (2006). Peer mentoring in post-secondary education: Implications for research and practice. *Journal of College Reading and Learning, 37*(1), 73–87.

Buechner, F. (1993). *Wishful thinking: A theological ABC.* New York: Harper One.

Buttimer, A., & Seamon, D. (2015). *The human experience of space and place.* New York, NY: Routledge.

Calleson, D. C., Jordan, C., & Seifer, S. D. (2005). Community-engaged scholarship: Is faculty work in communities a true academic enterprise? *Academic Medicine, 80*(4), 317–321.

California Campus Compact. (n.d.). Retrieved from www.cacampuscompact.org

Campus Compact. (2018). *The Thomas Ehrlich Civically Engaged Faculty Award.* Retrieved from https://compact.org/thomas-ehrlich-civically-engaged-faculty-award/

Carnegie Foundation for the Advancement of Teaching. (2012). *Community engaged elective classification.* Retrieved from http://classifications.carnegiefoundation.org/descriptions/community_engagement.php

Chait, R. (2002). *Why tenure? Why now? Questions of tenure.* Cambridge, MA: Harvard University Press.

Chan, A. W. (2008). Mentoring ethnic minority, pre-doctoral students: An analysis of key mentor practices. *Mentoring and Tutoring: Partnership in Learning, 16*(3), 263–277.

Choi, S. (2016, September 16). *Redefining citizenship*. Retrieved from https://www.huffingtonpost.com/steven-choi/redefining-citizenship_b_8146538.html

Colby, A., Ehrlich, T., Beaumont, E., & Stephens, J. (2003). *Educating citizens: Preparing America's undergraduates for lives of moral and civic responsibility.* San Francisco, CA: Jossey-Bass.

Committee on Institutional Cooperation. (2005). *Engaged scholarship: A resource guide.* Retrieved from http://www.cic.net/docs/default-source/technology/engaged_scholarship.pdf

Concordia College. (2018). *Concordia College faculty handbook*. Retrieved from https://cobbernet.cord.edu/files/resources/facultyhandbook.pdf

Cox, M. D. (2004, Spring). Introduction to faculty learning communities. In M. D. Cox & L. Richlin (Eds.), *New Directions for Teaching and Learning* (No. 97, pp. 5–23). New York, NY: Wiley.

Cranton, P. (1996). *Professional development as transformative learning: New perspectives for teachers of adults*. San Francisco, CA: Jossey-Bass.

Crenshaw, K. W. (1988). Race, reform, and retrenchment: Transformation and legitimation in antidiscrimination law. *Harvard Law Review, 101*(7), 1331–1387.

Crenshaw, K. (1991). Mapping the margins: Identity politics, intersectionality, and violence against women. *Stanford Law Review, 43*(6), 1241–1299.

Cruz, N. (1990a). A challenge to the notion of service. In J. C. Kendall & Associates (Eds.), *Combining service and learning: A resource book for community and public service* (Vol. 1, pp. 321–323). Raleigh, NC: National Association for Experiential Education.

Cruz, N. (1990b). *Principles of good practice in combining service and learning: A diversity perspective*. St. Paul, MN: Author.

Cullingford, C. (2006a). Mentoring as myth and reality: Evidence and ambiguity. In C. Cullingford (Ed.), *Mentoring in education: An international perspective* (pp. 1–10). New York, NY: Routledge.

Cullingford, C. (2006b). *Mentoring in education: An international perspective*. New York, NY: Routledge.

Daloz, L. A., Keen, C. H., Keen, J. P., & Parks, S. D. (1996). *Common fire: Lives of commitment in a complex world*. Boston, MA: Beacon Press.

Darder, A. (2015). *Freire and education*. New York, NY: Routledge.

Darder, A. (2017). *Reinventing Paulo Freire: A pedagogy of love*. New York, NY: Routledge.

Davis, D. J., Boyer, P., & Russell, I. (2011). Mentoring postsecondary tenure-track faculty: A theory-building case study and implications for institutional policy. *Administrative Issues Journal, 1*(1), article 6. Retrieved from www.dc.swosu.edu/aij/vol1/iss1/6

Deardorff, D. K., & Edwards, K. (2013). Framing and assessing students' intercultural competence in service learning. In P. H. Clayton, R. G. Bringle, & J. A. Hatcher (Eds.), *Research on service learning: Conceptual frameworks and assessment—Communities, institutions, and partnerships* (pp. 157–183). Sterling, VA: Stylus.

De Courcy, E. (2015). Defining and measuring teaching excellence in higher education in the 21st century. *College Quarterly, 18*(1). Retrieved from http://collegequarterly.ca/2015-vol18-num01-winter/decourcy.html

Deegan, M. J. (2017). Jane Addams, feminist pragmatism, and service learning. In C. Dolgon, T. D. Mitchell, & T. K. Eatman (Eds.), *The Cambridge handbook of service learning and community engagement*. Cambridge, UK: Cambridge University Press.

Delgado, R., & Stefancic, J. (2012). *Critical race theory: An introduction* (2nd ed.). New York, NY: New York University Press.

Denzin, N. K., & Lincoln, Y. S. (1994). *Handbook of qualitative research.* Thousand Oaks, CA: SAGE.

Desimone, L. M., & Pak, K. (2016). Instructional coaching as high quality professional development. *Theory Into Practice, 56*(1), 3–12.

Dewey, J. (1916). *Democracy and education.* New York, NY: Macmillan.

Dewey, J. (1927). *The public and its problems.* New York, NY: Henry Holt.

Dewey, J. (1933). *How we think: A restatement of the relation of reflective thinking to the educational process.* Lexington, MA: D.C. Heath.

Dewey, J. (1938). *Experience and education.* New York, NY: Kappa Delta Pi.

Dewey, J. (1976). *The school and society.* Carbondale: Southern Illinois University Press.

Diamond, R. M. (1995). *Preparing for promotion and tenure review: A faculty guide.* Bolton, MA: Anker.

Diamond, R. M., & Adams, B. E. (1993). *Recognizing faculty work: Reward systems for the year 2000.* San Francisco, CA: Jossey-Bass.

Diener, M. L., & Liese, H. (2009). *Finding meaning in civically engaged scholarship: Personal journeys/professional experiences.* Charlotte, NC: Information Age.

DiGirolamo, J. (2015). *Coaching for professional development.* Alexandria, VA: Society for Human Resource Management.

Doberneck, D. M. (2017a, January 10). *An annotated list of interdisciplinary community engagement journals.* Boston, MA: Campus Compact. Retrieved from https://compact.org/resource-posts/40226/

Doberneck, D. M. (2017b, January 5). *Journal section comparison table.* Boston, MA: Campus Compact. Retrieved from https://compact.org/resource-posts/journal-section-comparison-table/

Dorn, C. (2011). From "liberal professions" to "lucrative professions": Bowdoin College, Stanford University, and the civic functions of higher education. *Teachers College Record, 113*(7), 1566–1596.

Dostilio, L., & Perry, L. G. (2017). An explanation of community engagement professionals as professionals and leaders. In L. Dostilio (Ed.), *The community engagement professional in higher education: A competency model for an emerging field* (pp. 1–26). Boston, MA: Campus Compact.

Dostilio, L., & Welch, M. (2018). *The community engagement professional guidebook.* Sterling, VA: Stylus.

Dubb, S., McKinley, S., & Howard, T. (2013). *The anchor dashboard: Aligning institutional practice to meet low-income community needs.* Takoma Park, MD: Democracy Collaborative.

Dubinsky, J. M., Welch, M., & Wurr, A. J. (2012). Composing cognition: The role of written reflections in service-learning. In I. Baca (Ed.), *Studies in writing—Service-learning and writing: Paving the way for literacy(ies) through community engagement* (pp. 155–180). Boston, MA: Brill.

Dugal, S. S., & Eriksen, M. (2004). Understanding and transcending team member differences: A felt-experience exercise. *Journal of Management Education, 28*(4), 492–508.

Duke University. (2018). *Office of Assessment*. Retrieved from https://assessment.trinity.duke.edu

Dzur, A. W. (2004). Democratic professionalism: Sharing authority in civic life. *The Good Society, 13*(1), 6–14.

Eby, J. W. (2010). Civic engagement in faith-based institutions. In H. E. Fitzgerald, C. Burack, & S. D. Seifer (Eds.), *Handbook of engaged scholarship: Contemporary landscapes, future directions. Vol. 1: Institutional change* (pp. 165–180). East Lansing: Michigan State University Press.

Ehrlich, T. (2000). *Civic responsibility and higher education.* Phoenix, AZ: Oryx Press.

Engagement Scholarship Consortium. (2019). *Journals*. Retrieved from https://engagementscholarship.org/publications/journals

Eyler, J., Giles, D. E., & Schmiede, A. (1996). *A practitioner's guide to reflection in service-learning: Student voices & reflections.* Nashville, TN: Vanderbilt University.

Ewing, R., Freeman, M., Barrie, S., Bell, A., O'Conner, D., Waugh, F., & Sikes, C. (2008). Building community in academic settings: The importance of flexibility in a structured mentoring program. *Mentoring & Tutoring: Partnership in Learning*, 16(3), 294–310.

Finley, A., & McNair, T. (2013). *Assessing underserved students' engagement in high-impact practices: With an Assessing Equity in High-Impact Practices Toolkit.* Washington DC: Association of American Colleges & Universities.

Fish, S. (2003, May). Aim low. *The Chronicle of Higher Education*. Retrieved from http://chronicle.com/jobs/05/2003051601c.htm

Fitzgerald, H. E., Bruns, K., Sonka, S. T., Furco, A., & Swanson, L. (2012). The centrality of engagement in higher education. *Journal of Higher Education Outreach and Engagement, 20*(1), 223–244.

Fitzmaurice, M. (2010). Considering teaching in higher education as a practice. *Teaching in Higher Education, 15*(1), 45–55.

Flavell, J. H. (1979). Metacognition and cognitive monitoring: A new area of cognitive-developmental inquiry. *American Psychologist, 34*, 906–911.

Forchuk, C., & Meier, A. (2014). The article idea chart: A participatory action research tool to aid involvement in dissemination. *Gateways: International Journal of Community Research and Engagement, 7*, 157–163.

Freire, P. (1970). *Pedagogy of the oppressed* (M. B. Ramos., Trans.) New York, NY: Continuum.

Freire, P. (1998). *Pedagogy of freedom: Ethics, democracy, and civic courage.* Lanham, MD: Rowman & Littlefield.

Freire Institute. (2018). *Concepts used by Paulo Freire*. Retrieved from http://www.freire.org/paulo-freire/concepts-used-by-paulo-freire

Fricker, M. (2007). *Epistemic injustice: Power and the ethics of knowing*. Oxford, UK: Oxford University Press.

Furco, A. (2005). *Promoting civic engagement at the University of California.* Berkeley, CA: University of California, Center for Studies in Higher Education.

Furco, A. (2010). The engaged campus: Toward a comprehensive approach to public engagement. *British Journal of Educational Studies, 58*(4), 375–390.

Furco, A., & Holland, B. A. (2013). Improving research on service learning institutionalization through attention to theories of organizational change. In J. A. Hatcher, P. H. Clayton, & R. G. Bringle (Eds.), *Research on service learning: Conceptual frameworks and assessment* (pp. 441–470). Sterling, VA: Stylus

Garrott, L. (2009a). The professional journey: Neighborhood democracy. In M. L. Diener & H. Liese (Eds.), *Finding meaning in civically engaged scholarship: Personal journeys, personal experiences* (pp. 117–130). Charlotte, NC: Information Age.

Garrott, L. (2009b). The search for authentic citizenship. In M. L. Diener & H. Liese (Eds.), *Finding meaning in civically engaged scholarship: Personal journeys, personal experiences* (pp. 21–28). Charlotte, NC: Information Age.

Garvey, B., Stokes, P., & Megginson, D. (2018). *Coaching and mentoring: Theories and practice*. Thousand Oaks, CA: SAGE.

Gelmon, S., & Agre-Kippenhan, S. (2002, January). Promotion, tenure, and the engaged scholar: Keeping the scholarship of engagement in the review process. *AHHE Bulletin, 54*(5), 7–11.

Gelmon, S. B., Holland, B. A., & Spring, A. (2018). *Assessing service-learning and civic engagement: Principles and techniques* (2nd ed.). Sterling, VA: Stylus.

Glassick, C. E. E., Huber, M. T., & Maeroff, G. I. (1997). *Scholarship assessed: Evaluation of the professoriate*. San Francisco, CA: Jossey-Bass.

Glover, R. (2010, January). Principles of great design: Craftsmanship. *Smashing Magazine*. Retrieved from https://www.smashingmagazine.com/2010/01/principles-of-great-design-craftsmanship/

Gold, Y. (1992). Psychological support for mentors and beginning teachers: A critical dimension. In T. M. Bey & C. T. Holmes (Eds.), *Mentoring: Contemporary principles and issues* (pp. 25–34). Reston, VA: Association of Teacher Educators.

Guba, E. G., & Lincoln, Y. S. (1994). Competing paradigms in qualitative research. In N. K. Denzin & Y. S. Lincoln (Eds.), *Handbook of qualitative research* (pp. 105–117). Thousand Oaks, CA: SAGE.

Haas Center for Public Service. (2010). *Pathways of public service*. Stanford, CA: Stanford University.

Hafler, J. P., & Lovejoy, F. H., Jr. (2000). Scholarly activities recorded in the portfolios of teacher-clinician faculty. *Academic Medicine, 75*(6), 649–652.

Hanover Research. (2014, January). *Faculty mentoring models and effective practices*. Washington DC: Hanover Research. Retrieved from https://www.hanoverresearch.com/media/Faculty-Mentoring-Models-and-Effectives-Practices-Hanover-Research.pdf

Harding, A. (2018). *What is the difference between an impact and an outcome?* London School of Economics Blog. Retrieved from http://blogs.lse.ac.uk/impactofsocialsciences/2014/10/27/impact-vs-outcome-harding/

Harkavy, I. (2004). Service-learning and the development of democratic universities, democratic schools, and democratic good societies in the 21st century. In M. Welch & S. H. Billig (Eds.), *New perspectives in service-learning: Research to advance the field* (pp. 3–22). Greenwich, CT: Information Age.

Harkavy, I., & Benson, L. (1998). De-Platonizing and democratizing education as the basis for service-learning. In R. A. Rhoads & J. P. F. Howard (Eds.), *Academic service-learning: A pedagogy of action and reflection* (pp. 11–19). San Francisco, CA: Jossey-Bass.

Hart, T. (2009). *From information to transformation: Education for the evolution of consciousness*. New York, NY: Peter Lang.

Hartley, M. (2011). Idealism and compromise and the civic engagement movement. In J. Saltmarsh & M. Hartley (Eds.), *To serve a larger purpose: Engagement for democracy and the transformation of higher education* (pp. 27–48). Philadelphia, PA: Temple University Press.

Harward, D. W. (2012). Theoretical arguments and themes. In D. W. Harward (Ed.), *Transforming undergraduate education: Theory that compels and practices that succeed* (pp. 3–34). Lanham, MD: Rowman & Littlefield.

Hatcher, J. A. (2008). *The public role of professionals: Developing and evaluating the Civic-Minded Professional scale* (Doctoral dissertation). Available from ProQuest Dissertations and Theses Database, AAT 3331248 (https://scholarworks.iupui.edu/handle/1805/17469)

Hatcher, J. A., & Bringle, R. G. (1997). Reflections: Bridging the gap between service and learning. *Journal of College Teaching, 45*, 153–158.

Heffernan, K. (2001). Service-learning in higher education. *Journal of Contemporary Water Research & Education, 119*(1), 2.

Higher Education Research Institute. (n.d.). How service learning affects students. Retrieved from https://heri.ucla.edu/service_learning.html

Holland, B. (1999). From murky to meaningful: The role of mission in institutional change. In R. G. Bringle, R. Games, & E. A. Malloy (Eds.), *Colleges and universities as citizens* (pp. 48–73). Needham Heights, MA: Allyn & Bacon.

Holland, B. (2005, July 5). *Scholarship and mission in the 21st century university: The role of engagement*. Paper presented at the Australian Universities Quality Forum, Sydney, Australia. Retrieved from http://www.auqa.edu.au/

Holland, B. (2012, October 12). *Community engaged scholarship: Your teaching, research, and service "reconsidered."* Plenary presentation, University of Louisville, KY.

Holmes, S. L., Danley, L. L., & Hinton-Hudson, V. D. (2007). Race still matters: Considerations for mentoring Black women in academe. *The Negro Educational Review, 58*(1–2), 105–129.

Hondagneu-Sotelo, P., & Rashoff, S. (1994). Community service-learning: Promises and problems. *Teaching Sociology, 22*, 248–254.

hooks, b. (2003). *Teaching community: A pedagogy of hope*. New York, NY: Routledge.

Huber, M. T. (2002). Faculty evaluation and the development of academic careers. In C. L. Colber (Ed.), *Evaluating faculty performance* (New Directions for Institutional Research, No. 114, pp. 17–26). San Francisco, CA: Jossey-Bass.

Hutchings, P., & Wutzdorff, A. (1988). Experiential learning across the curriculum: Assumptions and principles. *New Directions for Teaching and Learning*, no. 35, 5–19.

Jasper, M. A. (1999). Nurses' perceptions of the value of written reflection. *Nurse Education Today, 19*(6), 52–63.

Jensen, K. (2016). The growing edges of beloved community: From Royce to Thurman and King. *Transactions of the Charles S. Peirce Society: A Quarterly Journal in American Philosophy, 52*(2), 239–258.

Jordan, C. (2007). *Community-engaged scholarship review, promotion and tenure package*. Peer Review Workgroup, Community-Engaged Scholarship for Health Collaborative. Retrieved from ttps://www.ccphealth.org/wp-content/uploads/2017/10/CES_RPT_Package.pdf

Jordan, C. (Ed.). (2009). Community-engaged scholarship review, promotion, and tenure package. *The Community-Engaged Scholarship for Health Collaborative, 20*(2), 66–86.

Jordan, C. M. (2010). Redefining peer review and products of engaged scholarship. In H. E. Fitzgerald, C. Burack, & S. D. Seifer (Eds.), *Handbook of engaged scholarship: Contemporary landscapes, future directions. Vol. 1: Institutional change* (pp. 295–305). East Lansing: Michigan State University Press.

Jordan, C. M., Wong, K. A., Jungnickel, P. W., Joosten, Y. A., Leugers, R. C., & Shields, S. L. (2009). The community-engaged scholarship review, promotion, and tenure package: A guide for faculty and committee members. *Metropolitan Universities, 20*(2), 66–86.

Juergensmeyer, E. (2017). Rhetorical advocacy and the scholarship of application. *Academic Labor: Research and Artistry, 1*, Article 7. Retrieved from http://digitalcommons.humboldt.edu/alra/vol1/iss1/7

June, A. W. (2008). A helping hand for young faculty members. *The Chronicle of Higher Education, 55*(3), A10–A12.

Kecskes, K. (2006). *Engaging departments: Moving faculty culture from private to public, individual to collective focus for the common good*. San Francisco, CA: Jossey-Bass.

Kellogg Commission. (2001). *Returning to our roots: Executive summaries of the reports of the Kellogg Commission on the future of state and land-grant universities*. Washington DC: National Association of State Universities and Land-Grant Colleges.

Kempers, M. (2001). *Community matters: An exploration of theory and practice*. Lanham, MD: Rowman & Littlefield.

Kezar, A., Drivalas, Y., & Kitchen, J. A. (2018). *Envisioning public scholarship for our time: Models for higher education researchers*. Sterling, VA: Stylus.

Kincheloe, J. L., & McLaren, P. L. (1994). Rethinking critical theory and qualitative research. In N. K. Denzin & Y. S. Lincoln (Eds.), *Handbook of qualitative research* (pp. 138–157). Thousand Oaks, CA: SAGE.

Kluckhohn, C., & Kelly, W. H. (1945). The concept of culture. In R. Linton (Ed.), *The science of man in the world crisis* (pp. 201–221). New York, NY: Columbia University Press.

Kolb, D. A., & Fry, R. (1984). *Experiential learning: Experience as the source of learning and development* (Vol. 1). Englewood Cliffs, NJ: Prentice Hall.

Kuh, G. D. (2008). *High impact educational practices: What they are, who has access to them, and why they matter.* Washington DC: Association of American Colleges & Universities.

Lage, M. J., Platt, G. J., & Treglia, M. (2000). Inverting the classroom: A gateway to creating an inclusive learning environment. *The Journal of Economic Education, 31*(1), 30–43.

Lawler, P. (2003, Summer). Teachers as adult learners: A new perspective. In K. P. King & P. A. Lawler (Eds.), *New Directions for Adult and Continuing Education* (No. 98, pp. 15–22). New York, NY: Wiley.

Lawry, S., Laurison, D., & Van Antwerpen, J. (2006). *Liberal education and civic engagement: A project of Ford Foundation's Knowledge, Creativity and Freedom Program.* New York, NY: Ford Foundation.

Liese, H. (2009). The civically engaged scholar: Identity, relationship, and the RPT process. In M. L. Diener & H. Liese (Eds.), *Finding meaning in civically engaged scholarship: Personal journeys, professional experiences* (pp. 77–85). Charlotte, NC: Information Age.

Lumpkin, A. (2011). A model for mentoring university faculty. *The Educational Forum, 75*, 357–368.

MacLennan, L. (2017). *Coaching and mentoring.* New York, NY: Routledge.

March, P. (2007). *Broader impacts review criterion.* Washington DC: National Science Foundation. Retrieved from https://www.nsf.gov/pubs/2007/nsf07046/nsf07046.jsp

Matsuda, M. J. (1987). Looking to the bottom: Critical legal studies and reparations. *Harvard Civil Rights–Civil Liberties Law Review, 22*, 323.

Mertens, J. B. (2009). Incorporating service-learning in quantitative methods economics courses. In C. A. Rimmerman (Ed.), *Service-learning and the liberal arts* (pp. 107–135). Lanham, MD: Lexington Books.

Meyerson, D.E., & Scully, M.A. (1995). Tempered radicalism and the politics of ambivalence and change. *Organizational Science*, 6, 585–600.

Mezirow, J. (1991). *Transformative dimensions of adult learning.* San Francisco, CA: Jossey-Bass.

Mezirow, J. (1999). *Transformative dimensions of adult learning* (2nd ed.). San Francisco, CA: Jossey-Bass.

Mezirow, J. (2000). *Learning as transformation: Critical perspectives on a theory in progress.* San Francisco, CA: Jossey-Bass.

Michigan State University. (2009). *Points of distinction: A guidebook for planning and evaluating quality research.* East Lansing, MI: University Outreach and Engagement, Kellogg Center.

Miller, C., & Harris, J. C. (2009). Conflicting agendas for scholars, publishers, and institutions. In A. N. Greco (Ed.), *The state of scholarly publishing: Challenges and opportunities* (pp. 9–27). New York, NY: Routledge.

Mitchell, T. D. (2008). Traditional vs. critical service-learning: Engaging the literature to differentiate two models. *Michigan Journal of Community Service Learning, 14*(2), 50–65.

Mitchell, T. D., Donahue, D. M., & Young-Law, C. (2012). Service-learning as a pedagogy of whiteness. *Equity and Excellence in Education, 45*(4), 612–629.

Mladenovic, M. (2012): *Mentoring in higher education*. Retrieved from http://milosm.info/Professor%20Milos%20Mladenovic%20publications/Mentoring%20in%20Higher%20Education%20-%20Mladenovic.pdf

Moely, B. E., Mercer, S. H., Ilustre, V., Miron, D., & McFarland, M. (2002). Psychometric properties and correlates of the Civic Attitudes and Skills Questionnaire (CASQ): A measure of students' attitudes related to service-learning. *Michigan Journal of Community Service Learning, 8*, 15–26.

Nilsen, P. (2015). Making sense of implementation theories, models and frameworks. *Implementation Science: IS, 10*(53). doi:10.1186/s13012-015-0242-0

Noe, R. A (2006). An investigation of the determinants of successful assigned mentoring relationships. *Personnel Psychology, 41*, 457–479.

Nyden, P. (2003). Academic incentives for faculty participation in community-based participatory research. *Journal of General Internal Medicine, 18*(7), 576–585.

Oden, R. S., & Casey, T. A. (2007). Advancing service learning as a transformative method for social justice work. In J. Z. Calderon (Ed.), *Race, poverty, and social justice: Multidisciplinary perspectives through service learning* (pp. 3–22). Sterling, VA: Stylus.

O'Meara, K. A. (2010). Rewarding multiple forms of scholarship: Promotion and tenure. In H. E. Fitzgerald, C. Burack, & S. D. Seifer (Eds.), *Handbook of engaged scholarship: Contemporary landscapes, future directions. Vol. 1: Institutional Change* (pp. 271–293). East Lansing: Michigan State University Press.

O'Meara, K., Eatman, T., & Petersen, S. (2015). Advancing engaged scholarship in promotion and tenure: A roadmap and call for reform. *Liberal Education, 101*(3), 52–57. Retrieved from http://www.aacu.org/liberaleducation/2015/summer/o'meara

Online Etymology Dictionary. (n.d.). *Competency*. Retrieved from http://www.etymonline.com

Palmer, P. J. (1987). Community, conflict, and ways of knowing: Ways to deepen our educational agenda. *Change: The Magazine of Higher Learning, 19*(5), 20–25.

Palmer, P. J. (1998). *The courage to teach: Exploring the inner landscape of a teacher's life*. San Francisco, CA: Jossey-Bass.

Palmer, P. J. (2000). *Let your life speak: Listening for the voice of vocation*. San Francisco, CA: Jossey-Bass.

Paulsen, M. B. (2002). Evaluating teaching performance. *New Directions for Institutional Research, 2002*, 5–18. doi:10.1002/ir.42

Pearson, N. (2002). Moving from placement to community partner. *Journal of Public Affairs, 7*, 183–202.

Peters, S. J. (2003). Reconstructing civic professionalism in academic life: A response to Mark Wood's paper, "From Service to Solidarity." *Journal of Higher Education Outreach and Engagement, 8*(2), 183–198.

Pigza, J. (2010). Developing your ability to foster student learning and development through reflection. In B. Jacoby & P. Mutascio (Eds.), *Looking in, reaching out: A reflective guide for community service-learning professionals* (pp. 73–94). Boston, MA: Campus Compact.

Popovich, N. G., & Abel, S. R. (2002). The need for a broadened definition of faculty scholarship and creativity. *American Journal of Pharmaceutical Education, 66*, 59–65.

Potter, M. K., & Kustra, E. D. H. (2011). The relationship between scholarly teaching and SoTL: Models, distinctions, and clarifications. *International Journal for the Scholarship of Teaching and Learning*, 5(1), Article 23. Retrieved from http://digitalcommons.georgiasouthern.edu/ij-sotl/vol5/iss1/23

Pratt, D. (2002). *Good teaching: One size fits all? Update on teaching theory.* San Francisco, CA: Jossey-Bass.

Price, M. (2017). *Scholarly identity mapping exercise.* Indianapolis: Indiana University–Purdue University at Indianapolis, Center for Service and Learning.

Prottas, D. J., Shea-Van Fossen, R. J., Cleaver, C. M., & Andreassi, J. K. (2017). Relationships among faculty perceptions of their tenure process and their commitment and engagement. *Journal of Applied Research in Higher Education, 9*(2), 242–254. Retrieved from https://doi.org/10.1108/JARHE-08-2016-0054

Ramaley, J. A. (2010). Students as scholars: Integrating research, education, and professional practice. In H. E. Fitzgerald, C. Burack, & S. D. Seifer (Eds.), *Handbook of engaged scholarship: Contemporary landscapes, future directions* (pp. 353–368). East Lansing: Michigan State University Press.

Reeb, R. N., & Folger, S. F. (2013). Community outcomes of service-learning: Research and practice from a systems theory perspective. In P. H. Clayton, R. G. Bringle, & J. A. Hatcher (Eds.), *Research on service-learning: Conceptual frameworks and assessment. Vol. 2B: Communities* (pp. 389–418). Sterling, VA: Stylus.

Register, S. J., & King, K. M. (2017). Promotion and tenure: Application of the scholarship of teaching and learning and the scholarship of engagement criteria to health professions education. *Health Professions Education, 4*(1), 39–47.

Rice, R. E. (1996). *Making a place for the new American scholar* (Working Paper Series, Inquiry No. 1). Washington DC: American Association for Higher Education.

Richard, D., Keen, C., Hatcher, J. A., & Pease, H. (2016). Pathways to adult civic engagement: Benefits of reflection and dialogue across difference in college service-learning programs. *Michigan Journal of Community Service Learning*, 23(1), 64–70.

Rimmerman, C. A. (2001). *The new citizenship: Unconventional politics, activism, and service* (2nd ed.). Boulder, CO: Westview Press.

Rockquemore, K. A. (2013, July 22). A new model of mentoring. *Inside Higher Ed.* Retrieved from http://www.insidehighered.com/advice/2013/07/22/essay-calling-senior-faculty-embrace-new-style-mentoring

Rogers, C. R. (1957). The necessary and sufficient conditions of therapeutic personality change. *Journal of Consulting Psychology, 21*(2), 95–103.

Rychen, D. S., & Salganik, L. H. (2001). *Defining and selecting key competencies.* Cambridge, MA: Hogrefe & Huber.

Saltmarsh, J. (2010). Changing pedagogies. In H. E. Fitzgerald, C. Burack, & S. D. Seifer (Eds.), *Handbook of engaged scholarship: Contemporary landscapes, future directions. Vol. 1: Institutional change.* East Lansing: Michigan State University Press.

Saltmarsh, J., & Hartley, M. (2011). *To a larger purpose: Engagement for democracy and the transformation of higher education.* Philadelphia, PA: Temple University Press.

Saltmarsh, J., Hartley, M., & Clayton, P. (2009). *Democratic engagement white paper.* Boston, MA: New England Resource Center for Higher Education.

Saltmarsh, J., Warren, M. R., Krueger-Henney, P., Rivera, L., Fleming, R. K., & Uriarte, M. (2015). Creating an academic culture that supports community engaged scholarship. *Diversity and Democracy, 18*(1). Retrieved from https://www.aacu.org/diversitydemocracy/2015/winter/saltmarsh

Sandmann, L. (2014). *Engaged scholarship: Preparing a case as scholarship.* Faculty development workshop presentation, University of New Hampshire, Durham.

Savage, H. E., Karp, R. S., & Logue, R. (2004). Faculty mentorship at colleges and universities. *College Teaching, 52*(1), 21–24.

Schnaubelt, T., & Schwartz-Coffey, C. (2016). Public service and civic engagement: Multiple pathways to social change. *Diversity and Democracy, 19*(3). Retrieved from https://www.aacu.org/diversitydemocracy/2016/summer/schnaubelt

Schon, D. (1983). *The reflective practitioner.* New York, NY: Basic Books.

Schon, D. (1987). *Educating the reflective practitioner.* San Francisco, CA: Jossey-Bass.

Schwandt, T. A. (1994). Constructivist, interpretivist approaches to human inquiry. In N. K. Denzin & Y. S. Lincoln (Eds.), *Handbook of qualitative research* (pp. 118–137). Thousand Oaks, CA: SAGE.

Schwartz, I. S., & Baer, D. M. (1991). Social validity assessments: Is current practice state of the art? *Journal of Applied Behavior Analysis, 24*, 189–204.

Seethaler, I. C. (2015). Feminist service learning: Teaching about oppression to work toward social change. *Feminist Teacher, 25*(1), 39–54.

Seifer, S. D., Wong, K., Gelmon, S., & Lederer, M. (2009). The Community-Engaged Scholarship for Health Collaborative: A national change initiative focused on faculty roles and rewards. *Metropolitan Universities, 20*, 5–21.

SENCER. (n.d.). Science Education for New Civic Engagements and Responsibilities. Retrieved from http://sencer.net

Siemers, C. K., Harrison, B., Clayton, P. H., & Stanley, T. A. (2015). Engaging place as partner. *Michigan Journal of Community Service Learning, 22*(1), 101–105.

Simon, L. A. K. (2011). Engaged scholarship in land-grant and research universities. In H. E. Fitzgerald, C. Burack, & S. D. Seifer (Eds.), *Handbook of engaged scholarship: Contemporary landscapes, future directions. Vol. 1: Institutional change* (pp. 99–118). East Lansing: Michigan State University Press.

Spitzberg, B. H., & Chagnon, G. (2009). Conceptualizing intercultural competence. In D. K. Deardorff (Ed.), *The SAGE handbook of intercultural competence* (pp. 2–52). Thousand Oaks, CA: SAGE.

Stanley, C. A., & Lincoln, Y. S. (2005). Cross-race faculty mentoring. *Change: The Magazine of Higher Learning* 37(2), 44–50.

Steele, M. (2017, April 21). *Principles and practice of mentorship: A learning relationship for both mentee and mentor.* Presentation at annual Northern Constellations conference of the Northern Ontario School of Medicine, Sudbury, Ontario, Canada.

Stoecker, R. (2016). *Liberating service learning and the rest of higher education civic engagement.* Philadelphia, PA: Temple University Press.

Strand, K., Marullo, S., Cutforth, N., Stoecker, R., & Donohue, P. (2003). *Community-based research and higher education: Principles and practices.* San Francisco, CA: Jossey-Bass.

Straus, S.E., Johnson, M.O., Marquez, C., & Feldman, M.D. (2013). Characteristics of successful and failed mentoring relationships: A qualitative study across two academic health centers. *Academic Medicine*, 88(1), 82–89.

Sturm, S., Eatman, T., Saltmarsh, J., & Bush, A. (2011). *Full participation: Building the architecture for diversity and public engagement in higher education.* New York, NY: Columbia University Law School, Center for Institutional and Social Change.

Sullivan, W. M. (2004). Can professionalism still be a viable ethic? *The Good Society, 13*(1), 15–20.

Sullivan, W. M. (2005). *Work and integrity: The crisis and promise of professionalism in America* (2nd ed.). San Francisco, CA: Jossey-Bass.

Swaner, L. E. (2012). The theories, contexts, and multiple pedagogies of engaged learning: What succeeds and why? In D. W. Harward (Ed.), *Transforming undergraduate education: Theory that compels and practices that succeed* (pp. 73–90). Lanham, MD: Rowman & Littlefield.

Tanner, K. D. (2012). Promoting students' metacognition. *CBE-Life Science Education, 11*, 113–120.

Tate, W. F. (1997). Critical Race Theory and education: History, theory, and implications. *Review of Research in Education, 22*, 195–247.

Tervalon, M., & Murray-Garcia, J. (1998). Cultural humility versus cultural competence: A critical distinction in defining physician training outcomes in multicultural education. *Journal of Health Care for the Poor and Underserved,* 9(2), 117–125.

Thakrar, J., Kenn, D., & Minkley, G. (2014). Across the continents: Engaging and questioning community. *Comparative Sociology, 13*(6), 773–792.

Theeboom, T., Beersma, B., & van Vianen, A. E. M. (2013). Does coaching work? A meta-analysis on the effects of coaching on individual level outcomes in an organizational context. *The Journal of Positive Psychology,* 9(1), 1–18.

Theobold, P. (1997). *Teaching the commons: Place, pride and the renewal of community.* New York, NY: Routledge.

Trigg, M., & Balliet, B. J. (2000). Learning across boundaries: Women's studies, praxis, and community service. In B. J. Balliet & K. Heffernan (Eds.), *The practice of change: Concepts and models for service-learning in women's studies* (pp. 87–102). Washington DC: American Association for Higher Education.

UNC Greensboro. (n.d.). *Leadership and civic engagement*. Retrieved from https://olsl.uncg.edu/community-scholarship/about-ces/

Van Cleave, T. J., & Cartwright, C. (2017). Intercultural competence as a cornerstone for transformation in service learning. In C. Dolgon, T. D. Mitchell, & T. K. Eatman (Eds.), *The Cambridge handbook of service learning and community engagement* (pp. 204–218). Cambridge, UK: Cambridge University Press.

Vogelgesang, L. J., Denson, N., & Jayakumar, U. M. (2010). What determines faculty-engaged scholarship? *The Review of Higher Education, 33*(4), 437–472.

Votruba, J. C. (1996). Strengthening the university's alignment with society: Challenges and strategies. *Journal of Public Service and Outreach, 1*(1), 29–36.

Votruba, J. (2011). Foreword. In H. E. Fitzgerald, C. Burack, & S. D. Seifer (Eds.), *Handbook of engaged scholarship: Contemporary landscapes, future directions. Vol. 1: Institutional change*. East Lansing: Michigan State University Press.

Vygotsky, L. (1978). Interaction between learning and development. *Readings on the Development of Children, 23*(3), 34–41.

Welch, M. (1999). The ABCs of reflection: A template for students and instructors to implement written reflection service-learning. *National Society of Experiential Education Quarterly, 25*(2), 23–25.

Welch, M. (2002). Promoting civically engaged scholarship through a study/action group. *Journal of Higher Education Outreach and Engagement, 7*(3), 111–120.

Welch, M. (2010a). O.P.E.R.A.: A first letter mnemonic and rubric for conceptualizing and implementing service-learning courses. *Australian Journal of Educational Research, 20*(1), 76–82.

Welch, M. (2010b). Shedding light on the shadow-side of reflection in service-learning. *Journal of College and Character, 11*(3), 1–6.

Welch, M. (2016). *Engaging higher education: Purpose, platforms, and programs for community engagement*. Sterling, VA: Stylus.

Welch, M. (2017). Reframing experiential education: A broader perspective of community engagement. *Experiential Learning and Teaching in Higher Education, 1*(1), 65–86.

Welch, M. (2018). Curricular engagement: In the eye of the whirlwind. In J. Saltmarsh & M. B. Johnson (Eds.), *The elective Carnegie community engagement classification: Constructing a successful application for first-time and re-classification applicants* (pp. 64–73). Boston, MA: Campus Compact.

Welch, M., & James, R. C. (2007). An investigation on the impact of a guided reflection technique in service-learning courses to prepare special educators. *Teacher Education and Special Education, 30*(4), 276–285.

Welch, M., & Koth, K. (2013). A meta-theory on the spirituality of service-learning in higher education. *Journal of College Student Development*, 54(6), 612–627.

Welch, M., Miller, P., & Davies, K. (2005). Reciprocal validity: Description and outcomes of a hybrid approach of triangulated qualitative analysis in the research of civic engagement. In S. Root, J. Callahan, & S. H. Billig (Eds.), *Improving service-learning practice: Research on models to enhance impacts* (pp. 119–139). Greenwich, CT: Information Age.

Welch, M., & Plaxton-Moore, S. (2017). Faculty development for advancing community engagement in higher education: Current trends and future directions. *Journal of Higher Education Outreach and Engagement, 21*(2), 131–166.

Welch, M., & Plaxton-Moore, S. (2018). A holistic framework for educational professional development in community engagement. In B. Berkey, C. Meixner, P. M. Green, & E. A. Eddins (Eds.), *Reconceptualizing faculty devopment in service-learning/community engagement* (pp. 27–58). Sterling, VA: Stylus.

Williams, P. J. (1991). *The alchemy of race and rights*. Cambridge, MA: Harvard University Press.

Wood, M. (2003). From service to solidarity: Engaged education and democratic globalization. *Journal of Higher Education Outreach and Engagement, 8*(2), 165–181.

Yamamura, E. K., & Koth, K. (2018). *Place-based community engagement in higher education: A strategy to transform universities and communities*. Sterling, VA: Stylus.

Yates, M., & Youness, J. (1997). *Community service and social responsibility in youth*. Chicago, IL: University of Chicago Press.

Yep, K., & Mitchell, T. D. (2017). Decolonizing community engagement: Reimagining service learning through an ethnic studies lens. In C. Dolgon, T. D. Mitchell, & T. K. Eatman (Eds.), *The Cambridge handbook of service learning and community engagement* (pp. 294–303). Cambridge, UK: Cambridge University Press.

Zlotkowski, E. (2015). Twenty years and counting: A framing essay. *Michigan Journal of Community Service Learning, 22*(1), 82–86.

ABOUT THE AUTHORS

Star Plaxton-Moore is the director of community-engaged learning at the Leo T. McCarthy Center for Public Service and the Common Good at the University of San Francisco (USF). Plaxton-Moore directs institutional support for community-engaged courses and oversees public service programs for undergraduates, including the public service and community engagement minor. She designed and implements an annual community-engaged learning and teaching fellowship program for USF faculty, and other professional development offerings that bring together faculty and community partners as colearners. Her scholarship focuses on faculty development for community-engaged teaching and scholarship, student preparation for community engagement, assessment of civic learning outcomes, and community engagement in institutional culture and practice. Plaxton-Moore holds an MEd from George Washington University and is currently completing coursework for an EdD in organizational leadership at USF. She is mom to two brilliant kids, Jackson and Stella, and spouse to Andrew Moore.

Marshall Welch has been active in the field of service-learning and community engagement for over 20 years, serving as a center director and assistant vice provost for community engagement in both public and private institutions of higher education. Welch is the coauthor of the National Inventory of Institutional Infrastructure for Community Engagement (NIIICE). He hosted the 2003 Conference on the Research of Service-Learning and Community Engagement and the first professional development retreat for center directors in collaboration with Campus Compact and has served on the board of the International Association for Research on Service-Learning and Community Engagement (IARSLCE). He is the author of numerous articles and chapters as well as books including *Engaging Higher Education: Purpose, Platforms, and Programs* (2016) and is the coauthor of *The Community Engagement Professional's Guidebook* (2018), both published by Stylus Publishing. He is now an independent scholar living in the Portland, Oregon, area.

INDEX

Assessing Service-Learning and Civic Engagement (Second Edition)

Principles and Techniques

By Sherril B. Gelmon, Barbara A. Holland, and Amy Spring

With Seanna Kerrigan and Amy Driscoll

This book offers a broad overview of many issues related to assessment in higher education, with specific application for understanding the impact of service-learning and civic engagement initiatives. This revised edition includes an additional chapter which explores recent changes in the assessment landscape and offers examples and resources for designing assessment strategies for community engagement in higher education. The original text includes narrative addressing assessment issues and strategies; detailed discussion of learning from multiple research projects performed over the past two decades about impact on multiple constituencies—students, faculty, communities, and institutions; and discussion of strategies for data collection, analysis, synthesis, and reporting. Specific assessment instruments for use with each constituency are provided, including suggestions for administration, preparation, and data analysis. This volume will be helpful for individuals seeking a comprehensive resource on assessment issues in higher education.

45 Temple Place
Boston, MA 02111

Subscribe to our newsletter: https://compact.org

Also available from Campus Compact

The Community Engagement Professional's Guidebook

A Companion to The Community Engagement Professional in Higher Education

By Lina D. Dostilio and Marshall Welch

This book is a companion guide to Campus Compact's successful publication *The Community Engagement Professional in Higher Education*. Lina Dostilio teams up with Marshall Welch to offer a rich and deep dive into the practice of higher education community engagement, breaking down the essential components of a community engagement professional's (CEP) work. From mentoring faculty research, leading campaigns to build civic engagement curriculum on campus, to managing the staff who support community engagement units, the authors tackle the breadth of the CEP's work by drawing on key resources and their own decades of experience in the field. Throughout the book, readers will encounter "Compass Points" that call for personal reflection and engagement with the text. These interactive moments combine with end-of-chapter questions to prompt thinking about a CEP's critical commitments and create a powerful and engaging tool kit that will be essential for any person doing community and civic engagement work on campus.

(Continues on preceding page)